PAKISTAN

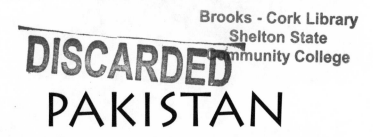
PAKISTAN

Fifty Years of Nationhood, Third Edition

SHAHID JAVED BURKI

Westview Press

A Member of the Perseus Books Group

Profiles/Nations of Contemporary Asia

This is the third edition of *Pakistan: A Nation in the Making.*

Copyright © 1986, 1991, 1999 by Westview Press, Inc.

Published in 1999 in the United States of America by Westview Press, 5500 Central Avenue, Boulder, Colorado 80301-2877, and in the United Kingdom by Westview Press, 12 Hid's Copse Road, Cumnor Hill, Oxford OX2 9JJ

Distributed in Pakistan by Pak Book Corporation, 21 Queen's Road, Lahore

Library of Congress Cataloging-in-Publication Data
Burki, Shahid Javed.
    Pakistan : fifty years of nationhood / Shahid javed Burki.—3rd ed.
        p.   cm.
    Includes bibliographical references (p.   ) and index.
    ISBN 0-8133-3621-X.
    1. Pakistan—History.   I. Title.
DS382.B89   1999
954.91—dc21   98-55927
                                                                                           CIP

Printed and bound in the United States of America

The paper used in this publication meets the requirements of the American National Standard for Permanence of Paper for Printed Library Materials Z39.48-1984.

10   9   8   7   6   5   4   3   2   1

To my children,
Emaad and Sairah

Contents

1 BIRTH: AUGUST 14, 1947   1

2 POLITICAL DEVELOPMENT: CONTINUING SEARCH FOR STABILITY   23

List of
Tables and Illustrations

Tables

Map

Acknowledgments

This third edition of my book has benefited from the comments of a number of scholars who reviewed the first two editions. Some scholars identified flaws that were easy to correct; other "flaws" were more difficult to address because they represented different ways of looking at Pakistan's economic, social, and political history. The first two editions were marred by a lack of attention to (1) the social status of women and (2) the evolution of the legal system. Some pointed out that the book did not note the precarious situation for women that was created by President Zia ul-Haq's efforts to introduce Islam into politics and economics. Some reviewers commented on the need to analyze the impact of an Islamic legal system on the political, social, and economic development of a system that had been inherited from the British. Some others questioned whether Pakistan had indeed succeeded in alleviating absolute poverty to the extent claimed in the first edition. Still others questioned the underlying message of hope that the second edition sought to communicate to readers.

The new edition of the book, which appears under a different subtitle, is an effort to accommodate these and many other comments. It also updates the story of Pakistan and brings it to the winter of 1998–1999, when a new political and economic order was being put into place. There is a great deal of new writing incorporated in this edition, and there are a number of people to whom I owe thanks for making it possible for me to reach new interpretations about the development of Pakistan. Their help came in the form of many conversations I had with them since the appearance of the first two editions. I owe a special debt to Babar Ali, Kamal Azfar, Shahid Hamid, Mahbubul Haq, Imran Khan, Farooq Leghari, Moeen Qureshi, Saeed Ahmad Qureshi, Mian Nawaz Sharif, Mian Shabaz Sharif, Najam Sethi, and Hasan Zaheer. I also owe a debt to the members of the caretaker administration I served following the dismissal of Benazir Bhutto in November 1996. I gained valuable insights into the way Pakistan was governed during the three months I spent in the country as finance minister on leave from the World Bank. I alone, of course, am responsible for any errors of fact and omission that remain.

Shahid Javed Burki

Map of Pakistan

INTRODUCTION

The circumstances—some political, some social, but many economic—that led to the creation of Pakistan as an independent state are discussed in the first chapter of this book. On August 14, 1947, Lord Louis Mountbatten, the last viceroy of British India, administered the oath of office to Mohammad Ali Jinnah as the first governor-general of Pakistan. The ceremony was held in Karachi, the capital of the new country. The same evening Lord Mountbatten flew back to New Delhi, and the following day—August 15, 1947—he was sworn in as the first governor-general of India. Thus, within a period of just over twenty-four hours, the British liquidated their Indian empire. Their departure was hurried and took a form not anticipated by many. The British had believed that when they left India they would hand over the administration to one successor government. Instead, they left two governments in charge of a partitioned India, one in Karachi and the other in New Delhi.

Pakistan, the smaller of the two successor states, was a political novelty—a country created to accommodate people who wanted to live separately because they followed a faith totally different from that of the majority of the country of their origin. A state created in the name of religion was a new political phenomenon, to be repeated only once again when the colonial powers withdrew from Asia and Africa. About one hundred countries have obtained independence in the years following World War II, but only one other—the state of Israel, created for the Jews of the diaspora—was established for religious reasons. But religion proved to be a weak basis for defining a nation's frontier. Pakistan, as it turned out, was established with problematic frontiers. The country was divided into two halves—or "wings," as they were called—but Islam failed to keep East and West Pakistan together for very long. In 1971, a quarter century after the country's birth, the eastern wing separated to form the independent country of Bangladesh. But the formation of Bangladesh left Pakistan with unstable frontiers. Even today, two of Pakistan's borders—the Durand line that runs between Afghanistan and Pakistan, and the "line of control" that now divides the old princely state of Kashmir between the territories "occupied" by India and Pakistan—have not been formally accepted by Pakistan's neighbors. With the war in Afghanistan against the occupation of the Soviet Union that lasted for ten years and the subsequent emergence of Islamic zealots who call themselves the Taleban (students) as the

virtual rulers of Afghanistan, Pakistan can expect its northern neighbor to continue to experience considerable turbulence for many more years. With people,
arms, goods, and commodities moving freely between Pakistan and Afghanistan,
the Durand line no longer works as the border. Would it be put back on the map
again? The situation on Pakistan's eastern border, in the Indian-held state of
Kashmir, also remains unsettled while both Pakistan and India, by testing nuclear
devices, have made the entire world nervous about the possibility of yet another
confrontation between the two countries over the future of this contested state.
Would Kashmir continue to remain divided? Would it merge with Pakistan?
Would India assume control over the entire state? Would the state become independent? These questions are being asked in both India and Pakistan.

Malleable frontiers are not the only reason for which Pakistan, even after more
than five decades of independence, remains a country in search of nationhood. It
continues to be politically unstable, without institutions that can be considered
viable. Since 1947, the country has tried about a half dozen different political systems and four formal constitutions, promulgated in 1946, 1956, 1962, and 1973,
respectively. General Zia ul-Haq's drastic amendment of the 1973 constitution
produced a political system that had little resemblance to the one operated by
Zulfikar Ali Bhutto.[1] At the time of independence, the administration of
Governor-General Jinnah drew constitutional authority from the Act of India,
passed by the British Parliament in 1935 and amended by the India Independence
Bill of 1946. These two bills gave nearly dictatorial powers to the governor-general. Jinnah's outlook, however, was democratic, and by the time he became governor-general, he was too ill to become a dictator. In addition, his successor,
Khawaja Nazimuddin, was too genial to make full use of the powers these two acts
had bestowed on him. Their successors—first Ghulam Muhammad and then
General Iskander Mirza—were considerably less scrupulous. Both used the acts of
1935 and 1946 to increase their power; accordingly, the constitution of 1956—the
first of the three formal constitutions to be introduced since independence—
adopted a parliamentary system in which the power of the head of state was
highly constrained. Not surprisingly, the 1956 constitution had a short life; it was
abrogated by General Ayub Khan, who went on to provide the country with a new
political system.

Ayub Khan's constitution, promulgated in 1962, introduced a presidential form
of government. Presidential elections were held in 1964, and even though Ayub
Khan was challenged by Fatimah Jinnah, the sister of Pakistan's founder, he won
an easy victory. Installed in March 1965 as Pakistan's first elected president, Ayub
Khan lasted in office for only four more years. In March 1969, following a spirited
and often violent campaign against him and his political system, he was thrown
out of office by General Yahya Khan, the commander in chief of the armed forces.
For the second time in eleven years (1958–1969), the country was without a constitution and under martial law. General Yahya Khan remained in office for thirty-
three turbulent, eventful months. He ordered elections to pick yet another

Constituent Assembly, but the polls resulted in the total polarization of politics in the country. The Awami League, a secessionist party, triumphed in East Pakistan, and the majority of the seats in West Pakistan were won by Zulfikar Ali Bhutto's Pakistan People's Party (PPP).

There were fundamental differences of opinion between the Awami League and the People's Party concerning the political structure that was needed for Pakistan. The differences could not be resolved, and the political situation deteriorated rapidly. By March 1971, only three months after the elections, East Pakistan was prepared to secede from the Pakistani Union. After nine months of an exceptionally bitter war, troops from West Pakistan surrendered to a combined force of Indian army and Bengali separatists, called Mukti Bahini; Bangladesh, the erstwhile East Pakistan, emerged as an independent state in December 1971.[2]

Discredited by its defeat in East Pakistan, General Yahya Khan's army went on to surrender political power in West Pakistan. On December 20, 1971, Zulfikar Ali Bhutto was sworn in as the president and chief martial law administrator—a strange combination of offices for a civilian politician who had campaigned for half a decade against military rule. It took Bhutto nearly twenty-two months to produce the country's third constitution. This one, introduced on August 14, 1973, was different from the constitutions of 1956 and 1962. Unlike the constitution of 1962 but like that of 1956, it created a parliamentary form of government; unlike both, however, it specified a bicameral legislature, with the upper house—the Senate—given the power to maintain the balance between the country's three smaller provinces and Punjab, the largest.

The first election under the new constitution was held four years later, in March 1977. The official results showed a landslide victory for Bhutto and his Pakistan People's Party—a result so lopsided that the opposition cried foul and launched a street movement against the government. The movement became violent, and the army had to be called in to restore law and order in the major cities. The army succeeded in controlling the agitation and, with its prestige thus restored, its commander, General Zia ul-Haq, removed Bhutto from office on July 5, 1977.

General Zia's coup d'état was the third in Pakistan's history, but there was a difference: He suspended but did not abrogate the constitution, and he did not immediately assume the office of the presidency. Fazal Elahi Chaudhury, the president from Bhutto's time on, was allowed to remain in office, and the assumption of power by General Zia ul-Haq was given a semblance of legitimacy when the Supreme Court declared that the extraordinary political developments that followed the elections justified the declaration of martial law. After remaining in office for a little more than seven years, General Zia asked the people of Pakistan to vote in a referendum on whether they approved of his efforts to Islamize Pakistan. It was implied that an affirmative vote not only would be seen as a vote of confidence in Zia but also would indicate the people's wish for him to continue in office for another five years. Very few people voted in the referendum—the rate of participation was less than one-quarter of the total registered voters—but the government declared it successful for the president and his policies. Having gained legitimacy for his rule, at least in his own eyes, Zia allowed the long postponed general elections to be held in February 1985.

The elections evoked an enthusiastic voter response and led to the induction of a civilian administration under Prime Minister Muhammed Khan Junejo that remained in office for slightly more than three years under General Zia's watchful eyes. Junejo persuaded Zia to lift martial law in December 1985 and accept a form of government in which executive powers were shared between the president and the prime minister. This system was inherently unstable; neither the military president nor the civilian prime minister was comfortable with it. Junejo was dismissed by the president in May 1988, and a caretaker government was appointed to hold general elections. There are good indications that Zia would have changed the system in favor of a presidential form of government prior to the elections. However, before he could implement his plans, he was killed in an air crash on August 17, 1988.

Zia's death and the general elections held in November 1988 brought the Pakistan People's Party back to power under Prime Minister Benazir Bhutto. The return of the Bhuttos to Islamabad (Nusrat Bhutto, Zulfikar Ali Bhutto's widow, was appointed the senior minister in her daughter's cabinet, and Asaf Ali Zardari, Benazir Bhutto's husband, became politically active behind the scenes) did not signal the end of the Zia era. Benazir Bhutto stayed in office for only twenty months; in August 1988 she was dismissed by President Ghulam Ishaq Khan on charges of corruption and mismanagement. Khan called for another general election, and in October 1990, the PPP was soundly defeated by a coalition of political parties sympathetic to Zia and his legacy. Another government was sworn into office in November 1990, under Prime Minister Mian Nawaz Sharif. This was the sixth administration to take office in the five years following Zia's decision to return Pakistan to some form of democracy.

In the spring of 1991, Pakistan seemed as far from defining its political identity as it had been in August 1947, the year of its birth. Over the years Pakistan has endured many crises: in October 1958, when the military, under General Ayub Khan, intervened in politics for the first time; in March 1969, when President Ayub Khan was forced out of office by popular opposition; in December 1971, when the country split into two parts and the "eastern wing" of East Pakistan became the independent country of Bangladesh; in July 1977, when Zia entered politics at the head of Pakistan's third military government; in April 1979, when Zulfikar Ali Bhutto, the prime minister deposed by the military, was hanged in Rawalpindi; in March 1985, when Zia returned some political power to a civilian government; in May 1988, when the power given to the civilians was resumed by Zia; in August 1988, when Zia was assassinated; in November 1988, when Benazir Bhutto became prime minister; and throughout the 1990s when Benazir Bhutto's Pakistan People's Party and Mian Nawaz Sharif's Pakistan Muslim League competed for power to the point that, on several occasions, people began to ask the question whether parliamentary government was a viable proposition for the country. There was not a single year in the decade of the 1990s when the country was not plunged into some sort of political crisis. Chapter 2 is the story of these developments.

Political turbulence was bound to affect economic development, but Pakistan's economy managed to grow at a respectable rate for the first four decades after the country achieved independence. In the fifth decade, the rate of economic growth slowed down to slightly more than the increase in the rate of growth of population. At this rate, poverty has begun to return to Pakistan. The ups and downs of the economy—periods of stagnation alternating with periods of remarkable dynamism—are discussed in Chapter 3, along with the growth of Pakistan's gross domestic product (GDP), which, in the fifty years since independence, has averaged over 5.4 percent per annum. At the time of independence in 1947, the provinces that were separated to form the two wings of the country—East and West Pakistan—were considerably poorer than those that remained in India. In 1999, in West Pakistan—the present-day Pakistan—according to one estimation, the average income per head of the population was twice as high as that in India and Bangladesh.[3] If not for the country's turbulent political history and its adverse effect on the economy, Pakistan today might have had a much higher level of per capita income. In 1991, the World Bank classified Pakistan as a low-income country—a country with a per capita income of less than the equivalent of US$500. Of the forty-two countries in this group, Pakistan had the highest per capita income in Asia—there were thirteen countries with a higher income level, all but four (Haiti, Sri Lanka, Yemen, and Indonesia) of them in Africa. By 1998, the last year for which this comparative data are available, Pakistan had begun to lose its preeminent position among the poor countries of the world.

In the late 1980s Pakistan had begun to exhibit many of the characteristics of a middle-income country: It was less dependent on agriculture than most low-income countries and had an industrial sector that was comparable in size and diversity to those in many middle-income nations; it had a vast reservoir of highly trained laborers; it had a large middle class numbering more than 30 million people; and it was as urbanized as the more developed countries of East Asia and the Middle East. In fact, Pakistan then could well have been placed among the middle-income countries with a per capita income of well over US$500. In the late 1990s, however, the expectation that Pakistan is on the verge of crossing the threshold to become a middle-income country has ceased to exist. In 1999, Pakistan was struggling to remain economically viable. For several months after it had carried out nuclear tests and the United States and some other industrial countries had imposed economic sanctions, it appeared that Pakistan would default on its external obligations.

Most of Pakistan's current economic problems are the result of poor management in recent years. As it has in politics, Pakistan has also experimented with several economic strategies. It tried many different economic systems. From 1947 to 1958, manufacturing was the politically favored sector. It received a great deal of government attention and a large amount of resources. Consequently, industries developed quickly during this period, but to the neglect of agriculture, the largest sector of the economy. The government of President Ayub Khan followed a different set of objectives; during his period, agricultural output increased at a rate not common in the Third World. Growing at a rate of nearly 7 percent per annum, the GDP growth was among the highest in the world. Then, under Prime Minister Bhutto's Fabianism, the economy was drastically restructured. Large industries, banks, and insurance companies were nationalized; the government also increased its presence in the sectors of health and education. Consequently, the economy lost the momentum it had picked up during the period of Ayub Khan. The government of General Zia ul-Haq adopted Ayub Khan's model of economic management but failed to reduce the size of the public sector. The rate of economic growth returned to the path it had followed in the 1960s. In 1988–1990, Prime Minister Benazir Bhutto undid most of what her father had done a decade and a half earlier and invited the private sector to participate once again in economic development. At the same time, she used the public sector for personal gain, a trend that was maintained by following administrations. The economy paid a heavy price for this abuse of power.

In developing this story, Chapter 3 explores the interaction between politics and the economy, the structural changes that have occurred in the economy since 1947, the problems the economy currently faces, the potential of the economy, and, finally, the policies that need to be adopted in order to restore economic health.

Chapter 4 deals with the problem of the low level of social development in Pakistan. Very low levels of literacy—particularly among women—and high rates of fertility pose problems that have to be solved in order to lay the basis for rapid economic growth in the future. Pakistan again faces the problem of mass poverty. For about fifteen years, from 1975 to 1990, Pakistan seemed to have solved the problem of absolute poverty. However, much of this accomplishment was the result of a massive inflow of capital from abroad, sent by millions of Pakistani workers living in the Middle East, Europe, and North America. The Gulf War forced the return of some of the workers from the Middle East while the demographic maturing of the Pakistani diaspora in Europe and North America brought about a decline in the amounts of money being remitted by them to their relatives still living in Pakistan. Now, as never before, Pakistan has to rely on its own resources to solve its economic and social problems.

Chapter 5 deals with the problem of poor governance and corruption that resulted in the dismissal of four prime ministers in twelve years by the presidents of Pakistan. That this has become a serious problem for the country was attested to by Transparency International, a Berlin-based nongovernmental organization dealing with these issues. In its annual report for 1996, Transparency International classified Pakistan as the second most corrupt country in the world. This chapter explores the reason for the persistence of poor governance and corruption in the country and suggests that a deep change in the culture of politics is the only viable solution to this problem.

The problematic frontiers that Pakistan was assigned to manage and defend from the time of its birth meant that relations with the outside world would necessarily become an extremely important preoccupation from the very first day of the country's existence. Chapter 6 reveals the nature of these frontiers, which bespoke uneasy relations with practically all neighbors—in particular, Afghanistan and the Soviet Union (while it existed) to the north, and India to the south. For a time, China also looked on with apprehension as Pakistan became an active member of several treaty organizations put together by U.S. Secretary of State John Foster Dulles. Relations with Iran remained warm until Ayatollah Khomeini came to power; thereafter, a degree of uncertainty prevailed as Pakistanis found their northwestern neighbor to be somewhat unpredictable. In view of their enormous wealth and Islamic fundamentalism, the rich oil-exporting countries across the Arabian Sea have also become important for Pakistan.

During its relatively brief existence, Pakistan has engaged in three major wars and a series of small skirmishes. The first two wars, in 1948–1949 and 1965, were fought over the disputed state of Kashmir; the third war, in 1971, was fought over Bangladesh; and periodic skirmishes have occurred between Pakistan and the Pathan and Balochi tribes that live in the "unsettled area" between Pakistan and Afghanistan.

The foreign relations of a country so preoccupied with its neighbors would naturally have a profound impact on both political and economic development. Chapter 6 continues with a description of the conduct of Pakistan's foreign policy and traces its impact on the country's political and economic growth.

A short concluding chapter pulls together the various strands from the six previous chapters of the book and assesses Pakistan's future prospects. The challenges facing the country are enormous; so, too, is its potential. Will Pakistan realize its potential? Or will it be overwhelmed by its problems? Only time will tell.

1

BIRTH: AUGUST 14, 1947

Mohammad Ali Jinnah and the Muslim League campaigned hard but not very long for the establishment of Pakistan as an independent state for the Muslims of British India. On March 23, 1940, at a crowded open meeting held in Lahore, Jinnah moved that the "Lahore Resolution" be adopted. The resolution demanded the creation of a country in which the Muslims of British India would be permitted to lead their lives according to their political, social, and religious culture. Jinnah, who came to be called Quaid-e-Azam (the Great Leader) by his large and devout following, was now convinced that India was inhabited not by one nation of Indians but by two nations—one Hindu and the other Muslim. The idea of Pakistan did not originate with him, however; Mohammad Iqbal, the "poet-philosopher," had suggested it earlier as an objective toward which the Indian Muslim community should begin to work. Having campaigned for Hindu-Muslim unity for more than two decades, Jinnah reached the same conclusion reluctantly and much later than Iqbal. Once he had reached it, he was prepared to employ all his formidable political skills and expertise to bringing about the partition of British India.

That a nation should be split in twain by a religious conflict was not new in the contemporary world. But the conflict of Hindus and Muslims ran to far greater depths than, say, the Catholic and Protestant conflict in Ireland. Not only religion but whole modes of life and attitude separated these two groups of people. Each was a permanent hereditary group, exhibiting no intermarriage (except at the highest and lowest social levels, and then only very rarely) or internal absorption. It is therefore not only for the sake of completing the historical record that the story of modern-day Pakistan should begin long before independence day on

1

August 14, 1947. Indeed, a historian must go back a number of years in seeking to understand how and why the Indian Muslims converted to the idea of Pakistan. The explanation for a number of developments—economic, political, and social—that were to occur later are to be found in the politics of this conversion.

The Muslims of British India

In the 1940s, when the demand for Pakistan gained momentum, some 100 million Muslims lived in British India, slightly more than one-fourth of the total population. Religion was the only thing these people shared; otherwise, there were vast differences of language, culture, and social and economic backgrounds between, say, the Muslims of the Punjab and those of Bengal. Within this one Muslim nation there existed at least three separate communities: one in the northwest (the provinces of Punjab, Sindh, and Northwest Frontier; and the princely states of Bahawalpur, Kalat, Kashmir, and Khairpur); the second in the northeast (the provinces of Bengal and Assam); and the third in the north-central part of British India (the United and Central Provinces; the provinces of Bihar and Orissa; Bombay, the capital city of Delhi; and numerous princely states scattered all over this part of the country). The first two communities constituted clear majorities in their areas: Of the total population of 60 million in the northwest, 60 percent professed Islam; of the 90 million in the northeast, some 55 percent were Muslims. Only in the north-central provinces were Muslims a small minority, no more than 20 percent of the total population. Muslims who belonged to this community were more educated, urbanized, and modernized than those in the other two; whereas agriculture was the principal source of income for the Muslims in the northwest and northeast, those in the north-central provinces depended mostly on government, law, medicine, commerce, and industry for their livelihood.

In many ways, the Muslims of the northwest had benefited from the British *raj* (rule). There was some threat of economic competition from the non-Muslims once the British lifted the protection they had provided, but this threat constituted only a minor worry. The Muslim landed aristocracy was powerful in the countryside; the religious leaders had a great deal of support in the villages as well as in the towns; and even the small urban community of Muslims had been reasonably well accommodated in the professions and public services. The Muslims in the northeast constituted a totally different socioeconomic class—a mirror image of the one in the northwest. They owned little land, did not have much education, and had not found a sure place for themselves in the modern administrative and economic institutions that the British had brought to India. Those in the northwest constituted the aristocracy of Indian Muslim society; those in the northeast made up its peasantry.

In between these two social and economic extremes were the Muslims of Delhi, the United and Central Provinces, Bihar, Orissa, and Bombay. These Muslims were descendants of the Mughul *raj*—sons, grandsons, and great grandsons of the families that, for more than two centuries, had served the Mughul administration in various capacities. The British conquest of India had hurt this elite the most; they were deprived not only of their traditional jobs but also of their social and cultural status. In 1857, this community made one disorganized but bloody attempt to regain the power it had lost to the British. The community called this uprising the War of Independence; the British labeled it the Indian Mutiny. The British put down the mutiny with considerable determination. The mutiny forced a fundamental change in the way the British governed India.[1] The East India Company—the trading company that had brought much of India under British rule—lost its charter to trade with and govern the territories it had acquired. The British government stepped into the company's place to directly administer India. London appointed a viceroy to rule India in the name of the Queen. "Before the Mutiny the ruler had been known as Governor-General of India, but now he was the monarch's Viceroy as well, to convey the rare distinction of his position. In the whole of the British Empire this official had only one superior: the monarch herself. Even the Prime Minister in London deferred to him on any occasion when they were together, for the Viceroy was uniquely the monarch's deputy. . . ."[2] The viceroys ruled India for ninety years, from 1857 to 1947, with the help of the elitist Indian Civil Service. The combination of these legacies of the British rule of India—a powerful executive who governed with the help of a strong, elitist bureaucracy—was to have a more profound impact on Pakistan's political and economic development than on that of Pakistan's sister country, India. The "viceregal model of governance"[3] was used by Pakistan in several ways for more than four decades following independence.

The mutiny's immediate impact was to socially and politically downgrade the Muslim community of north-central India. The new British-Indian administration dropped Urdu and Persian as official languages and replaced them with English. Because the Muslims had shown a considerable disdain for all things English, including the language, they suddenly found themselves functionally illiterate and unemployed. The place they vacated was quickly occupied by the Hindus. "The pliant and adaptable Hindu was not agitated by the scruples which had tormented the Muslims," wrote a contemporary British administrator. The Muslims stayed away—or, some believed, were deliberately kept away—from the British *raj*. "A hundred and seventy years ago," the British administrator went on to say, "it was impossible for a well born Mussulman to become poor; at present it is almost impossible for him to continue to be rich. . . . There is no Government office in which a Muslim could hope for any post above the rank of porter, messenger, filler of inkpots, and a mender of pens."[4]

Bringing the community out of this state of self-exile, therefore, became a major preoccupation with a number of Muslim reformers. The most successful of these was Sir Sayyid Ahmad Khan, who, having started his professional career as a minor government functionary, discovered that his people could not make much headway without modern education. For Pakistan—in terms of its creation as well as its political and social development—Sir Sayyid's educational program had two important consequences. First, those who accepted his outlook and his philosophy were able to find their way back into the economic and social life of modern India. The university that he founded in the town of Aligarh soon began to produce graduates who could easily move into the upper ranks of the British Indian Army as well as into the upper echelons of the rapidly expanding administrative system of the British *raj*. They could also enter the professions—law, medicine, banking, commerce, industry—that had helped the Hindus advance rapidly in British India. Hence this Aligarh generation not only provided the Pakistan movement with its leadership but, later, also provided the new country of Pakistan with its first ruling elite.[5]

The second important consequence of Sir Sayyid's efforts was that they helped at least one segment of the Indian Muslim community to change its identity from that of the Mughul society of the early nineteenth century, in which Muslims identified primarily with family and lineage (and, through these, with the Mughul political system), to the late-nineteenth-century product of colonial rule, Aligarh College, in whose hothouse atmosphere young Muslims discovered a common identity as Muslim students. Sir Sayyid and Aligarh College made it possible for the Muslims to discover a new political identity: Being a Muslim came to have a political connotation—a connotation that was to lead this Indian Muslim community inexorably toward acceptance of the "two-nation theory."

The other Muslim communities, those in the northwest and northeast, remained largely untouched by this movement of reform. Certain prominent families from these communities sent their sons to Aligarh; these sons, after graduation, seldom returned to their families. Aided by modern education and in full command of the English language, they usually found their way into government service—that is, into the many branches of the civil administration or into the army. Many Aligarh graduates from the northwest were to play very significant political roles in Pakistan. In these roles, they were to display a considerable amount of political and economic schizophrenia: From Aligarh they had learned the virtues of parliamentary democracy and laissez-faire economics, whereas in the social sense they continued to belong to a community that had been touched only marginally by Western political and economic thought. But the story of these later leaders of Pakistan belongs to a different chapter.

Although the leadership of the Pakistan movement came essentially from among the Muslim minority provinces of British India—Mohammad Ali Jinnah from Bombay; Liaqat Ali Khan, his principal lieutenant, from the United Provinces; Chaudhry Khaliquzzman also from the United Provinces; the nawab of Bhopal and the raja of Mahmudabad from two of the several princely states in and around the Central Provinces; and I. I. Chundrigar from Bombay—the Pakistan Movement would not have developed the force it did without winning the support of the Muslim-dominated provinces in the northwestern and northeastern parts of the country. The conversion of the Muslims from the Muslim majority areas to the cause of Pakistan was slow in coming; but once the idea caught on in Bengal, in parts of Assam, Punjab, Sindh, and Balochistan, and in the Northwestern Frontier Province (NWFP), the emergence of Pakistan became inevitable.

It was a different dynamic, however, that brought about the conversion of these three Muslim communities to the idea of Pakistan. Political frustration persuaded the Muslims of the north-central provinces to opt for the idea of Pakistan; religion played an important role in winning over the northwestern Muslims; and social and economic deprivation were the main reasons for the support eventually given by the northeastern Muslims to the demand for Pakistan. Each of these three dynamics deserves a further word of explanation.

The Muslims of North-Central Provinces

The advent of the British *raj* had very different consequences for the three Indian Muslim communities. What I have already said about one of these communities—the Muslim community of the north-central provinces—bears repetition. The collapse of the Mughul empire was eventually to take these Muslims of British India toward partial secularization and modernization. But there was a long period of agonized soul-searching in between—a period during which a number of Islamic revivalist groups fought, at times bitterly, with the modernists for control of the minds of this community. Success ultimately came to Sir Sayyid; his efforts brought the Muslims back from self-imposed exile.

During the first three decades of the twentieth century, the Muslim University at Aligarh had an extraordinary impact; thousands of its young graduates went into the fields of government, law, medicine, finance, industry, and commerce. These were new areas for the Muslims of India; but if the Muslims had not entered into them, they would not have been able to set up a modern political apparatus. Before the emergence of the Muslim League, political organizations among Muslims had taken the form of religious parties aiming at the revival of Islam. None of these parties had sought to play a secular political role. The Muslim League, under the leadership of Jinnah, provided a potent political weapon for the Muslims of India. There is, of course, no reason for which the establishment of a modern political party should have led the Muslims of India toward the partition of India. For more than three decades, the Muslim League had fought for the protection of Muslim rights within one Indian polity. It was only when the Muslims perceived that they could not gain these rights without establishing a state of their own that many of them—especially those in the north-central provinces—became attracted to the idea of Pakistan. According to a revisionist interpretation of Muslim aspirations in the period leading up to the creation of Pakistan, Mohammad Ali Jinnah's demand for the establishment of an independent Muslim state was tactical. The strategy adopted by Jinnah and the Muslim League was aimed at securing a prominent place for the Indian Muslim community within the political system that was to be established after the departure of the British. Such a role could not be justified solely by the number of Muslims, which according to the census of 1941 was about one-quarter of the total population of independent India. Jinnah argued on the basis of his "two-nation theory": The Muslims were not simply a large minority but a separate nation within India. The revisionist interpretation holds that Jinnah did not want an independent Pakistan and that he would have been very comfortable to live within a united India in which the constitution gave explicit protection to the rights and aspirations of the Muslim nation.[6]

There has been a great deal of debate as to whether the British administration in New Delhi or the provincial administrations set up by the Hindu-dominated Indian National Congress after the elections of 1937 discriminated against the Muslims. The rights and wrongs of this controversy are not important here; what does matter is that, in the early years of the twentieth century, many Indian Muslims came to feel the tension between their Indian nationality and the Muslim religion. This dilemma was posed by Maulana Mohamed Ali in 1930 in his customary style:

> Where God commands . . . I am a Muslim first, a Muslim second and a Muslim last and nothing but a Muslim. . . . But where India is concerned, where India's freedom is concerned, where the welfare of India is concerned, I am an Indian first, an Indian second, an Indian last and nothing but an Indian. . . . I belong to two circles of equal size but which are not concentric. One is India and the other is Muslim. . . . We belong to these circles . . . and we can leave neither.[7]

By the mid-1940s, a large number of Indian Muslims had convinced themselves, however, that their community would be at a serious disadvantage in a state under the political and economic control of non-Muslims. As already noted, modes of life and attitudes of mind separated the Indian Muslims from the non-Muslims, especially the Hindus. Two events, one in 1937 and the other in 1946, were to lend political color to this state of separateness.

After failing to get the agreement of various Indian groups (the Hindus, the Muslims, and the Princes) on a political solution to the "Indian problem," the British promulgated the Government of India Act of 1935. This act was described by the British as "their last and, in the event, most portentous essay in balancing and ruling India." At its core was the establishment of autonomy, with a representative parliamentary system of government, for eleven provinces of British India. These provinces—and also the princely states, it was hoped—were expected to join an all-India federation, which in turn was to have a representative parliamentary system. But the act failed to produce a political balance; when provincial elections were held in 1937 under its provisions, the Hindu-dominated Indian National Congress formed governments in eight of the eleven provinces. The Muslim League captured only 104 of the 489 seats reserved for Muslims, most of them in the north-central provinces. In the Muslim majority provinces, it performed very poorly; in Punjab it won only 1 of 86 Muslim seats, in Bengal, 37 out of 119 seats. Yet even this poor showing would not have sent the Muslim League on a separatist route if the Congress had managed to assuage Muslim fear in the minority provinces. It was expected that the Congress would include League representatives in the administration of the north-central provinces, where the League had shown considerable electoral success. This the Congress failed to do: The administration in the United Provinces included two Muslims, one from the Congress, the other a renegade Muslim Leaguer; in the Central Province, a deserting League member joined the administration; in Bombay, the Congress turned to an "independent" Muslim. "In the light of these consequences," noted a contemporary historian, "the Congress's policy, though politically understandable, was a blunder of the first order. It is often attributed to Pandit Nehru."[8]

Jawaharlal Nehru was also responsible for the political event in 1946 that confirmed to the Muslims of India that the creation of a separate homeland was the best possible outcome for them. Before concluding that it was not possible to leave the Indians a united India, the British made one more attempt to find a solution to the Indian problem. The government of Prime Minister Clement Attlee in London sent a three-man Cabinet Mission to explore with the leaders of India some possible ways to keep them together. Their exploration led to the formulation of the "Cabinet Mission Plan," which called for an Indian confederation of three units with the rather pedestrian nomenclature of A, B, and C groupings. Two of these groups of provinces were to be formed from the Muslim majority states and provinces in the northwest and northeastern parts of the country; the rest of India made up the third group.

What probably won the support of the Muslim League for this plan was the provision that after a decent interval of time—the duration of which was left undefined by the Cabinet Mission but generally believed to be fifteen years—any of these three groups could opt out of the federation. The Congress called this scheme "the plan to get Pakistan by the back door"; however, after the Muslim League had accepted it, the Congress also gave it its approval. According to Maulana Abdul Kalam Azad, a prominent Muslim who had stayed with the Congress, "The acceptance of the Cabinet Mission Plan . . . was a glorious event in the history of the freedom movement in India. . . . We rejoiced but we did not then know that our joy was premature and bitter disappointment awaited us."[9] Jawaharlal Nehru, by declaring in public within one month of Congress's acceptance of the plan that his party reserved the right to block the secession of any of the groups from the Indian union, killed Maulana Azad's joy and also the prospects of keeping India united.

Many historians have argued, in retrospect, that the plan was unworkable; that Nehru was justified in withdrawing his support; that, had the plan been implemented, the provision allowing federating units the right to secede would eventually have divided India into at least three states. It can also be argued in retrospect that the outcome the opponents of the plan had feared did come about: that, twenty-five years after the announcement of the plan, British India did split into three states; that, had the plan been accepted by Nehru and his colleagues, the emergence of Pakistan and Bangladesh would probably have been achieved with less bloodshed and less trauma; that, having spent fifteen years together within the framework of one federation, India, Pakistan, and Bangladesh, even as independent states, might have been able to preserve some areas of cooperation and collaboration.

The rapidly unfolding events of the summer of 1946—first the acceptance of the Cabinet Mission Plan by both the League and the Congress, then the unilateral rejection of some of its features by Nehru, and finally the League's total withdrawal from negotiations—left the Muslim leadership of the central provinces convinced that they had to work for the establishment of Pakistan. Jawaharlal Nehru's clumsy handling of the discussions with the Cabinet Mission confirmed the fears of these Muslims that their political, economic, and social rights would not be protected in a Hindu India.

The Muslims of Punjab and Bengal

The summer of 1946 was an important milestone on the way to Pakistan, but the creation of an independent Muslim state would require support from the provinces—especially the populous provinces of Punjab and Bengal—for the idea of Pakistan. Right up to this time, these provinces had withheld such support; now they quickly climbed on the Pakistan bandwagon. The circumstances that converted Punjab and Bengal to the idea of Pakistan were very different from those that had persuaded the Muslims of north-central India. Religion was the most important reason for Punjab; social reasons constituted the main impetus for Bengal. In these reasons lie the seeds for much that was to happen later in the areas of British India that now form the states of Pakistan and Bangladesh. Since this study is concerned with Pakistan, it will focus on the process that resulted in the acceptance by Pakistan's indigenous population of the concept of an independent Muslim state, with only a passing reference to the case of Bangladesh.

Islam does not separate religion from state. In the strict meaning of the term— at least in the sense that this term has come to be understood following Ayatollah Khomeini's revolution in Iran—Mughul India was not a Muslim state. But the Mughuls themselves did not always keep the affairs of the mosque separate from those of the state. Whenever and wherever religion was strong—in particular, whenever the institutions of religion were stronger than those of the state—the Mughuls were happy to bring about a fusion between the two. Such a fusion occurred in the rural area of the Punjab and other northwestern provinces of Mughul India. In the Punjab, the *khanqas* (local shrines generally run by hereditary leaders called *sajjada nashins*) thus came to be integrated into the complex system of administrative and political controls that the Mughul Court operated from Delhi. As one historian has noted, "By the end of the Mughul period, therefore, the religious influence of many of the *sajjada nashins* as custodians of the local outposts of Islam had become closely associated with their political influence as local outposts of the Muslim state."[10]

The British did not disturb this arrangement, continuing instead to rely upon the support of the landlords and *sajjada nashins* for controlling the countryside. This proved to be a wise policy. When the Muslims of the north-central provinces mutinied against the British *raj*, their co-religionists in the northwest not only re-mained loyal but also helped to put down the rebellion. But the northwestern provinces could not have remained impervious to the ferment that was taking place in the areas to their south—in Delhi and in the old Mughul province of Oudh. Within this ferment, the Muslims faced a choice between two divergent paths—a religious one, with the Muslims returning to the ways of Islam now that they had lost the umbrella of the Mughuls; and an adaptational one, in which the Muslims would be called upon to recognize and adjust to the changes that had oc-curred in their environment. Given the fact that the Muslims of Delhi and Oudh constituted an urban community with a high level of literacy, albeit one involving the Persian and Urdu languages, it is not surprising that the modernists under Sir Sayyid Ahmed Khan triumphed over those who sought the revival of Islam.

Having failed in the north-central provinces, the revivalists turned to Punjab and Sindh, where the Chisti Muslim order had founded a number of *khanqas* in the countryside. Had the British dismantled the arrangement that the Mughuls had used to bring their rule to the northwestern provinces, the revivalists would have caused a great deal of trouble for the *raj*. But the British had retained the sys-tem, and the new *khanqas* were obliged not to work against the best interests of the established order. Consequently, Muslim politics in the northwestern provinces remained dormant for more than a century after the incorporation of Sindh, Punjab, and the Northwestern Frontier Province into British India.

Jinnah and the Muslim League misread this situation. Being urban, modern, and relatively secular, they showed considerable distaste for the established order in the northwestern provinces. Whatever support they won was from the small community of urban Muslims of this area. Given that this part of British India was much less urbanized than the parts to which Jinnah and many of his more important colleagues belonged, their performance in the elections of 1937 is not surprising. As we have already seen, the League was able to win only one of the 87 seats reserved for Muslims in the Punjab legislature.

Jinnah's failure to obtain constitutional concessions from the Congress—his failure, especially, to get Muslim Leaguers included in the administration formed by the Congress after the election of 1937, combined with Jawaharlal Nehru's about-face on the proposals submitted by the Cabinet Mission—seemed to have convinced the Muslim leaders that their only alternative was to campaign for the establishment of Pakistan, that such a campaign could succeed only if the Muslims in the Muslim majority areas gave it their support, and that this support could be gained only on the grounds of religion. Thus, the failure of the Cabinet Mission Plan prompted the Muslim League to change its political language and to adopt a religious idiom. The protection of the economic, social, and political rights of the Muslims of India was no longer at issue; the concern now was the provision of a safe haven for the followers of Islam. With the use of this idiom, the Muslim revivalists were able to provide Jinnah and his Muslim League with an altogether new image. Jamaat Ali Shah, a prominent religious leader, answered criticisms of Jinnah by saying: "Think of Jinnah Sahib whatever you like, but I say that Jinnah Sahib is 'Wali Allah' [servant of God]."[11]

Even the nonreligious leadership took up the new slogan. Shaukat Hayat Khan, the son of Sir Sikander Hayat Khan who, as chief minister of Punjab, had kept Jinnah and the Muslim League at bay, found himself declaring that Pakistan would have a "government of the *Quran.*" The conversion of Punjab, and, with it, that of the other provinces of the northwest, was complete. Consequently, the League won a comfortable electoral victory in 1946. Moreover, this victory, along with the turn of events in Bengal, assured the Muslims the establishment of the state of Pakistan. As David Gilmartin has pointed out, "The most vital religious support for Pakistan came from the *sajjada nashins* of the revival shrines, who had long sought an outlet for expressing their religious concern in the political arena."[12] In the election of 1946, the Muslim League won 54 seats in the Punjab, equal to 65 percent of the total allotted to the Muslim population of the province. This was indeed a great triumph; nine years earlier, in the election of 1937, the League had gained only one seat.

The Muslims of the Northeastern Provinces

Social considerations prompted the Muslims of the north-central provinces to demand the establishment of Pakistan, as a separate homeland for the Muslims of India; religion, especially in its revivalist form, persuaded the Muslims of the northwestern provinces to embrace this idea a few years later; and a growing feeling of social deprivation was finally to win over the Muslims of the northeastern provinces.

The economic situation of the Bengali and Assamese Muslims was considerably weaker than that of the Muslims of other communities and was to become the main reason for their conversion to the idea of Muslim separatism. Now wise to the ways of Muslim politics in India, Jinnah was prepared to tailor his approach to the different circumstances of his co-religionists in different parts of the country. The large Bengali and Assami Muslim peasantry wanted protection from the predatory practices of the Hindu landlords. Jinnah's Muslim League was prepared to promise such protection. This it did by bringing into its fold A. K. Fazlul Haq, *Sher-e-Bangla* (the tiger of Bengal). He was to become one of the co-sponsors of the Lahore Resolution, which demanded the setting up of a separate homeland for the Muslims of India. But advocating "partition" as a way of protecting the rights of a minority community or the rights of a majority community if it was economically underprivileged—as were the Muslims in Bengal—was not something new for Fazlul Haq. He was one of the several politicians who had earlier convinced the British that the partition of Bengal into two provinces—the east dominated by the Muslims and the west dominated by the Hindus—was the only way to improve the economic circumstances of this Muslim community.

The British accepted the demand and Bengal was partitioned in 1905, a move that was to be bitterly opposed by the Hindu community. A movement was launched to get the British to annul the partition; it was called *swadeshi*, or "own country" agitation, because it encouraged not only the boycotting of British goods but also the production and use of Indian-made products. The *swadeshi* movement succeeded in its objective, and the British administration reunited the two parts of Bengal. Fazlul Haq was unhappy:

> I can assure the [British] officials that the Muslim community of Bengal can well survive the effects of even the most unsympathetic administrative measures and they will also survive the injustice done to them by the annulment of Partition. . . . I refer to the annulment, because I wish to protest against the manner in which the feelings of an entire community had been trampled under feet in utter indifference to the principles which have all along guided British rule in their country.[13]

The annulment was a bitter blow to the aspirations of the Muslims of Bengal. They had to wait another six and a half decades before they were able to attain what they maintained to be their legitimate right. The emergence of Bangladesh as an independent state in December 1971 gave the Bengalis what they had long aspired for: a political entity that allowed full expression of Bengali Muslim nationalism. But before this could happen, India had to be partitioned first on religious grounds. Only with the creation of Pakistan in 1947 was the emergence of Bangladesh made possible in 1971.

The annulment of partition provided the Bengali Muslim community with a political cause that lay dormant for nearly three decades. It was only in the late 1930s that the Bengali Muslims once again began to think in terms of partition and separation—this time not only for themselves, however, but for all Muslims of British India. Fazlul Haq joined Jinnah in drafting and sponsoring the Lahore Resolution. In presenting the resolution to the 1940 Lahore meeting, he reminded his audience of the long tradition of Muslim nationalism among the people of Bengal: "Though I am leading a coalition government in Bengal, I am Muslim first and Bengalee afterwards. . . . It was in Bengal in the year 1906 that the flag of the Muslim League was first unfurled, and now it is my privilege as the leader of Bengal to move the resolution for homeland of the Muslims from the self-same platform of the Muslim League."[14] The passage of the resolution on March 23, 1940, was the first step toward both the partition of British India and the emergence of Pakistan as an independent Muslim state. It was also the first step toward the establishment of Bangladesh, an independent country for the Muslims of Bengal.

Pakistan: The Unfinished Task

The state of Pakistan, therefore, was the product of a number of different aspirations expressed quite unambiguously by three rather different Muslim communities of British India. It was the extraordinary political genius of Mohammad Ali Jinnah that made possible the accommodation of these aspirations within one movement. Now the Bengalis, the Punjabis, and the Muslims of the United Provinces could work together resolutely toward one political objective—the attainment of Pakistan. For seven years—from the passage of the Lahore Resolution in 1940 to independence in 1947—all differences were brushed aside as Jinnah led his Muslim League to electoral victories in all the provinces that were important for the future state of Pakistan.

But what kind of country did the Muslims create for themselves in the old territory of British India? The new state was meant to achieve different things for different people: emancipation from the Hindu landlords of the peasantry of Bengal and Assam; the creation of new economic and political opportunities for the frustrated urban Muslim classes of Delhi, Bombay, and the United and Central Provinces; and establishment of an Islamic state for the *pirs* and *sajjada nashins* of Sindh, Punjab, and the Northwest Frontier Province. Could such aspirations find one political expression? Could a state be created to meet such different objectives? The answers emerged over the next few decades as Pakistan struggled to find a political meaning for itself. In the words of novelist Salman Rushdie:

> It is well-known that the term 'Pakistan,' an acronym, was originally thought up in England by a group of Muslim intellectuals. P for the Punjabis, A for the Afghans, K for the Kashmirs, S for Sind and the 'tan,' they say, for Balochistan. (No mention of the East West, you notice: Bangladesh never got its name in the title, and so eventually, it took the hint and seceded from the secessionists. . . .) So, it was a word born in exile which then went East, was borne-across or translated, and imposed itself on history; a returning migrant, settling down on partitioned land, forming a palimpsest on the past. A palimpsest obscures what lies beneath. To build Pakistan it was necessary to cover up Indian history, to deny that Indian centuries lay just beneath the surface.[15]

But the task was not easy; to this day it remains unfinished. Bangladesh—the eastern wing of a two-winged country—left in 1971 following a bitter conflict and civil war, and the western wing, modern-day Pakistan, once again began the arduous task of nation building. That task remains unfinished even as Pakistan celebrates its fifty-first birthday.

The Land and Its People

The geography of this new Pakistan helped in the task of nation building. Even though some of its borders remain undefined and disputed, its four provinces are contiguous to one another. This was not the case for Pakistan of 1947–1971, divided as it was between two roughly equal halves, one to the northwest and the other to the northeast of India. The center of gravity in such a fractured Pakistan, with so much Indian territory in between, did not lie within its own borders. It lay in India. The consequence was an excessive preoccupation with relations with India and an almost obsessive fear about Indian intentions toward it—factors that dictated not only Pakistan's external relations but its internal politics as well. The departure of Bangladesh from the Pakistan Union has dramatically changed the new country's geography and has moved the center of gravity to within the country's borders. Pakistan now behaves with somewhat greater confidence and assurance in conducting its relations with the outside world and in organizing its internal affairs.

This is not to say that a geographically contiguous Pakistan is linguistically and culturally homogeneous, however. There is a tendency on the part of the people of Punjab and those of Karachi—two communities that continue to dominate politics and Pakistan's economy—to avoid confronting the heterogeneity of Pakistani society, because the acceptance of such a notion would have a number of important political implications. However, the rise of Sindhi nationalism in the 1970s and 1980s compelled even these communities to recognize the social and economic divergence among the various groups that constituted the Pakistani society. As Sindhi nationalism became progressively more militant, it evoked a corresponding response from Punjab and the *muhajir* community of Karachi and Hyderabad. The *muhajirs* organized themselves into a highly effective political organization called the *Muhajir Quami Mahaz* (MQM), the National Refugee Front, that won all but one seat from Karachi in the National Assembly elections of 1988 and 1990. And the conflict between the central government of Prime Minister Benazir Bhutto and the Punjab administration of Chief Minister Mian Nawaz Sharif—throughout the twenty months the PPP government was in power (December 1988 to August 1990)—produced a powerful Punjabi backlash that surprised both Bhutto and her opponents in the elections of 1990. As discussed in Chapter 3, the 1997 elections practically finished Bhutto's Pakistan People's Party as a political force in Punjab, Pakistan's largest province and the one in which the People's Party initially developed and flourished.

The emergence of militant ethnic politics in Pakistan in the 1970s and 1980s, which caused a great deal of social and economic disruption, may paradoxically have made the task of nation building easier. The leaders of Pakistan could no longer pretend that the departure of Bengal produced a cohesive and homogeneous society that could be easily molded into a nation. The rise of the MQM, the reinvigoration of Punjabi nationalism, and the attention being given to the demands of the Pathan and Baloch nationalists have brought to the surface the forces that were initially suppressed by the Pakistan movement in the 1940s and the conflict between East and West Pakistan in the 1950s and 1960s. There is now a clearer definition of the obstacles that have to be crossed before Pakistan becomes a nation.

The heterogeneity the Pakistanis now clearly see in their society is a fact of history that goes back more than 5,000 years, even beyond the well-known Indus civilization. The recently discovered city at Rehman Dheri, north of Dera Ismail Khan, lying just west of the Indus, "is thought to have been in existence in 3200 B.C., a few hundred years before the cities of the Indus civilization, and to have been similar in culture to contemporaneous cities at Hissar and elsewhere in Iran, at Mundi Gjak in Afghanistan, and sites in Turkmenia (USSR)."[16] The Indus civilization that succeeded this early culture survived 800 years, from 2500 B.C. to 1700 B.C., and covered most of what is Pakistan today. This civilization manifested itself in at least two metropolitan centers—one at Mohenjo-Daro (near the modern city of Larkana in Sindh Province) and the other in Harappa (which lies between the Punjab cities of Lahore and Multan).

The Indus civilization appears to have suddenly vanished—at least that seems to be the conclusion drawn by archaeologists from the present state of knowledge. If its disappearance was indeed sudden, the implication is that a natural calamity occurred—perhaps a flood in the Indus Valley that washed away the many towns and cities that must have been part of this civilization. On the other hand, if the civilization disappeared over a period of time that stretched over several decades—maybe even a century—then the decay might have been brought about by soil deterioration. The soil's inability to produce enough food to sustain a certain level of population would have sent the people of the Indus Valley looking for new land.

Whatever the explanation for the disappearance of the Indus civilization, an intriguing hiatus exists between the prehistory of Pakistan and the dawn of its classical history. New archaeological findings, when they are made, will eventually close this gap and provide some further clues to the disparities in cultures and languages that persist to this day. Pakistan's classical history began with the conquest by Cyrus, king of Persia, and the founding of the Gandhara Empire that centered around Taxila, about twenty miles directly north of Islamabad. Cyrus brought his troops by land in the fifth century B.C., but later Persian incursions were made from the sea, using the Indus River to navigate toward the northwest. By the time of Alexander the Great's expedition in 327 B.C., the Persians controlled an area roughly contiguous to present-day Pakistan.

A curious development occurred after the Greek conquest of northern India: The southern section of the Indus Valley—the provinces of Sindh and Balochistan—came to be dominated by kingdoms centered around central India, whereas the northern sections—the provinces of Punjab and Northwest Frontier—were absorbed by the kingdoms of Indo-Greek origin. This division of the Indus Valley was curious in that it had little historical precedent. The natural tendency of all preceding civilizations and empires was to encompass the entire Indus plain. Perhaps even stranger is the fact that even after the Islamization of the area that now makes up Pakistan, this tendency was not corrected. The Pathan rulers of Afghanistan marched across the Indus Valley and the valleys of its tributary rivers toward central India, rather than down toward the sea. The Mughuls—successors to the Delhi Afghans—took the same route, from Kabul to Delhi, and only later did they attempt to bring the rest of the Indus Valley under their sway. The brief Sikh interregnum between the Mughuls and the British was made possible by the spread of political influence that moved in the opposite direction, from eastern Punjab northwestward toward Peshawar and Kabul. The British followed the Sikh route into modern-day Pakistan; they came from Delhi to Lahore, and from there they went on to Rawalpindi and Peshawar. It was quite a bit later that they moved into Sindh and Balochistan. When the British finally acquired Sindh, they preferred to administer it from Bombay rather than from Lahore, thus reinforcing the northwest-southeast political split of the Indus Valley.

The important political legacy left by this split was corrected only partially by the migration of millions of Indian Muslims who continue to call themselves *muhajirs,* or refugees, into the southern parts of Pakistan. It is difficult to understand why such an important fact of history has not attracted the attention of scholars. With no scholarly explanation available for this tantalizing break in the historical pattern, what can be attempted is, at best, speculative interpretation.

The question is why Pakistan's extraordinary geographical endowment was so neglected by the rulers and the people who held sway over it during most of recorded history. The civilizations that existed in prehistory appear to have exploited the commercial and military potential of the Indus River system. The system is extensive; viewed from the point where the Indus enters the Arabian sea, it has the shape of a fan, with six major tributaries reaching back into the foothills of the Himalayas. From River Kabul in the north to the Indus itself, and down to the south from Jhelum, Chenab, Ravi, Beas, and Sutlej, these rivers spread over an area of nearly 100,000 square miles. The land between them is flat and easily accessible, and the flow of the rivers is gentle and therefore easily manageable for both irrigation and navigation. For enterprising people, the rivers would have provided a remarkable network of communication and commerce; indeed, with this network as its basis, the entire area could have evolved into one political entity.

Why were these waters not used for the purposes just described? The only time the Indus system was used for navigational purposes occurred during the expeditions into India of the Persian kings and Alexander the Great, but even then the routes of advance—and to some extent also those of retreat—were over land rather than over water. Six centuries later, the Arab conquerors of Sindh also used the Indus, but not to its full potential. There were perhaps two reasons for this neglect of the rivers. The displacement of the partly maritime powers of Greece and Persia by the land-based Afghans and the Mongols from Central Asia may have caused the change from the use of rivers to that of roads for bringing in armies and administering the conquered territories. Or the destruction of the agricultural potential of the lower Indus Valley may have been responsible for the neglect of the river network. Conquering hordes did not bring in their own food supplies;

they depended on local output. They may have crossed the Indus and its tributaries and headed southeast toward the Gangetic plains because food was available there for their armies. Whatever the reason, the Indus Valley remained split for more than 2,000 years.

The split was accentuated by a system of communication that developed over the centuries. Its foundation was laid by Emperor Sher Shah Suri, who drove the Mughuls out of India for a long enough time to build what came to be called the Grand Trunk Road. The road connected the Khyber Pass with the Bay of Bengal—a distance of nearly 1,500 miles. The road, by linking Peshawar, Lahore, Amritsar, Delhi, Agra, Lukhnow, Allahabad, Patna, and Murshadabad, became the major artery of communication in North India. Using the Grand Trunk Road as the spine, the Sikh and British rulers of India built an impressive network of roads linking villages to market towns, market towns to cities, and military cantonments to the "forward areas." Even the difficult geographical terrain in the northwest was breached. But the network that was created had two different orientations, thus pointing up the differences between the northwestern and southeastern sections of the Indus Valley. The road system serving the Punjab and the Northwest Frontier Province had a northwest-southeastern direction, whereas that in Sindh and Balochistan had a northeast-southwest orientation. The two met in southern Punjab, in and around the city of Multan. Not surprisingly, therefore, of all the major cities of Pakistan, it is Multan that most easily and comfortably straddles the country's various cultures and languages. Saraiki, the language of the Multan region, is a hybrid of Punjabi, Sindhhi, and Balochi.

The railway system built by the British followed the highways. The main railway line ran from Peshawar in the northwest to Lahore and then on to Delhi and down the Ganges Valley. The Indus Valley was served by a subsidiary system, connecting the principal cities of Sindh (Karachi, Hyderabad, Sukkur) with the main urban centers of Punjab. But the Indus system was used lightly compared to the Peshawar-Lahore-Delhi line. Consequently, the port of Karachi, despite its proximity to Punjab, did not develop into the main port of entry for the northern provinces of British India; instead, this function continued to be served by Bombay.

Pakistan's geography and physical infrastructure—its rivers, ports, roads, and railways—did very little to integrate the Punjabis, Sindhis, Pathans, and Balochis into one nation. Even independence in 1947, and the integration of the four provinces into a single administrative unit of West Pakistan in 1955, failed to bridge the social, cultural, and economic gaps among the different nationalities. Integration of the economy was also slow. In short, geography did not help the process of nation building.

Art and literature, too, did little to unify and integrate. Although Urdu was adopted as the national language, it was not the principal language of the majority of the country's population. As shown in Table 1.1, Urdu was spoken by less than 8 percent of the population, whereas Saraiki, regarded as a secondary language, was

TABLE 1.1   Distribution of Households by Language, 1981 (in percentages)

	Punjabi	Pushto	Sindhi	Saraiki	Urdu	Balochi	Other
Punjab	78.7	0.8	0.1	14.9	4.3	0.6	0.6
Sindh	7.7	3.1	52.4	2.3	22.6	4.5	7.4
Northwest Frontier	1.1	68.3	0.1	4.0	0.8	0.1	25.6
Balochistan	2.2	25.1	8.3	3.1	1.4	36.3	23.6
Pakistan	48.2	13.1	11.8	9.8	7.6	3.0	6.5

Source: Government of Pakistan, *Statistical Pocket Book of Pakistan 1984* (Islamabad: Federal Bureau of Statistics, 1984), p. 61.

used by nearly one-tenth of the households. For two of the four provinces, the Northwest Frontier and Balochistan, the use of Urdu was insignificant.

Largely owing to state policy, "regional languages" (an inaccurate term, in the first place, as many of these languages were spoken all over the country) did not develop. In this respect, the situation in Pakistan was, and continues to be, totally different from that of India. The administrative reorganization of India in the 1950s along linguistic lines gave a tremendous boost to the regional languages, and a rich literature developed in them, especially after independence. The adoption of English as the working language of the union and state governments also lent support to the development of what is now called "Indian English" as well as to that of a new genre, Indian English literature. These developments did not take place in Pakistan, however. Urdu remained the main language of literature, but because its use was limited, Urdu literature produced very little of significance. The only exception was something Pakistanis call "protest literature," in which authors could express their deepest feelings through Urdu's fund of traditional poetic symbolism. Poetry became a powerful medium for conveying political messages, with Faiz Ahmad Faiz and Habib Jalib serving as two of its most influential practitioners.

Television, which went through a period of remarkable development in the 1960s and early 1970s, served for a while as a medium of expression for both literary and political impulses. "Television drama" attracted a good deal of talent and became a popular form not only in Urdu but also in Sindhi, Pushto, and Balochi. With the resurgence of Islamic fundamentalism, however, this art form was to suffer a serious setback. Since the late 1970s, state-controlled television has been used extensively for airing political and religious messages. But the use of television for these purposes as well as the government's liberal import policy had an unanticipated consequence: the extensive use of video cassettes for home entertainment. Even though the government attempted to stop the import of video cassettes, the presence of millions of Pakistanis in the Middle East, Europe, and the United States made it very difficult to enforce import controls. Video cassettes found their way into the remotest parts of the country as it was from these parts that the first wave of migration to the Middle East had originally come. Hundreds of video stores began to operate all over the country, not only in the major cities but also in small towns and villages. These stores stocked the latest Indian, U.S., and English movies as well as U.S. television programs.

The advent of the video cassette and strict enforcement by the government of morality laws led to the virtual demise of the once-active indigenous film industry. This industry had developed rapidly in the 1950s and 1960s in Karachi and Lahore and, at one point, was among the ten major film industries in the world. A code of censorship existed even then and was enforced with diligence, but it focused mainly on politics and less on moral issues. In the 1980s, the government revised the code as part of its Islamization program and began to enforce strict standards concerning story lines, costumes, music scores, and the onscreen relationship between the sexes. All this occurred while the Indian film industry was becoming more liberal and sophisticated. The Pakistani moviemakers were not able to withstand this competition, and dozens of studios were forced to close.

The fact that Pakistan inherited a fractured legal system from the British further complicated the task of nation building. The British adopted an eclectic approach in developing the legal infrastructure for the areas that were to later constitute the state of Pakistan. In the penal area they brought in new legislation to define crime and punishment, to regulate criminal proceedings, and to guide the courts with respect to the admissibility of evidence presented. The Penal Code, the Criminal Procedure Code, and the Evidence Act together became the backbone of the criminal system the British set up in the provinces of Punjab, Sindh, and the Northwest Frontier, but some geographical areas were excluded from the application of these codes. For instance, tribes in the Frontier Province and in the princely states of Balochistan were allowed to continue trying criminal offenses by *jirgas,* assemblies of elders, which meted out traditional punishments for the acts the tribal societies treated as criminal. Some of the tribal practices followed Quranic injunctions and some had even deeper roots, having been passed down from generation to generation since pre-Islamic times.

Even in the settled provinces of Punjab, Sindh, and the Northwest Frontier, the British did not separate the judiciary from the executive at the lower level of the legal and administrative systems. District officers also acted as Class I magistrates with powers to try all criminal cases that carried punishments of less than two years. These officers, most of whom came from the elitist Indian Civil Service, also adjudicated civil and revenue (financial) cases. The legal system, therefore, served to bestow the civil bureaucracy with vast powers, which the British used to keep India firmly within its grasp.

In the sphere of family law, the British were even more accommodating of traditional practices. They gave the Muslims, Hindus, Sikhs, and other religious groups the option to follow their own beliefs with respect to marriage, family relations, and inheritance. In defining property rights, the British were also willing to respect religious beliefs and interests. And they were not beyond protecting the interests of some religious communities by bringing in restraining legislation against the members of other communities. The most important legislation of this kind was the Land Alienation Act of 1901, which protected the Muslim peasantry of Punjab from Hindu moneylenders. Punjab's agricultural land was mostly in the hands of the Muslims, but a large number of Muslim peasants had become heavily indebted to Hindu moneylenders. The peasants' inability to service their debts began to result in large-scale foreclosures and consequent transfers of agricultural property from Muslims to Hindus. The British administration was concerned with this development because of the potential for religious conflicts, and they used the alienation act to prohibit nonagriculturalists from acquiring agricultural property, thereby saving the Muslim peasantry from succumbing to financial pressures.

The first important change in Pakistan's inherited legal system came with the promulgation of the Muslim Family Laws Ordinance in 1961—a part of the social revolution the government of General Ayub Khan instituted. The ordinance required every marriage under the Islamic law to be registered, every dissolution of marriage to be similarly recorded, and every case of a subsequent marriage while the previous marriage subsisted to be approved by an official Arbitration Council. According to a contemporary historian, "this piece of legislation . . . represents a significant step in the social evolution of Pakistan."[17]

The next major change in the country's legal system was made by General Zia ul-Haq's military government, but Zia's intent was different from Ayub Khan's. Whereas Ayub Khan had attempted to modernize Pakistan, Zia wanted to Islamize it. Ayub Khan concerned himself with those sections of the legal system he considered backward; among these, the most important were the laws pertaining to family relationships. Zia wanted a more sweeping change. Both ran into difficulties: Ayub Khan with the conservative elements in the society, Zia ul-Haq with those who regarded themselves as more progressive. Both left lasting impressions on the society and its legal system. Despite Zia's efforts at Islamization, Ayub Khan's Family Laws Ordinance remained on the books. And in spite of the opposition of the liberal forces, Zia's attempt to bring about greater conformity between the legal system and the requirements of Islam partially succeeded.

The most lasting legacy of Zia in this area is likely to be the institutionalization of the means to test the "repugnancy" of all laws with reference to Quranic injunctions. Until Zia's administration, the question of repugnancy had remained effectively unsettled. Pakistan's three constitutions (1956, 1962, and 1973) had preambles promising that all laws would conform to the Quran and Sunnah. The question of exactly what was meant by conformity and repugnancy was deliberately left vague because Islamic scholars since Prophet Muhammad had failed to define the exact meaning of an Islamic law. Instead of worrying about the meaning of Islamic laws, Zia set up institutions not only to test the validity of actual laws and pending legislation but also to practice Islamic laws. He created a parallel legal institution, the Sharia courts, that could try criminal, civil, and family cases according to traditional Islamic law rather than on the basis of the laws on the books. At the very apex of the legal system he established a Shariat bench that had the power to pronounce judgment on the Islamic purity of any piece of legislation referred to it.

Other legislation introduced by the Zia government significantly changed the administration of justice for a number of crimes. The Hudood Ordinance, promulgated in 1979, covered adultery, rape and prostitution (*zina*), bearing false testimony (*qazf*), theft, and drinking of alcohol. It prescribed Islamic punishments such as the amputation of hands for theft, stoning of offenders for sexual crimes, and lashes for consuming alcohol. Although none of these punishments were actually carried out in the twenty year period the ordinance has been on the books, its promulgation had the unanticipated effect of galvanizing a large segment of the country's female population.[18] (See Chapter 5 for a discussion of this subject.)

Prime Minister Mian Nawaz Sharif introduced a series of sweeping legal changes during his second term. The decisive victory of the Pakistan Muslim League in the February 1997 elections gave the Sharif government sufficient majority in both houses of the national legislature—the Senate and the National Assembly—to pass constitutional amendments that required two-thirds of majority for passage. The thirteenth amendment passed in April 1997, six weeks after Nawaz Sharif had assumed office, took away the president's power to dissolve the National Assembly and dismiss the prime minister. The fourteenth amendment, passed a few days later, barred members of the National Assembly and the provincial assemblies from crossing the floor by moving from one party to the other.

The most drastic legal change came with the introduction of the fifteenth amendment in August 1998. It authorized the "federal government . . . to take steps to enforce the Shariah, to establish *salat* [the form of prayer], to administer *zakat* [Islamic taxes], to promote *amr bil ma'roof* and *nahi anil munkar* [to prescribe what is right and forbid what is wrong], to eradicate corruption at all levels and to provide substantial socio-economic justice, in accordance with the principles laid down in the Holy Quran and Sunnah." The federal government was authorized to "issue directives for the implementation of these provisions . . . notwithstanding anything contained in the Constitution, any law or judgment of any Court." The opposition and the Human Rights Commission were quick to point out right after the amendment was moved in the National Assembly that the proposed constitutional change was aimed at giving dictatorial powers to the federal government in the name of religion. The introduction of the amendment did not find favor with *Dawn*, Pakistan's premier English-language newspaper. In an editorial published on August 30, 1998, a day after the government introduced the bill in the parliament, *Dawn* asked why Pakistani leaders continued to ignore the lessons of history. "The formula is a tired and tested one: when in trouble, mount the rooftops and in front of a disbelieving world raise the banner of Islam. By tabling the Fifteenth Constitutional Amendment which seeks to make the

Quran and the Sunnah the supreme law of the country, Prime Minister Nawaz Sharif has set out on the same slippery road, oblivious of the fact that other Pakistani rulers when beset by troubles which they could not handle, did the same but without obtaining what they had hoped to achieve."[19]

The picture that emerges from this quick overview is of an extremely heterogeneous society that is being persuaded to conform to a uniform linguistic, literary, cultural, moral, and legal standard, although the reaction to this attempt has not been severe given that the state has used persuasion rather than coercion. The code of behavior enshrined in the Quran and the Hadith has been used as the basis for this change, but the results of these efforts for the state cannot be viewed as highly satisfactory. The people might have been willing to respond to the teachings of Islam, but the remarkable openness of Pakistani society has served as a major distraction.

As is I discuss in a later chapter, Pakistan's educational sector is developing in a way that might introduce two very different sets of values: one liberal and oriented toward the west, the other looking to Islam for guidance. The effort by the government of Nawaz Sharif to introduce Islam into the society in an explicit way may encourage the conflict between these value systems to surface. It should also be emphasized that the Pakistani society has become open because of the emigration of millions of Pakistanis since the early 1970s. Despite the oil slump of the 1980s and the crisis created by Iraq's invasion of Kuwait in 1990, there remains a large pool of Pakistani workers in the Middle East. Estimates differ, but some 2 to 3 million Pakistanis—between 2.5 and 3.5 percent of the population—now live abroad. In terms of the proportion of total population, these Pakistanis constitute one of the largest groups of expatriates in the world. They are also affluent, having benefited enormously from the Middle East's turn of economic fortunes. They retain close contacts with their families in Pakistan. In short, they exercise economic, social, cultural, and political influences on Pakistan—influences that have grown considerably but have been neither fully appreciated nor adequately analyzed. These influences will have a profound impact on the development of the Pakistani nation and, indeed, constitute a recurrent theme of this work.

2

POLITICAL DEVELOPMENT: CONTINUING SEARCH FOR STABILITY

Pakistan achieved independence on August 14, 1947. On the morning of that day, Lord Mountbatten, the last viceroy of British India, swore in Mohammad Ali Jinnah as Pakistan's first governor-general. Three days earlier, on August 11, Jinnah had presided over the first meeting of the Constituent Assembly—an assembly of fewer than seventy people entrusted with the task of drawing up a legal framework for the new country. During most of that week, Jinnah, as the president of the Muslim League, had received hundreds of politicians at his residence. In a special meeting of the Constituent Assembly, the title of Quaid-e-Azam (The Great Leader) was conferred on Jinnah.

It was clear from all these activities that Jinnah interpreted the governor-generalship and the presidency of the Constituent Assembly as substantive jobs. They were not to be treated as honors bestowed on a man who had completed the task of founding an independent state for the Muslims of British India. That job done, Jinnah now turned to the task of providing the new country with political, economic, and administrative structures. The vigor that he displayed during this week of independence was remarkable not only on account of his age—born on December 25, 1876, Jinnah was now close to seventy-one years old—but also because, by August 1947, the disease from which he had secretly suffered had now reached an advanced stage. Not even his close political associates—including, perhaps, Prime Minister Liaqat Ali Khan—knew of the gravity of the governor-general's illness.

In retrospect, it made a great deal of sense for Mohammad Ali Jinnah to keep the news of his illness from his political associates when it was first revealed to him in 1945. Knowledge about Jinnah's illness might have slowed the process of British withdrawal from India that Louis Mountbatten had initiated soon after his arrival. Lord Mountbatten presided over the dissolution of British India in the conviction that it was in the interest of the Hindus as well as the Muslims to keep India united. His belief was shared by the Indian National Congress, which was the party of Gandhi, Nehru, and the majority of the Indian Hindu community. But Jinnah felt differently. He continued to argue with great passion—a passion that was viewed by his political opponents as characteristic stubbornness on the part of a man who could never compromise—that the Muslims of India would get less than a fair deal in a country in which they constituted only a small minority. As Mountbatten was later to admit, had he and the leadership of the Congress party known about Jinnah's illness, they would have played for time. Instead, after Jinnah's intransigence had convinced Mountbatten about the inevitability of India's partition, he advanced the date of independence from June 1948 to August 1947.

It is intriguing to speculate whether Pakistan would have emerged as a country if Mountbatten had kept to the original schedule. In any event, by the summer of 1948 the tuberculosis from which Jinnah suffered had taken its toll, and Jinnah had withdrawn to the hills of Balochistan to await death. It can be argued, though, that the social and economic dynamic responsible for much of the enthusiasm behind the Pakistan Movement would have continued to find expression even if Jinnah had died before the idea of an independent Muslim state had gained full acceptance by the British and the Hindus.

The same kind of argument can be made against another type of speculation: whether Pakistan would have found political stability if Jinnah, in the manner of Gandhi, had left the process of institution building—in particular the process of constitution making—in the hands of his lieutenants. Nehru in India did not have to wait for Gandhi's death before taking full political and administrative command. Sworn in as prime minister on August 15, 1947, Nehru had all the powers that that office implied. Liaqat Ali Khan, his counterpart in Pakistan, had little authority by comparison. Liaqat Ali Khan was to wait for another thirteen months—Jinnah died on September 11, 1948—but the mantle of political leadership that finally fell on his shoulders was much smaller than the one Jinnah had worn. The transfer of effective power to Liaqat Ali Khan during Jinnah's lifetime might have advanced the process of Pakistan's political development. Jinnah would have been at hand to persuade Liaqat's colleagues to follow the leadership of Jinnah's designated successor, just as Gandhi had done in India when Nehru was challenged by Sardar Vallahbai Patel.

As it happened, Liaqat found it very difficult to succeed Jinnah. Of the three jobs that Jinnah had held, only one—the presidency of the Muslim League—went to Liaqat. The other two went to two politicians from Bengal, Pakistan's "eastern wing." Khwaja Nazimuddin became the governor-general, and Maulvi Tamizuddin Ahmad was elected president of the Constituent Assembly. Moreover, by September 1948, some of the enthusiasm with which Pakistan's citizens had greeted the emergence of the country had dissipated. Bengal in the east and the smaller provinces of Northwest Frontier and Balochistan in the west had begun to show some restiveness at being excluded from decisionmaking by the groups that dominated politics in the capital city of Karachi. Thus, whereas Nehru had made use of postindependence euphoria to provide India with a constitution, Liaqat was still discussing the "basic principles" of constitution making in Pakistan.

This explanation of political instability in Pakistan—a situation that persists—puts great store on the acts of individuals and not enough on the dynamic underlying the political conflict that continues to this day. The explanation therefore calls to mind Mountbatten's belief that he could have prevented Pakistan's creation had he waited for Jinnah's death. Mountbatten failed to appreciate the force of the tension that existed between various religious and social groups in British India. Likewise, a number of scholars who have emphasized the role of individuals in shaping Pakistan's political history would do well to recognize that the area of discretion available to these individuals was not always very wide. Pakistan's history has been dominated by a succession of strong men; it has also been punctuated by political upheavals brought about by the attempts of these strong men to move against the wishes of more powerful and articulate groups in the society. Had Liaqat assumed political stewardship in August 1947 rather than thirteen months later, the drafting of the constitution might have proceeded with less difficulty. On the other hand, it is unlikely that this event alone would have produced political stability in Pakistan. The search for the cause of persistent instability has to go much deeper; it can be found only in the social, economic, and political dynamics of the very diverse society that, in 1947, with unexpected suddenness became the new state of Pakistan.

The Roots of Diversity

Diversity, initially, was caused by the movement of some 14 million people across the boundary that separated Pakistan from India during the 1947 partition of British India. Pakistan lost 6 million people and, in return, gained 8 million refugees from India. These refugees constituted two different streams. By far the most important of these as an influence on Pakistan's early economic and political development were the Muslims who came to Pakistan from Delhi, the United Provinces (the present state of Uttar Pradesh), the Central Provinces (now the state of Madhya Pradesh), Bombay, Gujarat, and the princely states of Bhopal, Hyderabad, and Junagarh. The second stream of migrants came from the eastern districts of Punjab.

The logic that Jinnah had pursued in getting the British and ultimately the Hindus to agree to the partition of India was turned against him when the time came to draw a boundary between the two countries. Both Punjab and Bengal had Muslim majorities, but not in all the districts of these two populous provinces. Accordingly, Jinnah, in order to obtain Pakistan, had to accept the partitioning of the provinces of Bengal and Punjab. When the boundaries were finally drawn—the exact boundaries came to be known two days after Pakistan and India had formally gained nationhood—a great number of Muslims were left in the Indian Punjab and Bengal, and a great number of Hindus remained in the Pakistani parts of the two provinces. The case of Punjab was complicated even further by the fact that the Sikh population was almost equally divided between the two parts of the province.

Mohammad Ali Jinnah accepted provincial partitions in the belief that both India and Pakistan would continue to have large minorities of Muslims and Hindus. He encouraged some Muslims to move from India to Pakistan, especially those with skills that his new country did not possess in great abundance. Both wings of Pakistan had primarily agricultural economies, and in both the levels of urbanization and literacy were low. He believed that the indigenous Pakistanis would not be able to provide the human capital that the new country needed; it had to be imported from the outside. Accordingly, Jinnah persuaded Muslim merchants, bankers, doctors, lawyers, and civil servants from the minority provinces to move to Pakistan, but he did not encourage an exchange of population on religious grounds. His famous inaugural speech to the Constituent Assembly on August 11, 1947, was received with a certain amount of incredulity by his followers. He said, in part:

> You may belong to any religion or caste or creed—that has nothing to do with the business of the state. . . . We are starting with this fundamental principle that we are all citizens and equal citizens of one state. . . . Now, I think we should keep that in front of us as our ideal and you will find that in the course of time Hindus would cease to be Hindus and Muslims would cease to be Muslims, not in the religious sense, because that is the personal faith of each individual but in the political sense as citizens of the state.[1]

How could Muslims cease to be Muslims and Hindus cease to be Hindus in the political sense when the religions to which they belonged were, in Jinnah's passionately held belief, so utterly different from one another? Was Jinnah giving up the two-nation theory, the ideological foundation of the state of Pakistan, once the new state had come into existence? Was the speech a clear signal to the people of Pakistan that the new state, though founded to preserve Islam in South Asia, was to be run on secular grounds? Was Jinnah providing a confirmation of the view shared by many of his opponents that he had cynically exploited the issue of religion to divide India? The speech raised all these and many other questions, but Jinnah failed to explain his statement. The explanation for what was said on August 11 is perhaps a simple one. Jinnah probably did not know that, even as he was speaking, millions of people were leaving their homes and moving in two different directions: Hindus and Sikhs to India, and Muslims to Pakistan. The transfer of population between independent India and Pakistan solved the political problem that Pakistan would have faced had a large number of Hindus and Sikhs stayed in Punjab and Sindh—the two provinces of the new Muslim country in which there were sizable communities of non-Muslims. The Pakistan that emerged as a result of this mass movement of people was religiously much more homogeneous than Jinnah or any of his associates had envisaged. Had Pakistan retained a number of religious minorities within its borders after independence—as would have been the case if the exchange of population had not taken place—its constitutional setup would have needed to accommodate religious diversity. It therefore made sense for Jinnah to speak on the political and constitutional problems that religious diversity could pose for a country that had been created on the basis of religion.

Jinnah was not alone in his ignorance; this movement of 14 million people had no precedent in history. Even the better-recorded movements in later times—Bengalis to India in 1971, Ethiopians to Somalia in the late 1970s, Cambodians to Thailand also in the late 1970s, Afghans to Pakistan in the early 1980s—did not involve so many people or occur over such a short period of time. After this movement had run its course, West Pakistan—the present-day Pakistan—had a very small non-Muslim population. If this migration had not occurred, the Muslims in Pakistan would have constituted 80 percent of the total population; the first census, taken in 1951, showed their population to be nearly 95 percent. One of the first acts of the Constituent Assembly was to give Pakistan a flag; the Assembly's choice was a simple one: It added a white strip—equal to 20 percent of the total flag area—to the flag of the Muslim League to represent the minorities in Pakistan. The census of 1951 revealed that the strip could have been much narrower: Even the members of the Constituent Assembly had not guessed the full impact of the exchange of refugees.

Both streams of migrants—that of the urban Muslims from the provinces of Uttar Pradesh, Madhya Pradesh, Bombay, and Gujarat; and that of the rural Muslims from the eastern districts of Punjab—were to profoundly influence Pakistan's future economic and political development. The migration of 1947–1951 would introduce the first element of flux into a society that was to remain remarkably fluid for a long time to come.

If the story of Pakistan's political development is to be told in chronological order, however, one must start with the entry into the country of urban Indian Muslims. The majority of the migrants from the urban areas of India were drawn to the cities of southwestern Pakistan, mostly Karachi and Hyderabad. Karachi, the birthplace of Mohammad Ali Jinnah, was chosen as Pakistan's capital. Since most of the people who had decided to migrate to Pakistan were doing so in order to benefit from the economic opportunities that were being opened up for them, it was logical for them to head for the capital city of the new country. In 1947, however, Karachi was not a big city; it was smaller than Lahore and did not have the infrastructure of a large urban center. Its capacity to absorb a great number of refugees was relatively small—even when the term *capacity* is understood in the loose way it is applied to the cities of the Third World. The migrants who could not be accommodated by Karachi went to Hyderabad, Sukkur, and other cities in its hinterland. By 1951, the year of Pakistan's first census, refugees accounted for 57 percent of Karachi's population, 65 percent of Hyderabad's, and 55 percent of Sukkur's. In all, the migrants from India in 1951 constituted 46 percent of the combined population of the twelve major cities of Pakistan.

Muhajir and Indigenous Cultures: The Constitution of 1956

The *muhajir* (refugee) culture, in most of its important manifestations, was different from the indigenous culture of Pakistan. The *muhajirs* came from an area that, following the Mutiny of 1857, had seen the political demise of most of the elite groups. The Mutiny and its aftermath left the nawabs (provincial governors) and the landlords without much wealth and political power. What emerged was a society remarkable in its egalitarian structure—a fact that contributed to the founding of a political party, the Indian National Congress, that very quickly turned into a political movement with a mass following. It was in this political environment that the urban Muslim community of north and central India began to seek a place for itself. The Muslim League, although founded by the nawabs and the landlords, was quickly taken over by the urban professional classes. Its structure, constitution, and working procedures were all "democratized." Consequently, following the creation of Pakistan, the refugees who had come from the cities of north and central India began to work for the establishment of some form of a representative political system—a variant, perhaps, of the Westminster model.

Although the Mutiny of 1857 helped to bring social and political modernization to much of north-central India, it had the opposite effect on the northwestern provinces. Punjab remained loyal to the British; the British administration, short of manpower, used troops from Punjab to restore order in many parts of India. Compensation for this help came in the form of *jagirs* (land grants), which were given to many families in Punjab. In this way, the British cemented their relationship with the Punjabi and, subsequently, the Sindhi landed aristocracy. The style of administration that evolved from this relationship was very different from the one that developed in north-central India. The administrations in Punjab and Sindh were each built around a strong executive; they approached most problems, political as well as economic, in a highly paternalistic manner. There was little scope for broad participation; even the judicial branch of the administration was under the control of the executive. The refugee and indigenous leaderships, therefore, were the products of two very different political cultures. A clash between them was inevitable.

There were other differences as well. For instance, the *muhajirs* desired a clear separation between religion and the state; Pakistan, having been founded to provide a sanctuary for the Muslim diaspora of British India, did not have to become a theocratic or a religious system. It was in this context that many refugee leaders interpreted Jinnah's speech of August 11. There was, however, a strong element within the indigenous leadership—an element responsible to some considerable degree for switching the sentiment in the provinces of Punjab, Sindh, and Northwest Frontier in favor of Pakistan—that sought to establish a system in conformity with the dictates of the Quran and Sunnah.

Differences also existed in the thinking on economics. The refugees, having come from urban areas, had little interest in using public funds to develop agriculture, even though agriculture was by far the most important economic resource of Pakistan. They had a stronger faith in private enterprise as well. Even though large-scale government procurement of all kinds of goods and commodities during World War II had enriched many refugee families, they had little other support from the British government. If anything, the mercantilist trade policy pursued by the British had reduced the access of the fledgling Indian industry to the large market in Britain. Urban India—including the Muslim merchant community—favored laissez-faire economics. The situation in Punjab, Sindh, and the Northwest Frontier Province was different; in these provinces the British administration had taken an active interest in building impressive and elaborate irrigation and agricultural marketing infrastructures. In addition, the Land Alienation Act of 1901 had curtailed entrepreneurial activity in Punjab's agriculture; specifically, it provided protection to the classes of people the British had designated as "agricultural" by declaring illegal all land transactions between them and those who were deemed "nonagriculturists." In this way, the urban business community, which was largely Hindu, was discouraged from taking over agricultural land from the largely Muslim peasantry.

Clashes between these two distinct cultures—the *muhajir* and the indigenous—were inevitable. One believed in secularism, liberal politics, and laissez-faire economics, the other in the establishment of an Islamic state and a state-managed economy. The first clash occurred over the question of reorganizing the Muslim League, the political party that under Mohammad Ali Jinnah's leadership had won the state of Pakistan for the Muslims of British India. A second clash came over the question of writing a constitution for the new country.

The Muslim League was divided into three factions. While Jinnah and Liaqat lived, the most powerful of these three factions was the one dominated by the *muhajirs* and led by Liaqat. Jinnah had kept himself above factional feuds within his party; moreover, his enormous standing in Muslim politics made it difficult for other factions to challenge him. Liaqat was a political figure of considerably smaller stature; when he assumed Jinnah's political mantle, the other two factions began to come into their own. One of these was made up of Muslim Leaguers from Bengal. Much less cohesive than the Liaqat group and plagued by divisions within itself, the Bengal faction suffered a humiliating electoral defeat in 1954 at the hands of a hastily constructed opposition representative of many different interests. This defeat eclipsed the Bengal faction in national politics for good. Accordingly, from 1954 to 1958, the battle for political spoils at the national level was fought between the other two factions: the *muhajirs* on the one hand, and the landed aristocracy and religious leadership on the other. From 1951 to about 1954 political power remained with the Liaqat faction. Then, between 1954 and 1957 the political pendulum swung widely, but by 1958 it finally came to rest on the side of the indigenous groups, when their representative, Malik Feroz Khan Noon, became prime minister. Although the army under General Ayub Khan struck before the new prime minister had had time to settle down, the advent of army rule did not eclipse the power of the indigenous faction. In fact, under Ayub Khan, this faction was to gain in power at the expense of the *muhajir* community.

The second clash between the two cultures took place on the floor of the Constituent Assembly. For four years, the Assembly had debated the constitution's "basic principles." For a state founded on the basis of religion—to protect the Muslims of India from being ruled by a non-Muslim majority—the definition of basic principles should not have presented a serious problem. But a serious problem it became; days were spent in debate on the issue of the role of religion in the conduct of the state and on the question of the rights of the federating provinces. As already indicated, the exchange of population between India and West Pakistan had resulted in the creation of one religiously homogeneous wing while the other wing—East Pakistan—retained a sizable Hindu minority. There could not, therefore, be an easy solution to the question of Islamization. And the *muhajirs*, given their more secular approach toward politics, further complicated the issue. Before 1954, they had constituted a formidable presence in the Constituent Assembly—a presence they used to keep at bay those who sought to turn the new country away from the Westminster mold of politics. The solution that was eventually found accommodated all three groups. The preamble to the constitution accepted Allah's sovereignty over man; all laws in Pakistan were to conform to the Quran and Sunnah; and the state would never place on the books a law that was repugnant either to the holy book or to accepted practice of the Prophet. This was clearly a declaration of intention, given that the constitution failed to set up a mechanism that could determine whether the legislative processes at the center or in the provinces ever produced un-Islamic legislation.

The question of protecting the rights of the federating provinces against possible encroachment by the central authority was resolved by incorporating a number of specific provisions in the constitution. The constitution borrowed heavily from the practice established in the India Act of 1935. The subjects of concern to the government were first defined and then divided into the categories of central, provincial, and joint responsibilities.

Except for the Islamization provision, there was little novelty in the constitution. Pakistan was to remain a member of the British Commonwealth under a president rather than a governor-general representing the British Crown. Members of the central and provincial legislatures were to be elected every five years. Effective power was to rest at the center in the hands of the prime minister, who was to be chosen by a simple majority of the national legislature; the provincial chief ministers were to be similarly elected and to be given responsibility for the subjects over which the constitution gave them jurisdiction.

Under the new constitution, General Iskander Mirza became the first president and Chaudhri Muhammad Ali was chosen the first prime minister. Ali was a *muhajir*, though not from the north-central provinces. Hence he did not belong to the group of urban *muhajirs* from the Indian provinces of Uttar Pradesh, Bihar, Delhi, and Maharashtra that had dominated Pakistan's politics in the early days. Rather, he was from Jullundur, a city in East Punjab that, in view of its Muslim majority, could easily have been a part of Pakistan. As a prominent member of the civil bureaucracy, Ali had been involved in organizing the administrative structure of the new state of Pakistan. In that capacity, he had worked closely with Liaquat Ali Khan, the first prime minister. Ali, therefore, was the perfect choice for making the transition from a political system dominated by the *muhajirs* to the one in which the indigenous leaders began to play an important role.

But the process of indigenization was not to proceed smoothly. The transition would have taken a long time inasmuch as the constitution of 1956 was more to the political and economic taste of the *muhajir* community. The transition was hastened by the formation in 1956 of the Republican Party, which brought together a number of prominent politicians native to West Pakistan and who had been kept out of power by the Muslim League. President Iskander Mirza was the new party's patron. The Republicans successfully challenged Chaudhri Muhammad Ali's Muslim League. Ali resigned, to be succeeded by Malik Feroz Khan Noon, who became prime minister. But the process of indigenization had proceeded much more quickly than was acceptable to those who had vivid memories of the way many leaders of the Republican party had opposed the creation of Pakistan. The ensuing political turmoil was brought to an end by General Ayub Khan's coup d'état. The coup, though organized in great secrecy, was not altogether unexpected. The army's entry into politics was greeted with a sense of relief by large segments of the population who had become tired of politicians' machinations.

The Ayub Khan Era

The Second Constitution

The settlement of refugees, the creation of the system of Basic Democracies, the formation of the Pakistan Muslim League, and the move of the country's capital from the *muhajir*-dominated city of Karachi to the army garrison town of Rawalpindi set the stage for the drafting of Pakistan's second constitution. The task was assigned to a small group of lawyers who produced a document radically different from the constitution of 1956. The new system of government was to be much more centralized, with the executive branch under the full control of an indirectly elected president. The president was to be chosen by an electoral college made up of 80,000 Basic Democrats, or union councillors. The powers of the central and provincial legislatures were severely restricted in that they had only a limited jurisdiction over money bills. The president could veto any legislation that came from the legislatures, but the legislatures were not given the power to override his veto. Two features of the old constitution survived in the new document. The system of parity was retained, with the seats of the central legislature divided equally between East and West Pakistan, and all laws were to follow the basic tenets of Islam.

Ayub Khan's political system had a great deal of flexibility: It was elastic enough to accommodate those groups that, benefiting from the remarkable economic progress being made at that time, wanted to follow it up with meaningful participation in political decisionmaking. The institution of Basic Democracies—not the new political parties, not even the constitution of 1962—gave the Ayub system much of its elasticity. This flexibility was lost when, for reasons that can only be speculated upon, Ayub began to withdraw support from the Basic Democracies and turned once again, as he had done during the first year of his administration, to the civil bureaucracy for managing economic as well as political affairs. But the civil bureaucracy had remained elitist, not only in its composition but also in its outlook.

This shift in Ayub Khan's political philosophy was probably produced by three sets of circumstances. The first was the presidential election of 1964, in which the parties in opposition to Ayub got together under the umbrella of a hastily structured political alliance with the rather unimaginative title of the Combined Opposition Party (COP) and put up Fatima Jinnah as their candidate. Miss Jinnah, the sister of the founder of Pakistan, was a reluctant recruit; however, having accepted the COP's offer, she proved to be an enthusiastic and tireless campaigner. Much of her support came from quarters whose residents had suffered under Ayub; of these none was more powerful than the merchant and industrial community of Karachi. The loss of monopoly over the industrial sector occasioned by the economic policies of the Ayub regime was reason enough to incite the opposition of this powerful group. Miss Jinnah, an opponent whose only strength was the strength of a symbol, lost the election, but Ayub's rather narrow margin of victory at the polls shook his confidence in the political system—even one with such limited participation.

Within a year of being reelected, Ayub Khan had allowed Pakistan to be drawn into armed conflict with India. The issue was Kashmir; from the evidence that has become available to date, it appears that Ayub reluctantly accepted the advice of some of his close associates—among them Zulfikar Ali Bhutto—that the time had finally come for finding a military solution to the problem that had plagued relations between India and Pakistan for nearly twenty years. Beginning on

September 6, 1965, the two countries fought a brisk war that lasted for seventeen days. When a cease-fire was finally declared, Pakistan found itself in a situation that was to have some unexpected consequences. But the most important outcome of this conflict was the open disaffection of many young generals with the conduct of the war. In such a situation, Ayub Khan found it increasingly difficult to persist with his political experiment.

Finally, perhaps because of these two pressures—the narrow victory in the elections of 1964 and the aftermath of the 1965 war with India—Ayub Khan's health gave way. In the spring of 1966, he traveled to the United States for open heart surgery. This prolonged illness demoralized him further. While recuperating, he had to surrender much of his power to a cabal of civil servants—a power he was ultimately unable to recover.

Economic downturn—the subject of a later chapter—also contributed to Ayub Khan's political problems. As so often happens in systems that do not provide channels for the expression of dissent and disapproval, the movement against Ayub Khan took the form of street agitation. It built up in intensity in the summer and fall of 1968. Despite several attempts to placate the opposition by granting them some form of participation without drastically altering the system, the agitation continued to grow in intensity. By the spring of 1969, the movement had been taken over by two exceptionally charismatic leaders—Zulfikar Ali Bhutto in West Pakistan and Mujib-ur-Rahman in East Pakistan. When Bhutto and Mujib refused to compromise, the military stepped in, demanded Ayub Khan's resignation, proclaimed martial law, abrogated the constitution, and appointed General Yahya Khan, the military's most senior officer, as president. But before turning to the events that dominated the second military government, we should pause to look at the Ayub period in some detail.

On the morning of October 7, 1958, General Ayub Khan, the army's commander in chief, removed the prime minister and his cabinet, dismissed the National Assembly, abrogated the constitution, dissolved all political parties, banned all political activity, and set himself up as the dictator with the title of chief martial law administrator. Twenty days later, the general staged another coup—this time one directed against Iskander Mirza, the president of the republic, who had originally invited Ayub Khan to take some of these draconian measures. October 27, 1958, marked the beginning of the era of one-man rule that was to last for several decades.

Ayub Khan moved quickly on several different fronts. Rehabilitation of refugees from the eastern districts of British Punjab was one of the issues given a high priority by his government. While the urban refugees based in Karachi and Hyderabad and the leadership indigenous to Pakistan were fighting over the shape of the constitution, the other groups of refugees—those from the eastern districts of partitioned Punjab—received little government attention or support. These refugees were mostly rural; upon coming to Pakistan they had scattered all over rural West Punjab and rural Sindh and had taken over the land previously owned and operated by the Sikhs and the Hindus. But the governments before Ayub Khan failed to give permanent title to the land that the refugees cultivated. The officer corps of Ayub Khan's army had a significant East Punjab representation; once the army had assumed control over the administration, it quickly formulated a program to permanently settle the refugees on the land they had occupied for more than a decade. A new department of rehabilitation was placed under the charge of General Azam Khan, one of Ayub Khan's more dynamic military associates. The settlement of the East Punjab refugee community not only revived activity in the sector of agriculture (a subject that will be touched upon in Chapter 3); it also introduced a new element into the already complicated political picture. The close association of this group with the army, particularly the officer corps, gave it a political prominence that would not have come to it had the old political structure been allowed to continue.

There was no place in the existing political structure for Ayub Khan and the constituency that supported him—hence the sense of purpose implicit in the harsh measures the general adopted: The constituency the armed forces represented had to be accommodated in the political system, and this could not be done without sweeping the table clean. Once that had been accomplished, Ayub Khan proceeded to take four steps, each one carefully planned and executed. In quick succession, the general set up a system of representative local government, created a new political party with members drawn mostly from the constituency that supported him, moved the country's capital from Karachi to Rawalpindi, and, finally, gave the country its second constitution.

The first of these measures was to create a system of local government with obvious appeal to the small landlords and middle peasantry of Punjab and the Northwest Frontier Province. Despite the settlement of some refugees in rural Sindh, the large landlord remained paramount in that province. The Basic Democracies, launched in 1960, constituted a system of interlocking local councils. Union councils, 8,000 in number, formed the base of the system. With an average membership of ten, elected on the basis of adult franchise, each union served a constituency of some 10,000 people. The union council's electoral district therefore typically included several villages. It was not easy for the large landlords to establish their personal control over such a vast area. For cases in which one politician held sway over a large area, Ayub Khan's government used the Elective Bodies Disqualification Ordinance (EBDO), promulgated to "weed out corruption and chicanery from domestic politics"—that is, to exclude undesirable politicians from taking advantage of the new system. The members of the union councils elected representatives to the tehsil councils, the next tier in the system; the members of the tehsil councils, in turn, sent representatives to the district councils and so on to the divisional and provincial councils. Whereas the union councils, including their chairpersons, were all elected representatives of the people, upper-tier councils featured a mixture of elected and nominated members. Nominated members were mostly bureaucrats serving in the area. Bureaucrats also chaired the tehsil, district, divisional, and provincial councils.

The system of Basic Democracies served well the purpose for which it had been set up; it not only gave a voice to the middle peasantry of Punjab and the Northwest Frontier Province but also converted Pakistan's powerful civil bureaucracy from an apparatus for maintaining law and order into a remarkable vehicle for promoting development.

Although the first election to the Basic Democracies system was held without political parties, Ayub Khan soon reached the obvious conclusion that a political system could not be run without parties. Lifting the ban on party formation, however, would have meant the revival of the parties that had held sway in the days before the coup d'état. The Ayub Khan constituency of small landlords, middle peasantry, and new industrialists of Punjab and the Northwest Frontier Province would have found it difficult to gain entry into, let alone exercise influence over, the old parties. Ayub Khan was too shrewd a politician to allow the resurrection of the old parties without first putting up a political umbrella under which to gather his own supporters. This he did by calling a convention of political leaders to reshape the Muslim League. Invitations went out not only to the old leaders but also to a number of new ones—namely, to the representatives of the various elements in the Ayub constituency. As could have been expected, the old Leaguers quickly renamed it the "Convention Muslim League"; they then went ahead and convened their own council of Muslim Leaguers, which resulted in the formation of the Council Muslim League. It was thus that Mohammad Ali Jinnah's party was split into two: not two factions existing within the framework of one party but two parties with different ideologies and different structures. The Council Muslim League was a hybrid formed from the Liaquat faction and the faction of landed aristocracy that had supported the creation of Pakistan. It was the old Muslim League but with a new name. The Convention Muslim League was a new phenomenon that was to become a permanent feature in Pakistan's scene—a political party without a pronounced ideology that could be relied upon to support the coalition of groups in power.

The third measure—the decision to move the country's capital from Karachi to the suburbs of Rawalpindi—was justified by the government on economic grounds. The federal government had grown in size over the last ten years, and the decision to locate the capital in Karachi had not been followed by any physical planning. The arrival of refugees had crowded the city; it would have been extremely expensive to build office space for the expanding government. Karachi also had a poor physical infrastructure. For this city of 2 million—Karachi's size at the time of Ayub Khan's coup d'état—drinking water had to be piped from more than fifty miles inland. The city had practically no agricultural hinterland; the food needs of the rapidly growing population had to be satisfied by supplies brought in from hundreds of miles away. And so the argument went. Although these considerations must have played a role in the decision to relocate the capital, the real motive was very different. Karachi was nearly a thousand miles from Rawalpindi, the headquarters of the Pakistan army. In addition, the city was dominated by the new merchant-industrial class toward which Ayub Khan and his military associates were, initially, considerably hostile. The home of the constituency Ayub Khan wanted to cultivate was located in the area around Rawalpindi. The district of Rawalpindi and the surrounding areas had been the recruiting ground for the British army in the nineteenth and early-twentieth centuries. The rapidly expanding Pakistan army had turned to the same areas in the search for recruits. For a military government, therefore, Rawalpindi was the ideal capital. General Yahya Khan, who headed the Capital Commission appointed by Ayub Khan to search for a new location for the seat of the central government, gave many economic reasons for recommending a site near Rawalpindi. As a serving army general, moreover, he was fully aware of the political significance of such a move.

Thus, Pakistan moved its capital from the city of Jinnah's birth to a city that was only forty miles from Rehana, the birthplace of Ayub Khan. The symbolism of this move was probably not lost on the people. By this action and others, Ayub Khan was signaling a clear break with the past—a new palimpsest was being spread to cover old and deep cracks.

These measures—resettlement of refugees, creation of a system of local government, and transfer of capital to the interior—set the stage for Ayub Khan's final political move, the promulgation of a new constitution. This last objective was accomplished on March 23, 1962, as if the choice of this particular day (it was on March 23, 1940, that the Muslim League, in an open meeting in Lahore, had adopted the Pakistan resolution) could somehow win the support of the people for the new constitution. But this was a naive expectation, given that the basic intent behind the new constitution was to put a great deal of distance between the government and the people. The Westminster model of parliament was abandoned in favor of a pale image of the French presidential system. The executive branch was to be all powerful. The president was to be elected not directly by the people but indirectly by the 80,000 Basic Democrats; and once elected, he could not be easily removed. The legislative branch—the National Assembly, the members of which were also to be elected indirectly—could initiate legislation but not enact it into law without the agreement of the president. On the other hand, the president had the power to ignore the wishes of the legislature on important matters; indeed, there were devices available to him by which he could enact legislation even if not approved by the Assembly.

In short, it was a lopsided constitution and, therefore, not a very popular one. It did not survive the departure of Ayub Khan from the political scene.

The Fall of Ayub Khan

Ayub Khan was an efficient administrator; he was also fully committed to the rapid development of the country's economy. But he was not a popular leader.

Field Marshal Ayub Khan was forced out of office by General Yahya Khan, the chief of staff of the armed forces, in the second military coup d'état in the country's history. It happened on March 25, 1969, a decade after Ayub Khan himself had engineered the ouster of President Iskander Mirza. The coup d'état by Ayub Khan was brought about by a general feeling of political malaise, by a near consensus among the politically aware segments of the population that the politicians had somehow failed in their duty to provide the country with a workable political system. By then, the military establishment had acquired a reputation for honesty, integrity, and efficiency—precisely the three virtues that the politicians seemed to lack. Accordingly, when the army intervened in October 1958, it was welcomed with some relief by the people who had watched with dismay the terribly undignified behavior of the politicians and the growing number of political parties they had professed to lead.

Once in power, however, the army, under Ayub Khan, lost some of its reputation for honesty, integrity, and efficiency. Ayub allowed his sons to leave the army and enter industry, a profession in which one of them proved to be remarkably successful. A number of senior officers were permitted to acquire large tracts of newly irrigated agricultural land in the province of Sindh, and many senior civil servants were suspected of enriching themselves by selectively dispensing licenses for industrial imports and for the establishment of new enterprises. After half a dozen years or so, the government began to lose its freshness; its claim that it had taken office to clean up the mess that had been left by the politicians after a decade of mismanagement no longer sounded very convincing. But Ayub Khan might have remained in office if he had not gone to war with India in the fall of 1965 and if he had not suffered a serious heart attack in the spring of 1968.

The 1965 Indo-Pakistan War interrupted the remarkable momentum of economic development that had begun with the assumption of office by Ayub Khan. Up until then, the rate of growth in Pakistan's economy was among the highest in the developing world. The war not only diverted toward military use the resources that would have otherwise gone into development; it also resulted in a sharp decline in the flow of external assistance. The nation was asked to tighten its belt and might have been willing to do so if tangible gains had been made on the battlefield. But the war ended in a state of confusion, with both India and Pakistan claiming victory. When the peace agreement was finally signed with India in the southern Soviet city of Tashkent, its terms left the impression that the advantage finally lay with India.

The Tashkent Declaration was to be the turning point in the political life of the administration of Ayub Khan. Zulfikar Ali Bhutto, Ayub Khan's foreign minister, left the government, giving the strong impression that what had not been lost on the battlefield was surrendered at Tashkent. India's policy toward Pakistan, he wrote after his departure from the government, "will shift from confrontation to cooperation, to the 'spirit of Tashkent.' She will now seek to convert Pakistan into her satellite by holding out inducements of peaceful cooperation."[2] This was a serious warning, people thought—a warning issued by a person who, as the former foreign minister, must understand the full implication of what he was saying. Zulfikar Ali Bhutto's words were to echo for a long time in the ears of those who had always believed that Pakistan had to be extremely vigilant if it was to protect its national integrity. By initially basing his campaign against Ayub Khan on the Tashkent Declaration, Bhutto was able to draw toward him the people who had become disenchanted with the military regime.

The final blow to Ayub Khan's authority came in early 1968, when a near-fatal heart attack put him out of office for several months. This was an opportunity for the military leader to use his own constitution; the constitution of 1962 had provided for just such an eventuality. In case of the president's severe indisposition, the task of running the government was to be assumed by the speaker of the National Assembly. The speaker at that time was Abdul Jabbar Khan, a politician from Bengal who had shown exceptional loyalty to Ayub Khan. Letting Jabbar Khan assume the presidency would have accomplished two things: It would have provided a test for the new constitution during a period of crisis, and it would have convinced the Bengalis that they were not condemned forever to be junior political partners at the national level. Instead, while Ayub Khan recuperated slowly, the reins of government were assumed by a small coterie of civil servants.

When Ayub Khan finally returned to office, he found that the political situation had changed quite dramatically. Zulfikar Ali Bhutto had formed a new party—the Pakistan People's Party—with the aim of returning power to the people within an economic and social framework that was vaguely defined as Islamic socialism. Bhutto was correct in his assessment that power had to be forcibly wrested from the military; the military would not willingly leave on its own. He also probably understood that discrediting Ayub Khan and his administration would not automatically transfer power to politicians such as himself. If Ayub Khan was forced to leave, he would probably hand over the administration to the generals. Some form of military government would have to intervene between the demise of Ayub Khan and his own ascendancy.

Bhutto played his cards well. Soon after leaving the government he began to tour the country, to get to know the people, to understand their frustrations. As he went from one city and province to another, he discovered that the economic slowdown of the time had begun to affect the people. Those most affected lived in the rural areas and had been hurt by a sharp decline in agricultural prices. Sensing this mood of unease, Bhutto began to formulate the program of his political party. His initial impulse was to use Pakistan's foreign policy as the centerpiece in his party's platform. Having met the people, he now knew that antipathy toward India, though a common sentiment, was not felt strongly enough by the people that they would risk their livelihoods—possibly also their lives—and come out into the streets to challenge the authority of the government. Other issues were of much greater concern to the people. Moreover, they could be convinced that Ayub Khan had failed to deliver on the promise to turn the country into a state fashioned on the principles of Islam and had failed also to distribute to the poor the benefits of economic growth that had occurred during his ten years in office. The government's extensive "decade of development" campaign thus provided the perfect background for Bhutto's campaign. As President Ayub Khan, the governors of the two provinces, and the ministers of the central and provincial governments crisscrossed the country underscoring the remarkable economic progress made in the 1958–1968 decade, Bhutto and his colleagues followed them everywhere, reminding the people how little they had benefited from all that the government said had been accomplished. Right in the middle of this debate, Mahbub ul Haq, the government's chief economist, went public with his "twenty-two-family hypothesis." In an address delivered in Karachi, Haq revealed that the principal beneficiaries of Pakistan's extraordinary economic performance were not necessarily the people in general but twenty-two industrial families in particular: "There exists a functional justification for inequity of income if it raises production for all and not consumption for a few. . . . The road to eventual equalities may inevitably lie through initial inequalities."[3] Haq had written in 1963 about the justification for the strategy around which the Second Five-Year Plan (1960–1965) had been built. But now, five years later, Haq asked for "standing economic theory on its head, since a rising growth rate is no guarantee against worsening poverty."[4] He regretted the fact that so little of the gains that Pakistan had made during Ayub Khan's development decade had been distributed to the people; the principal beneficiaries of the economic miracle were, as noted, a small group of industrial families including Ayub Khan's own. Haq's "twenty-two-family" speech came at a time when Bhutto had begun to focus the attention of the people on the unequal distribution of additions to national wealth. And the "twenty-two-family" slogan was just what Bhutto needed.[5]

Bhutto's campaign against inequality prompted the Bengali leadership to articulate their demands for provincial autonomy. Bengal had always felt discriminated against; for instance, it had always argued that the foreign exchange earned from the export of jute (which for a long time was Pakistan's major export earner but was produced only in the eastern province) had been used mostly in the western wing. Accordingly, the Bengali party known as the Awami League proclaimed a six-point program aimed at severely limiting the powers of the central government to defense, foreign affairs, and currency. "The power of taxation and revenue collection shall vest in the federating units," the Awami League demanded in its six points; moreover, ". . . there shall be two separate accounts for foreign exchange earnings of the two wings. . . . [The federating units will have the power] to establish trade and commercial relations, set up trade missions in and enter into agreement with, foreign countries."[6] And so on. It was ironic that the six-point program was announced in 1968 by Mujib-ur-Rahman at Lahore, the city in which, nearly three decades earlier, a motion for the Pakistan resolution had been made by another Bengali politician.

With the promulgation of the six-point program, the agitation against Ayub Khan acquired a new dimension. The pace of the opposition campaign quickened; what had started as an economic campaign in the small towns and villages of West Pakistan now assumed the form of a mass civil-disobedience movement.

Leader after leader was incarcerated (Zulfikar Ali Bhutto and Mujib-ur-Rahman, among others, went to jail), but the movement continued to gain momentum. In the early months of 1969, Ayub Khan summoned the leaders of the opposition after conceding that his 1962 constitution had to be abandoned in favor of a more representative system. He tried hard to reach an agreement, but Zulfikar Ali Bhutto, the man who by now had emerged as the most important political figure in West Pakistan, refused to cooperate. He wanted Ayub Khan's resignation, which finally came on March 25, 1969, when General Yahya Khan took up residence in the Rawalpindi presidency. With these developments began Pakistan's second military leadership. It lasted for thirty-three eventful months, during which the two wings of Pakistan fought an exceptionally bloody civil war prior to the emergence of the eastern province as the independent state of Bangladesh. In 1968, the Awami League's six-point demand for provincial autonomy had seemed preposterous to the leadership of West Pakistan. In December 1971, the same leaders were to concede much more.

The Yahya Khan Era

Within a few months of assuming power, Yahya Khan and his military colleagues dismantled the political system Ayub Khan had erected. There was a serious contradiction in their approach toward political management. Ayub Khan had begun to place some trust in politicians, at least in those who were prepared to accept his system of Basic Democracies, a high degree of centralization, and political parity between the two wings of the country. His successors kept all politicians at bay, in the belief that the mission they had set out to accomplish could be performed only if the military worked alone and without a great deal of close contact with the politicians. Even the civil service was made to play a secondary role in the new administration; a number of Ayub Khan's trusted civilians were sent home in keeping with the purge of the civil bureaucracy. Air Marshal Nur Khan, Admiral Abdul Ahsan, and Generals S. G. M. Pirzada and Abdul Hamid all wielded much more political power than Ayub Khan had assigned to his military associates. Accordingly, Yahya Khan established a semimilitary state, thus creating a precedent that was to be followed later on by General Zia ul-Haq.

But there was a contradiction in Yahya Khan's approach. At the time that he militarized politics, he also introduced a number of changes that returned the country to its pre-1955 situation, when politicians and parliamentary democracy had reigned supreme. The contradiction was to lead to a serious conflict between the military and the politicians.

To facilitate the return to parliamentary democracy, Yahya Khan instituted a number of very significant changes in the political setup. The scope and significance of these changes must have escaped the new military leadership. The principle of parity—that is, political equality between East and West Pakistan—was the foundation on which the constitutions of 1956 and 1962 had been erected. The larger population of East Pakistan was one reason why it had taken the politicians almost a decade to agree on the 1956 constitution. One-man-one-vote would have meant that a larger representation had to be given to East Pakistan in the national legislature. This the powerful political elites of West Pakistan were not prepared to accept. One possible solution was the principle of parity—the principle of "fifty-fifty," as it came to be called—which gave equal representation to the two wings of the country. But West Pakistan in the early 1950s was still not a "wing." Rather, it was made up of three provinces (Northwest Frontier, Punjab, and Sindh), a number of princely states (Bahawalpur, Kalat, and Khairpur being the largest among them), and the large centrally administered territory of Balochistan. The assembly of all these diverse administrative parts into "One Unit," or one wing, was therefore a precondition for the acceptance of the principle of parity. On September 30, 1955, West Pakistan's many administrative units were fused to form one province.

A decade and a half later, Yahya Khan decided to accept Bengal's demand for representation on the basis of population. Once this demand was accepted, preservation of the one unit of West Pakistan was no longer necessary. The smaller provinces in West Pakistan had never been very satisfied with the one-unit arrangement; for them it was both an administrative inconvenience and a political nuisance. Moreover, if the principle of parity was not to be the basis of the new constitution promised by Yahya Khan, retention of the one unit of West Pakistan was also no longer necessary. The military government accepted the argument; a One-Unit Dissolution Committee was set up to reorganize West Pakistan into the four provinces of Balochistan, Northwest Frontier, Punjab, and Sindh. These provinces, along with East Pakistan, constituted the five federating units, which shared power with the federal government under the provisions of a new constitution.

A Legal Framework Order, issued on March 30, 1970, outlined the manner in which the new National Assembly would be constituted and what its constitution-making duties would be. This assembly of 300 was to be elected directly by the people, with 162 chosen by East Pakistan and 138 by the four provinces of West Pakistan. General elections were to be held on October 5, 1970, and the National Assembly was to be given only 120 days to come up with a new constitution. If the Assembly could not complete the drafting of the constitution in the allotted time, it would be dissolved and another round of elections would be held. The president reserved the right to authenticate the constitution so that the document prepared by the Assembly did not contravene the five basic principles laid down in the Legal Framework Order. The Framework required that Pakistan be an Islamic state; that it have a democratic system, based on free and fair elections; that its territorial integrity be preserved for all time to come; that an earnest effort be made to eliminate economic disparity between the two wings of the country; and that the provinces be allowed maximum autonomy without rendering the federal government totally impotent.

TABLE 2.1   Results of the National Assembly Elections of December 1970

	East Pakistan	West Pakistan	Total
Awami League	160	–	160
Pakistan People's Party	–	81	81
Pakistan Muslim League	–	18	18
Jamaat-i-Islami	–	4	4
Others	2	35	37
Total seats	162	138	300

Source: Dawn (Karachi, December 8, 1970), p. 1.

Elections were held on December 7, 1970, two months later than the government had originally scheduled. The delay was caused by a cyclone that struck East Pakistan's coastal region on November 12 and wrought inestimable damage to life and property. It was reportedly the worst natural catastrophe in Pakistan's recorded history. The death toll was placed at more than 1 million, and all political activity came to a stop even in this intensely political province. For some reason, the central government was slow to respond; help from Islamabad arrived after international assistance had already begun to pour in. For the already suspicious Bengalis, this was yet another bit of evidence to demonstrate the indifference felt by their West Pakistani compatriots. Mujib-ur-Rahman's six-point program calling for complete provincial autonomy took on a new and urgent meaning. It was in this charged atmosphere that the people of East Pakistan went to the polls to elect their representatives to a new National Assembly.

But the election produced results that no one had anticipated (see Table 2.1). The most important of these was the emergence of two political leaders with two very different mandates. Mujib-ur-Rahman's mandate was to negotiate for East Pakistan a degree of autonomy—a mandate that bore a remarkable resemblance to the one Mohammad Ali Jinnah had received from the Muslim community of British India in the elections of 1946. In retrospect, it is now clear even to the people of West Pakistan that, after the December 1970 election, there was no turning back for Bengal. The election set the Bengalis on a route that was to take them toward complete independence a year later. An entirely different political campaign resulted in the triumph of Zulfikar Ali Bhutto in West Pakistan. Bhutto's political program aimed at the total restructuring of Pakistan's economy. People were promised socialism: state control over the commanding heights of the economy and equal access by all people to such basic needs as food, health, education, and shelter. Mujib-ur-Rahman had won support on the basis of a program that asked for provincial autonomy, whereas Bhutto won support on the basis of individual economic and social equality. There was nothing in common between the two programs; there was even less in common between the political figures who had espoused them.

Mujib-ur-Rahman was essentially a provincial politician with few interests aside from those related to his constituency. He was not a sophisticated man; he did not understand economics and did not care much about foreign affairs. His primary aim was the betterment of the people of East Bengal. In pursuit of this aim, he had joined Jinnah's Muslim League and taken an active part in the Pakistan Movement. Over the years, as he began to project the interests of East Pakistan, the size of his constituency expanded enormously.

Zulfikar Ali Bhutto's political initiation had occurred much later than Mujib's and under very different circumstances; he had been picked by General Ayub Khan to represent Sindh in the cabinet. When Bhutto was introduced to politics, he had no personal constituency of his own and did not develop one for as long as he remained with Ayub Khan. It was only after he resigned his job as foreign minister and began to tour the country that he developed a personal following. As with Mujib, the size of Bhutto's following increased very rapidly but, in contrast to Mujib, people were attracted to Bhutto for the novelty of the cause that he had begun to espouse. Bhutto's type of populism was not a new phenomenon in Third World politics. Very deliberately he had fashioned his style and his idiom after such Third World leaders as Sukarno, Nkrumah, Peron, and Castro. But for West Pakistan, this populist approach was a new development; until that time, West Pakistani politicians had followed a very low-key approach toward politics, preferring to negotiate among themselves rather than to use popular support to further their aims and ambitions. Bhutto was a new kind of leader. Accordingly, the constituency that he cultivated for himself was new—a constituency that had waited a long time in its search for a leader. Once the leader arrived on the scene, the constituency was galvanized into action very quickly, but when he left the scene, the constituency still remained. Like Peronism, Bhuttoism was to survive Bhutto.

It was inevitable for the forces of Mujib and Bhutto to collide—and, indeed, the collision came soon after the election results were announced. After the election, East and West Pakistan had acquired leaders of their own; their very different mandates had been legitimized by the people. Mujib wanted autonomy for East Pakistan; Bhutto wanted restoration of civilian rule and a restructuring of the economy. Neither was interested in sitting down for 120 days in the National Assembly in order to draft a constitution in line with the broad principles laid down in Yahya Khan's Legal Framework Order.

Events moved quickly after the elections. The new National Assembly was convened to meet on March 3, 1971, but Bhutto decided to boycott the meeting, arguing that he needed to reach an understanding with Mujib on important constitutional issues before he and his associates could go to the National Assembly. Yahya Khan's first response to Bhutto's ultimatum was to postpone the first meeting of the National Assembly, an action that prompted Mujib to order his followers not to cooperate with the military government. By the first week of March, Islamabad's writ no longer ran in Dhaka, and Pakistan's flag had begun to be replaced with that of the Awami League.

On March 7, Mujib-ur-Rahman laid down new conditions for participating in the deliberations of the National Assembly. There is still speculation as to whether he could have been swayed from taking the path of full secession even at this late stage. According to those who so speculated, General Yahya Khan and his political associates in West Pakistan—in particular, Zulfikar Ali Bhutto—would have had to be more accommodating toward the Awami League, accepting it as the majority in the National Assembly and its leader, Mujib-ur-Rahman, as the prime minister. It was perhaps with this possibility in mind that Mujib, in a short speech of only eighteen minutes (and thus unusually precise for Mujib) announced that the Awami League intended to stop short of full secession. This was a risky course to take, for the very large crowd—large even for a political rally in Dhaka's racecourse ground—expected Mujib to go the full distance. Mujib's conditions were not accepted, however, and after a couple of weeks of tense negotiations, Yahya Khan launched "operation searchlight" against the Awami League. Mujib-ur-Rahman was arrested and taken to West Pakistan, and a number of his close associates escaped to Calcutta, India, to form a government in exile. The operation commenced on March 25 and lasted until December 17, when, helped by the Indian armed forces, the *Mukti Bahini* (Bengali freedom fighters) forced Pakistan's army to formally surrender in a public ceremony, took over Dhaka, and established the independent state of Bangladesh.

The Bhutto Era

The Emergence of Bhutto

"Give people democracy and look what they do with it. The West in a state of shock, the sound of one wing flapping, beset by the appalling notion of surrendering the government to a party of swamp aborigines, little dark men with their unpronounceable language of distorted vowels and slurred consonants; perhaps not foreigners exactly, but aliens without a doubt. . . . The final defeat of the western forces, which led to the reconstitution of the East as an autonomous (that's a laugh) nation and international basket case, was obviously engineered by outsiders: stone washers and damn-yankees, yes. The Chairman visited the United Nations and . . . stormed out of the General Assembly, handsome, intemperate, great. 'My country hearkens for me!' . . . and returned home to take up the reins of government in what was left of the land of God."[7]

The chairman in *Shame*, Salman Rushdie's fictional history of Pakistan, is, of course, Zulfikar Ali Bhutto. Bhutto had joined the government of Yahya Khan as deputy prime minister shortly before the surrender of the Pakistan army to the Indian forces in Dhaka. In that capacity he had traveled to New York to negotiate a peaceful solution to the crisis in East Pakistan. A day before the army's surrender, he had stormed out of the meeting of the Security Council, tearing into shreds the resolution offered by Poland to end the fighting in Pakistan's eastern wing. He vowed a "thousand years' war" with India as he left the Security Council chamber. This extraordinary scene, viewed by millions of people on television in

Pakistan, was to burnish in their minds an image of a remarkable patriot refusing to submit even as his own forces were about to surrender to an invading army. This performance won Zulfikar Ali Bhutto the support even of those who had not voted for him in the election of December 1970. It also won him the admiration of young army officers who had felt humiliated by the conduct of the generals. As Bhutto traveled back to Rawalpindi, these officers staged a silent coup against their senior colleagues. General Yahya Khan was persuaded to resign the presidency, and Bhutto, upon his return, was sworn in as president and chief martial law administrator of what was left of Pakistan.

The Constitution of 1973

The Bhutto era lasted for five and a half years, during which the economy was restructured, the public sector was given a great deal of prominence, Pakistan's approach to the outside world was redefined on the basis of a relationship with India that no longer sought equality with it, and a new consensus was developed on constitutional issues among different political players. It was a period, therefore, of remarkable dynamism—a period during which a great deal was accomplished. It might have lasted much longer than it did but for the serious flaws in the character of the man who guided the country during this period of adjustment and change. On July 5, 1977, Bhutto was ousted from power by the military, which took control once again not out of political ambition but because of the tensions generated by Bhutto's treatment of other political leaders, their parties, and their platforms. For instance, Asghar Khan, one of the prominent opposition politicians, actually invited the military to intervene and restore a democratic order to the country. Bhutto's economics and foreign policy are the subjects of later chapters; this chapter reveals the nature and scope of the political consensus that formed the basis of his constitution—the constitution of 1973, the third in Pakistan's history.

The principle of parity between two wings of roughly equal size was the basis of the constitutions of 1956 and 1962. With Pakistan now divided into four very unequal parts, there was no easy solution to the problem of power sharing between the center and the provinces. The domination of Punjab was feared by the smaller provinces. Punjab had nearly 60 percent of the population and a large representation in the armed forces; it also produced well over one-half of the GNP. Sindh, second to Punjab in size and wealth, had an enormous untapped agricultural potential; although irrigation had arrived in Punjab in the early decades of the twentieth century, Sindh's virgin soil was still in the process of being "colonized" by farmers, many of whom were either immigrants from Punjab or retired army officers. Sindh had also accommodated another set of migrants—namely, those who had come to Pakistan from the cities of India in the aftermath of the partition. These migrants—the *muhajirs*—settled in the major cities of Sindh (in Karachi, Hyderabad, Sukkur, and Khairpur) and had little contact with the political culture of rural Sindh. That culture was dominated by large landlords—the *weidaras*—one of whom was Zulfikar Ali Bhutto himself. The Northwest Frontier Province was as heterogeneous as Sindh; within its borders lived Pathans as well as Punjabis. The Pathans were divided into two groups—those of the "settled districts" (the districts that had accepted the British *raj* and its laws) and those of the tribal areas in which *pukhtunwali* (the local Pathan law) was still followed. The Punjabis had an important economic presence in the cities of Peshawar and Abbotabad. Finally, there was the province of Balochistan, which, though smallest in size in terms of population, had a landmass twice the size of Punjab. Balochistan was the poorest of the four provinces, but it had potential riches—some known, some still unknown. It was certainly rich in natural gas and had vast deposits of coal and marble in addition, perhaps, to iron, gold, and copper. The Balochis, not unlike the Pathans, were a fiercely independent people. They, too, had rejected the "civilizing" influence of the British *raj*, preferring to live under their own code. But there was one important difference of great political significance between the Pathans and the Balochis: The tribal Pathans lived in small independent communities that were highly egalitarian, whereas the Balochis were divided into tribes, each under the control of the powerful *sirdar* (chief).

The Pakistan that emerged in 1971, therefore, was a colorful mosaic of many different peoples. They spoke a number of different languages—Punjabi, Sindhi, Baruhi, Pushto, Balochi, Urdu, Saraiki, and so on—and belonged to many different cultures. These differences had remained submerged for as long as Bengal was a part of Pakistan; then the question of finding a viable solution to the sharing of power between the two wings had occupied all political attention. With Bengal now gone, the focus shifted to West Pakistan's internal differences.

The trauma of defeat in East Pakistan may have made it possible for the politicians of West Pakistan to agree to a new constitution. Bhutto convened the National Assembly to meet in Islamabad on April 4, 1972. The Assembly was made up of 139 members—138 elected from West Pakistan and Nurul Amin, one of the two non-Awami Leaguers who had been returned in East Pakistan. On October 20, 1972, only six months after the first meeting of the Assembly, a constitutional accord was signed by the leaders of the different political parties. The constitution was authenticated by President Bhutto on April 12, 1973, and came into force on August 14 of the same year. Thus Pakistan, on its twenty-sixth birthday, acquired its third constitution. The constitution represented a consensus on three matters: the role of Islam in politics, the sharing of power between the federal government and the federating provinces, and the division of responsibility between the president and the prime minister.

Bhutto would have preferred a presidential form of government, one not too different from that of Ayub Khan, but he was persuaded to accept a modified parliamentary system. The modification was intended to protect the prime minister from frivolous changes in party loyalty of the type that had paralyzed govern-

ments in the period before Ayub Khan. Under the procedures of the new constitution, the exercise of considerable political will was required in order to remove
the prime minister. A vote of no-confidence against the prime minister was made
virtually impossible, at least for ten years. Once the constitution had been put into
force, Bhutto stepped down from the presidency and became the prime minister.
Fazal Elahi Chaudhury, a small town politician from Punjab of no great standing,
was appointed president.

The fears of smaller provinces about Punjab domination were assuaged by the
creation of a bicameral legislature—a Senate with equal provincial representation
and an Assembly with seats distributed according to population—as well as by
Bhutto's solemn word that he would not interfere with the workings of the
provincial governments in which his Pakistan People's Party (PPP) did not have a
majority. Accordingly, when the constitution came into force, two non-PPP governments were put into place—one in Peshawar, the capital of the Northwest
Frontier Province, and the other in Quetta, the capital of Balochistan.

The third consensus—the one concerning the role of Islam in government and
in politics—took Pakistan much beyond the intent embodied in the constitutions
of 1956 and 1962. "Islam shall be the State religion of Pakistan," declared the new
constitution, using a phrase that had not occurred in the previous constitutions
and one that was to have a profound impact in the future. The new constitution
also laid down the course of action to be followed by the country in its relations
with the outside world. This was an unusual area to be covered in a constitution,
and the need for incorporating it was not clear. In particular, the constitution required that the state "shall endeavour to preserve and strengthen fraternal relations among the Muslim countries based on Islamic unity."

Soon after the adoption of the constitution, it became clear to the opposition
that Bhutto did not really intend to abide by the consensus he had reached with
them. The opposition governments in Balochistan and the Northwest Frontier
Province were openly discriminated against; their leaders were frequently criticized for being unpatriotic; and, finally, on February 12, 1974, the government of
Balochistan was dismissed on charges of having incited the people of that
province to rebel against central authority. The government in the Northwest
Frontier Province resigned in sympathy with its counterpart in Balochistan.

On May 24, an amendment in the constitution gave the executive the authority
to declare illegal any political party found "operating in a manner prejudicial to
the sovereignty or integrity of the country." This power was to be exercised with
the approval of the Supreme Court, and, as demonstrated by later events, the
court was ready to oblige. This power was used to ban the National Awami Party,
by now the only effective opposition to the People's Party, and one other step was
taken toward Bhutto's unstated but by now obvious objective of turning Pakistan
into a one-party state. The final step toward this ultimate goal would be another
general election, which would put the People's Party in total command of the

TABLE 2.2 Results of the National Assembly Elections of March 1977

	Punjab	*Sindh*	*Frontier*	*Balochistan*	*Total*
Pakistan People's Party	108	32	8	7	155
Pakistan National Alliance	8	11	17	–	36
Pakistan Muslim League	–	–	1	–	1
Total seats	116	43	26	7	192

Source: Dawn (overseas weekly) (Karachi, March 13, 1977), p. 6.

National Assembly. The election for the National Assembly was slated for March 7, 1977, and that for the four provincial assemblies was slated for March 10.

The Elections of 1977

Opposition was fragmented and in retreat when, on January 7, 1977, Zulfikar Ali Bhutto announced the intention of his government to hold general elections for the national as well as the provincial assemblies. But the remarkable speed with which the opposition was able to organize itself into a fairly cohesive force—a force that was given the name of Pakistan National Alliance (PNA) for the purpose of contesting the elections—must have surprised Bhutto. The PNA, launched on January 11, 1977, was a collection of nine political parties ranging from Jamaat-i-Islami on the right to the National Democratic Party (previously called the National Awami Party) on the left. The opposition was able to put together a program that seemed attractive to many; it also campaigned hard, drew very large crowds to its public meetings, and, on the eve of the elections, seemed in a position to capture a significant number of seats in both the national and the provincial assemblies. Nobody expected the PNA to win, not even its leaders, but most political observers expected it to improve its position in the legislatures. It was therefore with surprise and dismay that the PNA and its supporters heard the results on the morning of March 8. Of the 192 seats contested, only 36 (or 18.8 percent) went to the PNA. The Punjab result seemed most surprising of all, in that the opposition won only 8 out of 116 seats (see Table 2.2).

The opposition cried foul and took to the streets. Once again, elections had generated tensions that the politicians found impossible to cope with; demonstrations occurred daily, fired upon first by the police and then, when the law-and-order situation deteriorated further, by the armed forces. Bhutto now faced a situation not too dissimilar from the one Ayub had confronted in 1969. In fact, he adopted the same approach. Opposition leaders were summoned and talks were begun, but, once again, the army intervened. The army took Bhutto and the leaders of the PNA into custody, and General Zia ul-Haq announced that fresh elections would be held within ninety days. The army's operation was called "fair play."

The Fall of Bhutto

Although forced out of power on July 5, 1977, Bhutto continued to dominate Pakistan's politics for another twenty-one months. During most of this time, he remained in prison. His first incarceration was in the nature of "protective custody," having been ordered by General Zia ul-Haq to save Bhutto from the people's wrath "in a political climate which is distinctly hostile to the former Prime Minister." But the political climate began to improve; on July 17, less than two weeks after the coup d'état, Bhutto addressed a large meeting of his followers on the lawn of his improvised prison. The time for launching movements such as the one that had removed him was over, he declared: "The time had come for a revolution." Released from custody soon afterward, he hesitated only for a moment before advising his supporters that he would participate vigorously in the elections promised for October 1977 by the military regime.

According to a Pakistani journalist who closely followed the course of events that occurred after the assumption of power by the military, Bhutto's visits to Karachi and Lahore, the two principal cities of Pakistan, attracted large crowds; but "irrespective of the continuing popularity . . . the local press, including some newspapers that used to be almost lyrical in his praise, are daily discovering two or more of his misdeeds."[8] Freed from the shackles of government control, the press displayed considerable enthusiasm in investigating abuses of power during the Bhutto years. These investigations resulted in a clamor for "accountability," a process that began with a case lodged in Lahore's High Court that accused Bhutto of participating in a conspiracy to murder a political opponent. The court proceedings not only focused on the criminal charge brought against the former prime minister but also dwelt at length on the way Bhutto had administered Pakistan during his years of stewardship. To help the debate along, the government published a number of white papers detailing his administration's misdeeds. These investigations and the people's reaction to them demonstrated vividly how polarized Pakistan's society had become. General Zia articulated the middle-class response: "I said to him 'Sir'—I still called him that—'Sir, why have you done all these things, you whom I respected so, you who had so much' and he only said that I should wait and he would be cleared. It was very disappointing." Bhutto's followers labeled the campaign against the deposed prime minister a vendetta of the social classes that had suffered under him and promised that "nothing could avert their skinning."[9] This was a reference to the PPP's manifesto for the October elections, which resolved to "skin alive the capitalists and other property owners."[10]

Bhutto's judgment that time would clear his name proved wrong. The Lahore Court announced its verdict on March 19, 1978, finding him to be an "arch culprit" in the ambush of November 1974. The purpose of that ambush had been to kill Ahmad Raza Kasuri, a one-time political protégé turned opponent. The court then ordered Bhutto's execution.

The execution was delayed for more than a year while Bhutto's lawyers explored all possible legal avenues to save their client's life. The final legal pronouncement came on March 31, 1979, when the country's Supreme Court refused to review their earlier verdict. On April 4, 1979, Zulfikar Ali Bhutto was hanged at the Rawalpindi jail.

The Zia Era

General Zia ul-Haq was not well known outside army circles when he wrested power from Zulfikar Ali Bhutto and put Pakistan under martial law.[11] He had been selected a year earlier by Bhutto to become the chief of staff of the army, succeeding General Tikka Khan, a loyal supporter of the prime minister. Zia's coup d'état on July 5, 1977, surprised Bhutto and most political observers in Pakistan. Nobody guessed then that this little known, self-effacing general would move against a popular political leader, manage to stay in active politics for more than eleven years, and would finally depart from the political scene involuntarily. Public discontent had forced Ayub Khan, Pakistan's first military president, to leave office; Yahya Khan, the second army officer to occupy that office, had been dislodged by his military colleagues. Zia ul-Haq survived several agitations against him and also managed to retain the loyalty of the army officer corps.

However, the Zia era ended as unexpectedly and as suddenly as it had begun. He was killed in an air crash on August 17, 1988. With him died a number of senior army generals; among them was General Akhtar Abdur Rahman, chairman of the Joint Chiefs of Staff, who, as the director general of the Interservices Intelligence (ISI), had masterminded the resistance put up by the Afghan *mujahideen* against the Soviet occupying forces. Also killed was Arnold Raphal, the U.S. ambassador to Pakistan. The crash, near Bahawalpur, a city in south Punjab, occurred in suspicious circumstances. It was investigated by the U.S. FBI, the military and civil intelligence agencies of Pakistan, and by a special commission established for this purpose by Ghulam Ishaq Khan, Zia's successor as president. All investigations reached the same conclusion: Zia's plane, an army C-130, crashed as a result of an explosion in the cockpit. The explosion was caused by a bomb placed in the plane while it was parked at the airport near Bahawalpur. Zia's assassins had succeeded in penetrating the tight security net that was in place while he was in Bahawalpur. That is as far as the investigators were able to proceed; none of the investigating teams was prepared to speculate about the identity of the assassins.[12]

General Zia ul-Haq, in power for more than eleven years, had been able to reshape Pakistani politics, society, and culture in several ways. He brought Islam into politics, used political manipulation rather than consensus building to stay in power, created a place for the military in the political system, and slowed to a crawl the development of political parties in the country. Was Zia a reluctant recruit to politics, pushed on to the political stage by a set of circumstances over which he had no control? Or was he an exceptionally shrewd individual who was successful in camouflaging his political ambition while he was the chief of staff of the army and who outwitted his opponents once he placed himself in power?

Islam and Pakistan's Political Development

The objective of the armed forces' "operation fair play"—the army maneuver that led first to the intermittent incarceration of Zulfikar Ali Bhutto and then, with the logic of events, to his eventual execution—was to hold elections and bring democracy back to the country. The promise was that elections would be held within ninety days of the army's intervention. The elections were postponed, however, so that the process of accountability could be completed—a process by which Bhutto and his associates were to give a full account to the people of the reasons for which they had managed the country's economy and polity in the way that they had. The account was given by Bhutto in a number of appearances before the High Court of Lahore and the country's Supreme Court; it was also given in a book entitled *If I Am Assassinated. . .* , which he wrote while awaiting execution of the death sentence.[13] The process, as noted, was completed on April 4, 1979, when Bhutto was hanged in Rawalpindi, but the elections—this time promised for November 1979—were postponed again, as, in the words of General Zia, they would not have produced "positive results." The positive results the general sought were to prepare the way for the establishment of a truly Islamic order in Pakistan.

This was not a new objective, suddenly adopted by the military after Bhutto had fully accounted for all his sins. Rather, it was an objective that General Zia had clearly underscored in his first speech after assuming power and declaring martial law. At that time he had praised the "spirit of Islam" that had inspired the opposition movement against the Bhutto government, and had concluded: "It proves that Pakistan, which was created in the name of Islam, will continue to survive only if it sticks to Islam. That is why I consider the introduction of an Islamic system as an essential prerequisite for the country."[14]

Zia's approach to Pakistan's political development once again raised an important question: Was Pakistan created in order to set up an Islamic state in the Muslim majority areas of British India, or was it the consequence of a political movement that aimed to set up a country in which the Muslims of British India could live without fear of Hindu domination? This question was first posed to Mohammad Ali Jinnah when he launched his campaign for Pakistan, was asked a thousand times during the several periods of constitution making, and was being raised again as the military under Zia wrestled with the problem of finding a durable political order. What is the answer?

Jinnah provided two rather different interpretations as to why he had wanted an independent state for the Muslims of India. "How would you describe the 'vital principles' of Pakistan?" he had been asked in 1944 by Beverly Nichols, a journal-

ist from Britain. In five words Jinnah had answered, "The Muslims are a Nation."
He went on to say,

> You must remember that Islam is not merely a religious doctrine but a realistic and
> practical code of conduct. I am thinking in terms of life, of everything important in
> life. I am thinking in terms of our history, our heroes, our art, our architecture, our
> music, our laws, our jurisprudence. . . . In all these things our outlook is not only
> fundamentally different but often radically antagonistic to the Hindus. We are differ-
> ent beings. There is nothing in life which links us together. Our names, our clothes,
> our foods—they are all different; our economic life, our educational ideas, our treat-
> ment of women, our attitude to animals . . . we challenge each other at every point of
> the compass.[15]

Islam, according to this interpretation, was not just a religion but a code of
conduct. If Pakistan was being created for Islam, it must fully follow its dictates,
not only in religious terms but in all aspects of life—political, cultural, economic,
and social. Jinnah seemed to be arguing for the establishment of a truly Islamic
state in Pakistan.

In his first statement to the Constituent Assembly in August 1947, however, he
had seemed to take a different line. As earlier noted, he had talked about religion
as being a personal faith and had hoped that in the course of time in Pakistan
"Hindus would cease to be Hindus and Muslims would cease to be Muslims." Had
Jinnah changed his mind between 1944 and 1947 on the very important issue of
the role of Islam in shaping institutions in Pakistan? After all, in 1944 Pakistan
was only an idea; but in 1947 it was a reality that Jinnah confronted as the governor-general and president of the Constituent Assembly. As with the earlier question on the meaning of Pakistan, this question, too, has no clear answer.

But the dilemma that General Zia ul-Haq and his associates faced was a real
one. "Pakistan is like Israel, an ideological state," the general said in 1981, as he began to reshape Pakistan's political and some parts of its economic and judicial systems. "Take out Judaism from Israel and it will collapse like a house of cards. Take
Islam out of Pakistan and make it a secular state; it would collapse. For the past
four years we have been trying to bring Islamic values to the country."[16]

Numerous attempts to resolve this dilemma were made after 1979, following
Bhutto's execution and Zia's decision to stay in power. In February of that year, a
system of Islamic courts was introduced to enforce a new set of *shariat* laws,
which defined the punishments for adultery, false witness, theft, and consumption of alcohol. Prescribed punishments included lashes, amputation of hands
and limbs, public hanging, and death by stoning. The courts were also empowered to test whether existing laws were Islamic—a provision that, predictably, resulted in a great deal of legal activity, including a case filed and personally argued
by a retired justice of the Supreme Court challenging the entire concept of representative democracy. The former justice argued that what was permitted under
Islamic law is an *amir* (ruler) and a *shura* (an assembly not necessarily chosen by

the people). The *amir* could remain in power for as long a time as permitted by the *shura*.

On August 30, 1979, the Political Parties Act of 1962 was amended by a presidential ordinance requiring all existing political parties to register with the Election Commission, to publish formal manifestos, and to submit their accounts for audit. There was the strong implication that a political party could be denied registration if its manifesto did not explicitly include Islamic provisions. Then, in October, a twelve-member committee of "scholars, jurists, *ulema* [Islamic scholars], and prominent persons from other walks of life" was appointed to formulate and present to the government recommendations for the structure of an Islamic government system. This committee of wise men failed to reach a consensus on the precise way to Islamicize the political structure. But their failure did not deter the government. On March 24, 1981, General Zia, on his own authority as chief martial law administrator, promulgated a Provisional Constitutional Order. The main provisions of this order concerned the setting up of a Federal Council (Majilis-e-Shura) "consisting of such persons as the president may, by order, determine" to "perform such functions as may be specified in an order made by the president." There was promise of political activity in the future, but only those parties that had previously registered with the Election Commission were to be permitted to participate. By implication, this provision debarred Bhutto's Pakistan People's Party from future political activity, since the PPP had failed to register. To make doubly sure that future politics would be confined to those groups and organizations acceptable to the military, the order gave the president the power to dissolve any such organization or group that in his opinion "has been formed or is operating in a manner prejudicial to the sovereignty, integrity, or security of Pakistan."

The order also sought to discipline the judiciary, which in the past had shown some wayward tendencies. All court judgments against earlier orders of the government were retroactively invalidated, and the military courts and cases brought before them were specifically excluded from the jurisdiction of all other courts. Finally, the judges were ordered to take a new oath of office to abide by the new order; those who refused to accept the wording of the new oath—and this group included the chief justice of the Supreme Court—were dismissed.

The various provisions of the order established a system advocated by such Islamic scholars as Maulana Maududi. These scholars had long contended that parliamentary democracy was not strictly compatible with the practice followed during the time of Prophet Muhammad and the four caliphs that succeeded him. But other scholars have disagreed with this interpretation of absolute obedience to the ruler. According to Fazlur Rahman, those who have clung to this orthodoxy "devised nothing to control the absoluteness of the ruler himself. The *shura* or the consultative body enjoined by the Quran and ingrained in Arab life could have been developed into some kind of effective institution, but nothing was done in this direction."[17]

The conduct of the *shura* confounded its critics; its members, even though they gave general support to the president and his administration, were more critical than anybody had expected. The government treated the *shura* more seriously than seemed possible under the provisions of the order that established it in the first place.

This experiment with a limited form of democracy apparently encouraged General Zia ul-Haq to take the next step—replacement of the *shura* with an elected assembly. The *shura* had worked well as an effective consultative body, but it soon became obvious that the people wanted something much more representative than a handpicked assembly of political notables.

The Politics of Manipulation

General Zia ul-Haq's attempt to Islamicize Pakistan's political system was seen by several opposition leaders as a way of slowing down the promised return to civilian rule. These leaders assembled their "defunct" parties under a new umbrella organization called the Movement for the Restoration of Democracy (MRD), which was launched in February 1981. Eleven parties, including Zulfikar Ali Bhutto's Pakistan People's Party and several rightist parties were included in the MRD. Zia responded to these pressures on August 12, 1983, by announcing a detailed blueprint for the restoration of democracy.

The fact that President Zia announced his blueprint on August 12 rather than August 14—the date on which Pakistan had gained independence—indicated the pragmatic approach he was to adopt throughout this period. The president must have known that his political opposition, the Movement for the Restoration of Democracy, had decided to launch a movement against the military government on independence day. A speech delivered two days in advance of the MRD announcement took a great deal of wind out of the opposition's sails.

In the political journey that began on August 12, 1983, and continued right up to his death on August 17, 1988, President Zia seemed to stop a number of times as if to see whether the direction in which he was moving was indeed the right one. When he paused to reflect on the course of his journey, he seemed to be aware only of the distance he had traveled, not of the distance that remained to be covered. During these pauses en route to his final destination, he did not convey the impression of a man in a great hurry. However, General Zia did not reach the end of his constitutional odyssey; his job was still unfinished when he died.

The speech of August 12, 1983, was vintage Zia in that he expressed a firm intention to move toward some form of democratization without indicating what form that democratization would ultimately take. Spelling out the details of the structure he wanted to evolve would only have brought criticism and opposition and, therefore, doubt and uncertainty. It is quite possible that the general and his colleagues had not made up their minds about the exact way they wanted to achieve *some* transfer of power to the politicians. The failure to inscribe concretely the system the generals wanted to produce was probably less the outcome of a deliberate plan than the product of their uncertainty as to what would ultimately be acceptable to the people and the armed forces. A number of details were vague: Left unclear, for instance, were the questions as to whether the constitution of 1973 would be the basis for the promised elections; whether a framework would be created within which the armed forces would be allowed to play a legitimate political role and, if so, whether the army leaders themselves would be subject to some checks and balances; whether the federal structure of the 1973 constitution (which the Bhutto government had never allowed to come into existence) would be given real life and a genuine attempt would be made at the devolution of political and economic power to the provinces; and, perhaps most important of all, whether the "defunct" political parties would be allowed to resurrect themselves and, if so, whether the old politicians would be permitted to participate in politics once again. The answers to some of these tantalizing questions emerged in due course, but not as part of a grand design; they came as reactions to various kinds of pressures that were exerted on the government by its supporters and its opponents during this period of evolution. General Zia ul-Haq favored political manipulation over consensus building to prolong his rule and to keep his opponents off balance.

The announcement of August 12, 1983, did not, of course, satisfy the established political forces, particularly those from the province of Sindh. The reports from the intelligence agencies that must have persuaded General Zia to hasten the announcement of his framework turned out to be accurate. Two days after the general's speech, the Movement for the Restoration of Democracy decided to vindicate its title by asking the people to launch a "popular" campaign to restore democracy to the country. The campaign's formula was essentially the one that had been tried with much success before—in the agitation against Ayub Khan in 1968–1969, in the Bengali secessionist movement in 1970–1971, and in the campaign against Zulfikar Ali Bhutto in 1977—but this time the politicians failed and the government survived. Taking its cue from the past, the MRD ordered its leaders to seek arrest and its followers to agitate in the streets. In order to avoid antagonizing the people who were not supporters of the MRD, and in the hope of winning them over to the opposition, those who responded to the MRD's call were encouraged to be selectively violent—to aim their anger not at public property but at government personnel. And in order not to provoke too violent a response from the armed forces, the MRD seemed to direct its campaign at the civilian authorities rather than at the men in uniform. Close contacts were established with the foreign media to spread the news of mass arrests and sporadic violence from one part of the country to another.

The movement took an ugly turn in the rural areas of Sindh, the province of Zulfikar Ali Bhutto. For nearly three months, opposition forces fought street battles with the police. By the end of November, when it was all over, the government admitted that more than 60 persons had been killed and that it had jailed nearly 5,000 supporters of the MRD. The opposition's estimate of casualties and incarceration was naturally much higher, but by the end of the year it, too, had accepted the fact that much steam had gone out of the campaign.

The campaign failed because it did not spread to all parts of the country; it did not spread because the movement, at a fairly early stage, acquired an objective other than the restoration of democracy. In particular, under the leadership of Ghulam Mustafa Jatoi, a veteran PPP leader, the MRD sought to redress the provincial grievances felt deeply by a large number of Sindhis against the Punjab-dominated administration at Islamabad. Subsequently, the campaign was given a further twist when, in a speech delivered before the *Lok Sabha,* the lower house of the Indian parliament, Indira Gandhi gave it her support. She told the Indian parliament that her government could not remain indifferent to what was going on in Pakistan and that she fully supported those who were working for the restoration of democracy in that country. Even if there had been some chance that the MRD movement would spread to the populous province of Punjab, the Gandhi statement killed it. From then on, the movement acquired a very strong provincial overtone; in effect, it was confined to the rural areas of Sindh.

The MRD leadership did not recognize, perhaps, that the military had gained a considerable competence in handling localized demonstrations and that their movement would not prove to be an exception. The agitation cost many lives, but it finally petered out. A movement can prove to be fatal for the political authority if it acquires mass popular appeal, as had happened in the case of anti-Ayub and anti-Bhutto campaigns. But that movement has only a limited impact if its objective becomes confined to a set of issues with a narrow appeal. This is essentially what happened to the MRD campaign against General Zia.

The movement did serve some purpose; however: It persuaded General Zia ul-Haq that his plan for the restoration of democracy had to include some safeguards for ensuring that the process, once set in place, did not run off course. Changes in direction had occurred before, as, for instance, when Ayub Khan failed to contain the forces he had unleashed by agreeing to amend his constitution. A similar derailment of the process had occurred when General Yahya Khan held elections as a part of his design to restore democracy. General Zia's solution to the problem was a simple one: Unlike Generals Ayub and Yahya before him, he gave a clear signal to the nation that he had every intention of being the central figure in any system that finally evolved from his political experiments.

Accordingly, on November 30, 1984, and to a somewhat surprised nation, General Zia announced his decision to hold a national referendum. In the referendum, held on December 19, the voters were asked to say "yes" or "no" to the following question:

Whether the people of Pakistan endorse the process initiated by General Mohammad Zia ul-Haq, the President of Pakistan, for bringing [the] laws of Pakistan [into] conformity with the injunction of Islam as laid down in the Holy Quran and Sunnah of the Holy Prophet (Peace be upon him) and for the preservation of the ideology of

Pakistan, *for the continuation and consolidation of that process* and for the smooth and orderly transfer of power to the elected representatives of the people. [Emphasis added.][18]

It was made clear that affirmation by a simple majority of the votes cast would be seen as a mandate to General Zia ul-Haq to remain in office for another five years. In the words of one political commentator:

> The referendum exercise, which came as a bolt from the blue, was said by official quarters to stem from two compulsions. First, if the issue of the President's election was not settled before the elections to the Parliament, then there was every possibility that the elected [members] would not remain loyal to the President and ensure his own [subsequent] election . . . the argument being that if the nominated members of the Majilis-e-Shura, who were dependent [in] their positions entirely on the goodwill of the government, can also on occasion differ from the official line, then there was a greater probability that the elected parliamentarians would be more independent and therefore difficult to manage.[19]

Under this logic, it was essential for General Zia to ensure his own election before embarking on that of the national and provincial legislation. Accomplishing this through a referendum avoided the awkward problem of using the 1973 constitution under which the president's election followed that of the assemblies. A mandate under the 1973 constitution would have meant convening the assemblies elected in 1977—an election that his government had claimed all along was repudiated by the people. Referendum was the only course, but even that solution posed legal problems inasmuch as a direct question about the president's tenure in office would have been in conflict with the 1973 constitution. Hence the question that was asked had to be phrased indirectly with the reference to Islamization.

Other than the legal problem, the reference to Islam had a strategic purpose. It was hoped that the people would find it difficult to respond negatively to General Zia's continuation in office for five more years if he was seeking a mandate for further Islamization. An additional problem concerned the elections in India that had been scheduled for December 25 by Rajiv Gandhi, the new Indian prime minister. Given the size of the electorate and the enthusiasm with which it always participates, elections in India have always attracted a great deal of attention in the Western democracies. Therefore, some display of democracy in Pakistan before the Indian election was considered to be essential if the support the country needed from its friends in the United States and Europe was to be retained.

The referendum was held on December 19, and, according to the results announced by the government, President Zia received the mandate he had sought. Some 62 percent of the 34 million voters were said to have cast their ballots; of these 98 percent said "yes." In other words, more than 60 percent of the electorate had voted to keep General Zia in office for another five years. But, not unexpect-

TABLE 2.3   Voter Participation in the Elections of 1985 (in percentages)

	Assemblies	
	National	Provincial
Punjab	59.6	61.8
Sindh	44.6	49.8
Northwest Frontier	38.8	47.6
Balochistan	35.1	46.6
Total percentage of registered voters	52.9	56.9

Source: "Elections show a high turnout," Muslim (Islamabad, March 2, 1985), p. 1.

edly, the result was contested by the opposition, which estimated the turnout of the electorate to be no more than 10 percent of the total. "We will not respect or recognize Zia as president, and we will not accept the results of the rigged election," announced the leadership of the MRD after the Election Commission had announced the results. Another agitation was announced "to bring down Zia but keep the country together."[20] But the opposition, caught off guard by the government's decision to hold a referendum, was not able to mount the promised agitation, and Zia's process of democratization continued at the pace he had prescribed for it.

Elections were held on February 25 for 217 National Assembly seats and on February 27 for 483 seats in the four provincial assemblies. In all, 5,007 candidates participated. Competition for provincial assembly seats was keener than for the seats in the National Assembly: On the average, there were 8 candidates for every provincial assembly seat, but only 5 for the National Assembly. Out of an electorate of nearly 33 million, 18.5 million cast votes for the provincial seats and 17.3 million cast votes for the candidates for the National Assembly. Voter turnout was impressive: nearly 53 percent for the National Assembly and nearly 57 percent for the four provincial assemblies. For both elections, voter participation was highest in Punjab and lowest in Balochistan—an indication, perhaps, of the relative development and modernization of the provinces (see Table 2.3).

The results—particularly the unexpectedly large turnout of voters in all parts of the country—pleased the government's critics and its foreign supporters. "The longest-serving martial law regime in Pakistan's history has finally managed to hold its first general elections in a manner that was peaceful and fair beyond any doubt. . . . On top of it, the voter turnout has been beyond all expectations even if it is still less than the official turnout figure given for the referendum," wrote the editor of the Muslim, an independent and influential newspaper published in Islamabad.[21] According to the Wall Street Journal, as well, the results were encouraging: "The Reagan administration has encouraged General Zia to move toward civilian rule. This week's elections made some small progress toward that goal."[22]

General Zia ul-Haq's effort to restore civilian rule gained some credibility inside as well as outside the country, and set into motion a process that could no longer be easily manipulated. The exercise in limited democracy produced a number of surprises for the regime, some of which will still influence the course of political development in the country. Perhaps the most important outcome of the election was the electorate's failure to strongly endorse the government's move to Islamicize the society.

Jamaat-i-Islami, the party that had relentlessly pursued the cause of Islamization through the years and was known to be close to General Zia, did very poorly. Even though political parties were not allowed to participate in the elections, the Jamaat let it be known that it supported sixty candidates for the National Assembly. Of these only eight were elected, of whom four were from the cities of Karachi and Lahore. The only rural support the party received was from the Northwest Frontier Province, which returned four Jamaat followers. In light of this outcome, the new leadership was inclined to be more cautious in pursuing the goal of Islamization.

The new political leadership was also very conservative in managing the economy, as suggested by the first budget presented to the new National Assembly. The budget outlined a conservative economic philosophy in which the government's role in economic management was to be severely limited. Instead, private enterprise was to be "provided full opportunity to lead the economy toward new heights."[23] The large rural sector of the economy was not to be burdened with direct taxation, and the incidence of tax on nonrural incomes was lowered to promote individual effort and enterprise. In presenting the budget, Mahbub ul Haq, the new finance minister, was responding to the ideological shape of the new Assembly.

The pronounced swing to the right was the direct consequence of the remarkable comeback of the rural aristocracy to the center of Pakistani politics. A large majority of the national and provincial assembly seats was captured by rural notables—landlords, religious leaders, and scions of prominent families. The rural elite's restoration to political power was facilitated by the ground rules laid down by the government for the elections. Political parties, if allowed to participate in the elections, would have brought some voter discipline. After all, it was the immense popularity of the leftist Pakistan People's Party that had resulted in the virtual elimination of the rural aristocracy in the elections of 1970. In the absence of the discipline normally exercised by political parties, voter choice was polarized. In the rural areas a very large number of voters ended up supporting village notables.

The same lack of discipline produced an entirely different result in the cities. There the electorate cast essentially a negative vote—that is, a vote against the government and many of its policies. The voters of Islamabad elected a former air force officer over the minister of information largely because they did not like the heavy hand the government had laid on the media, particularly the state-controlled television. In campaigning against the government's management of the economy, a relatively unknown political figure defeated another minister in the large industrial city of Gujranwala. And in Rawalpindi, the city's mayor, who had identified himself with the government, lost to a young student leader. The reason: voter dissatisfaction with the state of urban services. These and other outcomes produced a set of new urban politicians who were elected to the assemblies with no clear mandate other than to change the way the government was conducting itself. Once again, the absence of political parties—and, therefore, of any clear economic or political ideology—meant that the majority of the representatives from urban areas would openly challenge the government without providing an unambiguous alternative of their own. The defeat of Khwaja Mohammad Safdar, the government's nominee for the speakership of the National Assembly, was the first manifestation of their negative approach to politics. On March 21, two days before the new constitutional system became operative, Safdar was defeated by Fakhr Imam, a young politician whose only attractive feature at that time was his willingness to oppose the government's candidate.

Thus, the elections of February 1985 produced national and provincial assemblies in which rural notables had a strong presence and urban representatives who, although defiant, were politically adrift. The lack of political focus of the members from the urban areas was to have a profound influence on the course of events in the months following the elections.

On March 2, three days after the completion of the electoral process, President Zia promulgated an order that introduced sweeping changes in the constitution of 1973. The purpose behind most of the changes was to concentrate political power in the hands of the president. Article 90 of the 1973 constitution had stipulated that "the executive authority of the federation shall be exercised in the name of the President by the Federal government consisting of the Prime Minister and the Federal ministries which shall act through the Prime Minister who shall be the chief executive of the Federation." According to the amended article, "the executive authority of the federal government shall vest in the President and shall be exercised by him either directly or through officers subordinate to him." A new provision was added to further strengthen the hands of the president. It stipulated that "if any question arises whether any matter is or is not a matter in respect of which the President is by the Constitution empowered to act in his discretion, the decision of the President in his discretion will be final, and the validity of anything done by the President shall not be called [into] question on the ground that he ought or ought not to have acted in his discretion."

General Zia's decision to drastically amend the constitution was criticized on grounds of legality and timing. Sheikh Anwarul Haq, the former chief justice whose court had upheld Zulfikar Ali Bhutto's death sentence and also provided the coup d'état of July 5, 1977, with a legal cover under the "doctrine of necessity," now spoke against Zia's tampering with the 1973 constitution. He said that his court had viewed the martial law proclaimed then as a temporary measure adopted to restore law and order and democracy. The president's interpretation of the court's decision, according to the retired judge, far exceeded the judges' original intention.[24] In questioning the timing of the announcement, the Executive Committee of the Jamaat-i-Islami found it "shocking that just when the freshly elected assemblies were going to meet, the constitution had been amended arbitrarily." According to the Jamaat, the correct approach would have been to entrust the amendment bill to the National Assembly.[25] Although the issue of legality and timing were of concern, the concentration of executive power in the hands of one man was the real focus of most of the criticisms against the president's action. "Everybody is at his [the president's] mercy and he is at the mercy of providence alone," declared a contributor to the *Muslim*.[26] "The real essence of what will happen on March 23 when the new constitution is enforced is the replacement of Zia the military ruler by Zia the new civilian autocrat. He may be shedding his army uniform but he is keeping his absolute power," said the *Times* of London.[27]

General Zia did not shed his uniform on March 23 when he handpicked Muhammed Khan Junejo as prime minister. Junejo, a veteran politician from Sindh, had served as a minister in one of the cabinets Zia had formed after taking over the presidency. Once sworn in, the prime minister went on to display remarkable independence. He dropped all but one general from the cabinet, and, more important, went on to announce to the public that democracy and martial law could not coexist. This assertion of independence and its tolerance by General Zia and his military colleagues helped the prime minister establish a political base independent of the military, thereby finally leading the National Assembly to give him a unanimous vote of confidence when it met for its first formal session. Having been confirmed by the legislature, the prime minister came into his own, thus advancing by one further step the process of civilianization. For the process to be completed, however, one further step had to be taken: the introduction of political parties.

It made good political sense for General Zia to insist on partyless elections; he was certain that Zulfikar Ali Bhutto's Pakistan People's Party would win a large number of seats—possibly a majority in the National Assembly—if the elections were held on the basis of political parties. Because the Bhutto family had not forgiven the generals for staging a coup d'état against Zulfikar Ali Bhutto in July 1977 and then allowing him to be executed in April 1979, a PPP victory at the polls would have been suicidal for the army. Accordingly, the elections were held without the participation of the political parties. Once the national and provincial legislatures commenced their formal business, however, it soon became clear that unless the political parties disciplined the members, the results would be totally chaotic. As one minister put it during the opening day of the National Assembly's budget session in May, "We don't have one party, or ten parties, or twenty parties; we have two hundred parties. Each member of the assembly considers himself responsible only to himself, not to any other person, let alone to a higher authority."[28] The conduct of the National Assembly in its first full session and that of the provincial assemblies (given that three such assemblies—those of Balochistan, Punjab, and the Northwest Frontier Province—demanded the lifting of martial law) convinced the regime that political parties had to be restored in some form or other. The first move was to create an "official group" in the National Assembly consisting of two-thirds of the Assembly's membership. The official group, formed in the summer of 1985, facilitated the passage in the fall of two critical pieces of legislation—the Indemnity Bill and the Political Parties Act. General Zia ul-Haq had made it clear to the members of the national legislature that unless they provided the martial law regime with a bill that would provide legal protection to his administration for *all* actions taken during the eight years of martial law, it would be impossible for the military to hand over power to a civilian successor. There were several precedents for the form of blanket indemnity sought by General Zia, including, for instance, its use in Brazil and Turkey before the military administrations in the two countries surrendered power to politicians. After a long and surprisingly candid debate, the National Assembly passed the Indemnity Bill.

In addition to indemnity for the actions taken during the martial law period, General Zia insisted on the creation of a new framework within which political parties would be allowed to function. The main purpose of such a framework was to allow the chief executive in the post–martial law period—in this case President Zia ul-Haq—some control over the formation or dissolution of political parties. Equipped with this power, General Zia could keep a watchful eye on Zulfikar Ali Bhutto's Pakistan People's Party (PPP). The leaders of the PPP—in particular, those who lived in exile in Europe, including Bhutto's wife, his daughter, Benazir, Mumtaz Bhutto (Zulfikar Ali Bhutto's cousin), and Ghulam Mustafa Khan—not only remained hostile to General Zia but also refused to accept the constraints on their behavior as prescribed in the Indemnity Bill. Accordingly, the military needed some additional protection, and this it sought within a legal framework designed to guide the working of political parties. The Political Parties Act was passed by the National Assembly on December 9, 1985. Its most important feature was the requirement that a political party could function only if it was registered with the Election Commission; moreover, in obtaining registration, the party had to accept Pakistan's Islamic ideology and commit not to do anything that would "defame or bring into ridicule" the army or the judiciary. The Election Commission was given the authority to ban a party if it strayed from such a commitment.

Having equipped the executive with this power, General Zia ul-Haq was finally in a position to send the armed forces back to their barracks. This he did on December 30, 1985, thus indicating—or so it seemed then—the end of the third and longest period of military rule in the country's thirty-nine-year history. In lifting martial law, General Zia went much further than many had expected in returning Pakistan to civilian rule. Martial law courts were closed, the constitution (albeit in its amended form) was restored in full, and human rights were revived without qualification. As the *Economist* put it: "President Zia has even restored the section which says that anybody tampering with the constitution is guilty of treason: some members of the opposition hope, if they ever win power, to try him on that charge."[29]

The changes introduced on December 30 contained one other surprise: President Zia announced that he was staying on as chief of staff of the army. It had been widely believed that the top job in the army would go to General Khalid Mahmud Arif, Zia's close associate and friend and now the deputy chief of staff. The decision to keep the job for himself introduced an interesting twist in the evolution of the new political system. By keeping the armed forces involved in the evolution of the system, Zia was guarding against the possibility of another military takeover in case the experiment with democracy failed. As one member of the parliament put it: "For eight years politicians accepted Zia as president by virtue of being COAS [chief of the army staff]. Now the army should let him be COAS for a few years because he is our president."[30]

Under the protective umbrella provided by these legislations, Zia ul-Haq's civilian associates were prepared to begin some form of institutional politics. On January 8, 1986, Prime Minister Junejo announced the revival of the Pakistan Muslim League, a political party with a long and checkered history. The party had known many forms: Under Mohammad Ali Jinnah it brought independence to Pakistan in 1947, only to be discredited as a party of merchants and rural oligarchs in the turbulent years of 1954–1958. Along with all other political parties, the Muslim League was dissolved when Ayub Khan brought Pakistan under martial law in 1958. The League was revived again in 1962 under the leadership of General Ayub Khan, but a number of old "Leaguers" stayed out of the official party to form their own group—namely, the Council Muslim League, so called because the decision to revive the Muslim League was taken by a council of Leaguers. The two "Leagues" clashed in the presidential election of 1964: General Ayub Khan was the candidate of the (official) Muslim League, whereas Fatima Jinnah, the sister of Pakistan's founder, was put forward by the Council Muslim League. Ayub Khan won in a bitterly fought campaign with Zulfikar Ali Bhutto, who acted as the general's campaign manager and led the charge against the opposition. However, when Bhutto left Ayub Khan's government two years later, he decided to form his own party: the Pakistan People's Party. In the parliamentary elections of 1970, the PPP won 87 seats—against the Muslim League's 18—out of a total of 135 seats reserved for West Pakistan.

One can well understand why General Zia was unenthusiastic about letting fall the mantle of an official party on a political association with such an unglamorous past. But it is also not too difficult to surmise the reasons for which Prime Minister Junejo decided to bring the Muslim League back. Not only was the name of the party well known in Pakistan; it had also meant different things to different people at different times. In the exceptionally fluid period following martial law, the political process would indeed be more effectively begun on the basis of a party with a known name, even if its program and ideology were undefined.

Prime Minister Junejo had his way not only on the question of the revival of the Muslim League but also in the formation of the federal cabinet. Ushered into office on January 28 was a new cabinet in which a number of technocrats (among

whom Mahbub ul Haq, the finance minister in the martial law government, was
the most prominent) lost their jobs.[31] A number of loyal members of the Muslim
League were rewarded by being included in the cabinet. The new cabinet of
twenty-two ministers and thirteen ministers of state carried a strong Junejo im-
print and was one more indication of the relative independence with which the
prime minister was now able to act. General Zia was prepared to accept this new
relationship: It was important for the success of his political experiment that
Prime Minister Junejo should be seen to have emerged out of the general's
shadow. General Zia appreciated the fact that in the political environment that
prevailed in early 1986, a prime minister who was seen as closely tied to the military would quickly lose all credibility. That the prime minister faced a difficult situation was very quickly brought home to the military, now watching the flow of
politics from their barracks. Held at Lahore on February 5 was the first political
rally to be organized by the opposition, at which a number of politicians opposed
to General Zia's political order reiterated their determination to restore the 1973
constitution in its unamended form.

The durability of the system introduced by Zia was tested by a series of events
in 1988. The system may have worked if Zia had shown greater willingness to accommodate Junejo. Zia did not; he became increasingly restive as Junejo began to
assert the limited amount of authority allowed him under the amended constitution of 1973. The first major conflict between the two centered on the question of
Pakistan's Afghan policy. Zia and the Interservices Intelligence favored a military
solution. They believed that only a military victory over Kabul would put power
in the hands of the *mujahideen* leaders supported by Pakistan. Junejo was in favor
of a negotiated settlement, arguing that the Soviet willingness to withdraw from
Afghanistan had presented Pakistan with an opportunity that would be impru-
dent to ignore. To force Zia, the army, and the ISI to accept a negotiated solution
to the Afghan problem, Junejo convened an all-party conference in Rawalpindi in
March. Zia was not invited to attend, but all other major political leaders, including Benazir Bhutto of the Pakistan People's Party, were summoned to Rawalpindi.
The conference endorsed Junejo's approach; encouraged by the political consensus thus formulated, the prime minister authorized signing the Geneva accord
with Afghanistan. (See Chapter 5.)

Junejo's attempt to exert some control over military discipline and appointments was even more difficult for Zia to swallow. On April 11, a large ammunition dump at Ojhri, an army camp in the suburb of Rawalpindi, blew up, raining
scores of missiles and projectiles on the city and neighboring Islamabad.
Hundreds of people were killed. Two enquiry commissions were set up, one by
Prime Minister Junejo and the other by the army. The prime minister's commission held the Interservices Intelligence responsible for the explosion and the resulting deaths. The commission suggested that the prime minister call for the resignation of General Akhtar Abdur Rahman—who was director general of the ISI
when the Ojhri camp was being stocked with ammunition—as well as that of Lt.

General Hamid Gul who succeeded Rahman. President Zia was not prepared to accept this recommendation in part because the two generals were very close to him and in part because the prime minister was moving into territory—military affairs—where Zia did not want him to tread. But Muhammed Khan Junejo did not stop at this. As defense minister he held up the promotion of a couple of generals considered to be close Zia associates and suggested to Zia that the time may have come for the president to give up his position as the chief of army staff.

Zia was convinced that something deeper lay behind these moves by his hand-picked prime minister than a simple assertion of a role that was assigned to him by the constitution. He decided to move against Junejo; the plans for the prime minister's dismissal were formulated while he was out of the country visiting China and Japan. Junejo returned to Islamabad on May 29, and while he was addressing a press conference at the airport, another batch of journalists were on their way to hear Zia's proclamation dismissing the prime minister and his cabinet. Zia also dissolved the national and provincial assemblies and promised that elections would be held within a period of ninety days, as stipulated in the constitution.

Zia used constitutional grounds to dismiss Junejo, basing his decision on what he viewed as the incompetence of Junejo's administration, its willingness to tolerate corruption, and its failure to promote Islamization of the society. In actuality, Zia was unhappy with the system he had created; he expressed his regrets when I met him a few days before his death. He told me:

> It was a mistake on my part to have accepted the advice of some of my colleagues that a parliamentary system of some kind is the only political system that would work in Pakistan. I should have gone for a presidential form of government. After all, it is working in other countries. I am also not so sure whether a federation based on four provinces is suitable for Pakistan. We should perhaps divide the country into twenty or so administrative units but have a unitary form of government at the center.

Zia had clearly given up on his system. Although he had promised elections within ninety days of his dismissal of Prime Minister Junejo, it is unlikely that he would have kept his promise. Had Zia lived, he would have attempted to change the political system, having concluded that a Westminster type of democracy is not suited for Pakistan.

Military in Politics

Senior military officers have participated in Pakistani politics ever since the country came into existence, but only during Zia ul-Haq's rule did the military's involvement became institutionalized. Field Marshal Mohammad Ayub Khan used the military to spring into politics but did not bring the entire armed forces into the political structure. He severed formal links with the army when he became president on October 27, 1958, and General Mohammad Musa was appointed to replace Ayub Khan as commander in chief. General Mohammad Musa was expected to manage the army's affairs on his own, but Ayub Khan felt confident enough about the army's loyalty to him to entrust its day-to-day management to the new commander in chief. Ayub turned his energy to the country's political and economic development. For a few years after the coup d'état of October 1958, he continued to rely on some of his army colleagues for advice on political matters and for managing some of the important sectors of the economy. For instance, Lt. General Mohammad Azam Khan was made responsible for settling the millions of refugees who had arrived in Pakistan from India soon after independence in 1947 but had not yet been assigned property rights over the houses they lived in, the businesses they owned, or the land they cultivated. Once Azam Khan had successfully handled this difficult task he was sent to East Pakistan as governor. East Pakistan had remained restive and sullen under military rule. Azam Khan's assignment, which he took up in 1960, was to gain legitimacy for the army's role in that province.

Ayub Khan believed that his intervention in politics would be treated with credibility only if his administration was able to manage the economy more efficiently than the previous civilian administration and at the same time succeeded in improving social services for the lower class. Lt. General Wajid Ali Burki, who had earned a reputation for the very competent management of the army's medical services, was put in charge of the portfolios of Health, Social Welfare, and Labor. Burki was now expected to put his expertise to work on the civilian side. Lt. General Khalid Sheikh was appointed to look after railways and communications. Generals Azam, Burki, and Sheikh were all from the army. Ayub Khan did not turn to the other military services, the air force and the navy, to help him run the country.

Having assigned his army colleagues to a number of sensitive positions, Ayub Khan wasted little time in developing close links with a number of civilian advisers. Some of these people were professionals such as Manzur Quadir, a prominent lawyer, who guided Ayub Khan on constitutional matters. Some were from the landed aristocracy such as Malik Amir Mohammad Khan, the nawab of Kalabagh who became Ayub Khan's closest political adviser after being appointed governor of West Pakistan in 1960. Some were bureaucrats such as Altaf Gauhar, who handled information and propaganda for the military regime, and Mohammad Shoaib, who became the principal architect of Ayub Khan's model of economic development. Azam Khan was later replaced by Abdul Monem Khan, a Bengali politician, and Burki and Sheikh were dropped from the cabinet after the promulgation of the new constitution. By March 1962, Ayub Khan had completed the task of appointing civilians to his administration.

General Yahya Khan came into office considerably less prepared than his predecessor, Ayub Khan. His move into politics was precipitated by a serious crisis: The growing movement against Ayub Khan had turned violent, and the army, called in to restore order, was not inclined to save Ayub Khan's political system for him.

Yahya adopted a different approach toward the armed forces' role in politics. Throughout his tenure as president, he did not bring in civilian advisers to help him deal with the political problems that confronted him as Ayub Khan had. Instead, he kept the initiative with his military staff. Lt. Generals S. G. M. Pirzada and Abdul Hamid remained his closest political advisers, and they counseled him to completely disband the system created by Ayub Khan.

Yahya Khan had planned the move against Ayub Khan in full consultation with the other service chiefs, Air Marshal Malik Nur Khan, chief of staff of the air force, and Admiral S. M. Ahsen, chief of staff of the navy. It was Nur Khan, the "outspoken" chief of the air force, who was deputed by the military brass to inform Ayub Khan that he had lost the confidence of the armed forces. Once martial law was declared, Yahya Khan brought in other service chiefs to help him administer the country. Nur Khan was brought in to manage the social sectors by becoming a member of the all-military "administrative council" that initially seized power from Ayub Khan. Later, Nur Khan was appointed governor of West Pakistan. Admiral S. M. Ahsen, who had handled the portfolios of Finance, Planning, Industry and Commerce in the council, was dispatched to Dhaka to become the governor of East Pakistan.

Yayha Khan's unsuccessful presidency can be blamed in part on the way he handled civil-military relations. Because he kept himself distant from the politicians he was unable to gauge the political mood of the country. This distance led him to make a number of grievous political mistakes including the sudden dismantling of the political system that had evolved during the Ayub era and the decision not to start a dialogue with East Pakistan immediately after the electoral triumph of the Awami League, the province's main political party. At the same time, because he depended on the counsel of only a few military advisers, Yahya Khan did not ensure the loyalty of the top echelon of the army establishment. Following the defeat of the army in East Pakistan, senior officers of the army were quick to distance themselves from Yahya Khan and were prepared to turn over the administration to a civilian, Zulfikar Ali Bhutto.

General Zia ul-Haq was also not as well prepared as Ayub Khan to shoulder political responsibility, and he was not quite sure of his ability to inspire confidence among the senior officers of the armed forces. Accordingly, he followed an approach that was to lead ultimately to the acceptance of a permanent political role for the armed forces. Zia also drew a number of important lessons from history. By far the two most significant of these was to confine political participation to the army and not to all the branches of the military, and to institutionalize rather than individualize the army's political involvement. Zia's decision to involve only the army was also dictated by the fact that Air Marshal Zulfiqar Ali Khan, the chief of staff of the air force at the time of Zia's coup d'état, was close to Zulfikar Ali Bhutto. Zia kept him and Admiral Khalid Janjua, the chief of staff of the navy, in the dark when he and his corps commanders decided to move against the prime minister. In depending on the army's command structure for political support rather than on individual senior officers, Zia avoided the pitfalls that cut short the political careers of Field Marshal Ayub Khan and General Yahya Khan. During his eleven years in office, Zia was able to face a number of political crises that were no less significant than those that brought an end to the presidency of Ayub Khan.

General Zia involved senior army officers in politics much more than either Ayub Khan or Yahya Khan had. Zia engaged officers as commanders of formations, as staff officers in the Army General Headquarters, and as members of his personal staff. It became a common practice for the corps commanders to meet in Rawalpindi to be briefed on political matters and to advise Zia. This practice (begun informally while "Operation Fair Play"—the decision to impose martial law, depose Zulfikar Ali Bhutto, and then hold elections in October 1977—was being planned) became routine as Zia took a number of other steps following the July 1977 coup d'état. Operation Fair Play was planned with the help of Lt. General Faiz Ali Chishti, the corps commander of Rawalpindi.[32] However, a number of subsequent steps—such as the decisions to postpone national elections promised as part of Operation Fair Play, to arrest Bhutto and put him on trial for the attempted murder of a political opponent, to hang Bhutto following the Supreme Court's rejections of his appeal—were all taken with the approval of the senior officers of the army. Although he brought in senior officers for political work and advice, Zia did not depend on one single group. He moved them around various command and staff positions, was reluctant to grant extensions in service beyond the age of mandatory retirement, and was generous in appointing superannuated senior officers to important civilian and diplomatic assignments.

These practices strengthened the army's institutional involvement in politics. Zia could have followed the approach of his predecessors because Lt. Generals Chishti and Khalid Mahmood Arif embodied the type of advisers retained by Ayub Khan and Yahya Khan during their respective administrations. According to Chishti, "Gen. Zia was lucky to have Maj. Gen. Arif as his lifelong confidante. He had experience as a Martial Law Officer during Yahya's regime and handled matters efficiently."[33] General Arif became Zia's chief of staff after proclamation of martial law in July 1977, was promoted to the rank of a full general and appointed vice chief of army staff in March 1984, and was retired from army service after the completion of his three-year term. In March 1987, Zia chose General Mirza Aslam Beg to succeed Arif as the vice chief of army staff. He took Lt. General Chishti into the first martial law cabinet but allowed him to leave the administration in March 1980. He appointed army generals as provincial governors in 1978: Lt. Generals Sawar Khan in Punjab, S. M. Abbasi in Sindh, Fazle Haq in the Northwest Frontier, and Rahimuddin Khan in Balochistan. Sawar Khan stayed in Punjab for two years and in March 1980 was brought to the army's general headquarters in Rawalpindi and appointed vice chief of army staff. In 1984, Lt. General Abbasi was replaced by Lt. General Jahandad Khan as governor of Sindh, and Lt. General S. F. S. K. Lodi took over from Rahimuddin Khan as governor of Balochistan. A number of senior officers were appointed to diplomatic positions, including Lt. General Ejaz Azim who became Pakistan's ambassador to the United States in 1980. Neither Ayub Khan nor Yahya Khan had involved so many senior army officers in political and administrative work. By doing so, Zia ul-Haq not only created a powerful constituency for himself in the army but also created a strong vested interest for the armed forces to remain in politics.

Zia's induction of the army into politics was not confined to the appointment of army officers to senior political and administrative positions. Anxious that he should not be caught by surprise on the political front, Zia entrusted the task of domestic political intelligence to the Interservices Intelligence, an agency that had been created essentially to coordinate and analyze information gathered by military attachés in Pakistan's diplomatic missions. The ISI turned out to be extremely effective in this role and was responsible for keeping Zia one step ahead of the opposition during the movements launched against him in 1983 and 1985. The ISI also managed the flow of arms and financial assistance from the United States, China, and Saudi Arabia to the *mujahideen* fighting the Soviets in Afghanistan. Zia appointed Lt. General Akhtar Abdur Rahman, another trusted army associate, to head the ISI. Under Rahman, the ISI became actively involved in all aspects of Pakistan's Afghan policy. It not only guided the *mujahideen* in the formulation of military strategy against the Soviet troops but also advised Zia and the foreign office on the position Pakistan should take in resolving the Afghan crisis. In March 1987, Zia moved Lt. General Rahman out of ISI, promoted him to the rank of full general, and appointed him chief of joint staffs. Major General Hamid Gul replaced Rahman as the director general of ISI. Rahman was with Zia in the air force plane that crashed on August 17, 1988, killing the president and several of his senior military associates.

The structured form of the army's involvement in politics made it possible for Zia's successors to quickly transfer power to a civilian president following the Bahawalpur plane crash. General Aslam Beg had traveled to Bahawalpur in a different plane; he learned of the crash and Zia's death while he himself was flying back to Rawalpindi, the army headquarters. Once in Rawalpindi, Beg convened a meeting of the senior army officers who were in the city; consulted the corps commanders on the telephone; summoned Ghulam Ishaq Khan, the chairman of the Senate, to army headquarters; and as indicated in the constitution of 1973 asked him to assume the presidency. Upon becoming president, Ishaq Khan appointed Aslam Beg chief of army staff, a position Zia ul-Haq had held for more than eleven years. Admiral Iftikhar Sirhoey was appointed chairman of the Joint Chiefs of Staff in place of General Akhtar Abdur Rahman. The institutional form of consultation with the senior army officers that Zia had practiced throughout his eleven-year tenure made possible the clean transition within a few hours of the president's death. What has been described as "the self-abnegatory role of the armed forces, rare in the tenuous political situations of the Third World," was not that at all. The military stepped out of the political limelight confident that it now had the formal institutional structure that would permit it to move back in again if the situation so demanded.

Although not wishing to move back, the military found itself facing a serious dilemma as a result of the elections of 1990. The PPP had not gained a majority but was the largest single party in the National Assembly. If democracy was to be brought back to the country, Benazir Bhutto, the party's chairperson, had to be called to form a government in Islamabad and become prime minister. Could she be trusted? The military's answer to this question was to continue the arrangement that had been put into place following Zia ul-Haq's death. They came to be known as the "troika." The term "troika" had come into currency in the early months of 1989 and was used to describe the informal grouping made up of the president, the prime minister, and the army chief of staff (COAS) that governed Pakistan after the death of General Zia ul-Haq. The troika as an informal governing arrangement evolved over time as a response to the twists and turns in the country's political history. From 1989 to 1996, Pakistan saw six troikas, each with its own peculiar dynamics and each with a different distribution of power among its three members.

The first troika came into being gradually as Pakistan adjusted to the situation caused by the death of President Zia ul-Haq. Zia's death had left an immense political vacuum that had to be filled somehow. Of the two formal positions that he had held, that of army chief of staff went to General Aslam Beg, who was Zia's deputy at the time of his death. Ghulam Ishaq Khan, chairman of the Senate, took over as acting president. But in appointing a caretaker administration to function until an elected government could be put into place, he did not nominate a prime minister. Ishaq invited Aslam Beg to participate in the deliberations of the caretaker administration, thus laying the ground for the formation of the troika. However, the third member of the arrangement was still to take office.

The tacit agreement reached between President Ishaq Khan and General Beg on the one hand and Benazir Bhutto on the other reduced her freedom. Bhutto agreed to be guided by Ghulam Ishaq Khan and Aslam Beg in the areas they considered critical for Pakistan's security. These included nuclear policy, in particular decisions with respect to the development of a nuclear bomb and the capability to deliver it; the country's stance toward Afghanistan and Kashmir; and relations with India. Bhutto also agreed to let the army look after its own affairs. The troika thus evolved into an institution for overseeing decisionmaking in the country.

From 1988 until December 1998, Pakistan saw many changes in the membership of the troika but the informal institution retained its importance. However, with the resignation of President Farooq Leghari as president and the election of Muhammad Rafiq Tarar, Prime Minister Nawaz Sharif has concentrated so much power in his hands that the troika arrangement became redundant.

Pakistan's Military Presidents:
A Comparative Analysis

Pakistan's three military presidents, General (later Field Marshal) Ayub Khan (1958–1969), General Yahya Khan (1969–1971), and General Zia ul-Haq (1977–1988), attempted to find a workable solution for Pakistan's political problems. Their approaches differed considerably. Ayub had well-developed ideas about the type of political system that could be made to work in Pakistan: He was convinced that Western political ideas could not take root in the political soil of Pakistan. As earlier noted, he experimented with his system of Basic Democracies in which the people were allowed only a limited amount of participation. But the system did not work, and his willingness to tinker with what he had created only encouraged his political opposition to ask for more changes. Ultimately, they sought the resurrection of the parliamentary system that Ayub Khan had dispensed with in 1958. But this outcome was not acceptable to the armed forces and their partners in the powerful civil bureaucracy. They responded with another coup d'état, the second in the series.

General Yahya Khan, unlike his predecessor, became a political leader by accident, inasmuch as he happened to be commander in chief of the armed forces at the time of the collapse of Ayub Khan's government. Since the aim of the anti-Ayub movement was the resignation of the president, it must have been clear to the movement's leaders that the military would not accept a constitutional transfer of power in case the president agreed to resign. If the provisions regarding succession in the constitution of 1962 had been followed, the speaker of the National Assembly would have succeeded the president in case of the president's resignation. In 1962, Abdul Jabbar Khan—a Bengali politician of little significance—was the speaker. The politicians seemed quite content with another martial law, which is why they called off the movement the moment that martial law was declared. It would appear that General Yahya Khan's decision to put the country under martial law had little to do with personal ambition; any other general in his position would probably have behaved in much the same way.

Yahya Khan came into office without any political program. His first impulse was to entirely dismantle the system erected by Ayub Khan; after all, that was the demand of the politicians. His second impulse was to resist with all his might the workings of the political dynamic released by his earlier actions. Yahya Khan went from one crisis to another, becoming more and more inflexible along the way. By the time he left the presidency, Pakistan was in political shambles, its "eastern wing" having finally left the union.

Zulfikar Ali Bhutto, Yahya Khan's successor, was a civilian politician who moved into the President's House in Rawalpindi on the basis of an unambiguous mandate that he had earned from the people in the election of 1970. During the Bhutto years, Pakistan's political development moved in a direction opposite to the one taken during the Ayub period. Ayub Khan, having used the military to assume power, tried very hard to gain legitimacy. Bhutto was able to displace the military because he had been elected by the people, but his particular way of managing the political system lost him all his legitimacy. By the spring of 1977, Bhutto had also lost the support of a large part of his original constituency and had totally alienated his opposition. The result was a political movement even more violent than the one that had dislodged Ayub Khan eight years earlier. As had happened before, the commander of the armed forces stepped in to remove a discredited system and an unpopular politician. General Zia ul-Haq's coup d'état—much like those of General Ayub Khan and General Yahya Khan—was seen then not as the product of personal ambition but as a political imperative. Although General Zia was politically as ill-prepared as General Yahya had been, he was willing to experiment and innovate. Like Yahya Khan, he went from one political crisis to another, but, unlike his predecessor, he managed not to be overwhelmed by them.

General Zia ul-Haq's approach to Pakistan's political problem was much different from those of his two military predecessors. Ayub Khan had behaved like a master architect with a carefully worked out design before the first shovel of political dirt was removed from the ground. In 1954, he worked out the system that was put into effect between 1958 and 1962. When the ground began to shake under the structure, General Ayub's approach was to strengthen what he thought were its weak points. But the structure continued to crack; it was wobbling by the time General Yahya Khan moved in to take command of it. General Khan decided to pull it down altogether without any idea as to what could be erected in its place. Within a few weeks of assuming control, he found himself without a political shelter. It was Yahya Khan's civilian successor, Zulfikar Ali Bhutto, who took up the task of putting up another political structure in the place that had been left devastated by General Yahya Khan.

Metaphorically speaking, General Zia ul-Haq did not immediately move into the house his civilian predecessor, Prime Minister Zulfikar Ali Bhutto, had built. Instead, he was content to stay in the Army House, even after assuming the presidency many months after the coup d'état of July 5, 1977. During his sojourn in the Army House, he continued to remodel the structure he had inherited from Bhutto. By the time he had inducted civilians back into the government, Pakistan had acquired a political system that was considerably different from the one Bhutto had fashioned in 1973. The changes were brought in gradually and involved a great deal of experimentation. But the structure that finally emerged in the summer of 1985 in which the politicians were prepared to accept a political role for the military might survive longer than any of those Pakistan has tried during the course of its turbulent political history.

There are four discernible periods in the political maturation of Pakistan's third military president. The first ranged from 1977 to 1979, during which time the objective seems to have been to use existing political institutions to transfer power to civilian leadership. The process was complicated by the remarkable resilience exhibited by Zulfikar Ali Bhutto and the persistence of the political phenomenon that can only be described as Bhuttoism. To deal with this problem, General Zia adopted a risky solution, but one that, in his mind, was really the only viable one: physical elimination of Zulfikar Ali Bhutto.

The second period started after Bhutto's execution in April 1979 and lasted until the summer of 1983, during which time Zia, not unlike Ayub Khan before him, began to seek ways to legitimize his military government. He tried a number of methods, including incorporation of some of the anti-Bhutto forces in a civilian-cum-military government; rule by diktat, with the civilian bureaucracy playing the role of a surrogate political party; Islamization of the economy and the society in the belief that faith would provide the glue to hold together a country that had been created on the basis of religion in the first place; a limited amount of popular participation through the establishment of a system—or, rather, four systems, one for each of the four provinces—of local government; and, finally, an emphasis on improving economic management, as if to suggest that the legitimate purpose of the government in a developing nation is not necessarily to administer in accordance with the wishes of the people (no matter how these wishes are articulated) but to improve the people's economic well-being.

Experience proved all of these methods to be seriously flawed. The anti-Bhutto forces, especially those that were willing to work with the government, represented a small section of the population. The close proximity of a few politicians to the military served only to diminish their appeal—a fact that weighed heavily in the elections of 1985, when a number of government supporters failed to win seats in the national legislature. The resurrection of the military-civilian bureaucratic model pursued by Ayub Khan during the first half of his tenure (1958–1962) also proved to be a nonviable solution, even though the military in the late 1970s was much more broad-based in its social composition than it had been during that early period. Islamization was a move that proved popular with some segments of the society, but these segments would have supported the military anyway. Indeed, the national and provincial elections of February 1985 demonstrated that the government's relentless drive toward Islamization only caused the Islamic parties to fare even less well than they had in the previous elections. The establishment of local governments was a move in the right direction but only a small step toward the creation of a *reasonably* representative form of government. Economic development, especially when it produced benefits for all segments of the population (as it did during much of Zia ul-Haq's political stewardship), was again welcome to the people. As Ayub Khan was to discover after his own very successful experiment with economic development, however, an increase in GDP satisfies the people but does not substitute for political development. An average rate of growth of more than 7 percent per annum from 1958 to 1966 did indeed keep people reasonably satisfied; but they became restive when the growth rate dropped below 5 percent in the 1966–1969 period. As we shall see later on, a remarkable rate of economic growth was also experienced during the first six years of the Zia presidency, but in the seventh and eighth years the economy began to falter. It was either by design—following a lesson learned from history—or purely by chance that Zia began to civilianize his regime during this period.

The fact that General Zia ul-Haq did not persevere with any of these indirect methods for gaining political legitimacy for his regime attests to his astuteness as a politician. From 1982 on, his cabinet had mostly military officers, retired civil servants, and technocrats. The few politicians who remained were included not so much to bring legitimacy as to ensure that the regime did not lose total contact with the established political groups. The government continued its efforts to evolve a viable system of local government and to Islamize the economy, but, once again, the motives for doing all this were not necessarily political.

The lesson that General Zia learned from these experiments was that he had to organize a system in which people could directly participate in order to ensure a degree of political tranquility. Indeed, the launching of the Movement for the Restoration of Democracy in 1981 had sent a strong signal to the president that the political opposition now considered itself strong enough to challenge him directly. The movement's initial success, particularly in the province of Sindh, appears to have convinced the president and his military colleagues that they had to seek a political solution to Pakistan's persistent constitutional problems.

The third phase in Zia's political evolution began with the president's speech of August 12, 1983, in which he presented a blueprint for the restoration of constitutional government. This blueprint was very rough in that the only item spelled out clearly was that the president expected the process to be completed by March 23, 1985—namely, the forty-fifth anniversary of the adoption by the Muslim League of the "Lahore Resolution" asking for the establishment of a separate homeland for the Muslims of British India. During this period General Zia ul-Haq, by taking a number of steps (many of which were not contemplated in advance), was to bring Pakistan to the threshold of another constitutional experiment. The fourth phase began in the summer of 1987 when Zia realized that a parliamentary system could not accommodate a strong president. His dismissal of Junejo on May 29, 1988, was the first step toward the establishment of a presidential form of government, which he would have introduced had he lived.

A Series of Failed Administrations

The First Ghulam Ishaq Khan Interregnum

Ghulam Ishaq Khan became acting president following the death of Zia ul-Haq on August 17, 1988. Khan was faced with a difficult task: He had to keep the army at bay. To do that he had to demonstrate to senior officers that a return to formal democracy, a necessary outcome of the elections scheduled for November 1988, need not sacrifice the armed forces' principle interests. These interests included the continued flow of large amounts of budgetary resources to the military, support by the government of the nuclear weapon development program, Pakistan's continued involvement in the *mujahideen* struggle against the regime of President Najibullah in Afghanistan, and the maintenance of a hard position toward India. The army leadership was also nervous about the possible return of the People's Party to power under Benazir Bhutto, whose father had been dispatched to the gallows by their predecessors. Ghulam Ishaq Khan had his own concerns as well. He had held a number of senior economic positions under Zulfikar Ali Bhutto and had become persuaded that a number of economic problems faced by Pakistan could be traced back to the policies adopted by Prime Minister Bhutto. As Zia ul-Haq's finance minister, Ishaq Khan had worked hard to revive the economy from the near-recession induced by Bhutto's policies. He was now worried that a return by the People's Party would prove economically ruinous once again. Ishaq, a former civil servant, was also apprehensive about the PPP's attitude toward the bureaucracy. It was Zulfikar Ali Bhutto who had dissolved the elitist Civil Service of Pakistan (CSP) of which Ishaq Khan was a member. The CSP's place was taken by an ad hoc structure to which members of all services as well as political appointees could be inducted. This system of "lateral entrants" had demoralized the CSP and in the opinion of many, including the acting president, had also lowered the quality of service offered by the civil bureaucracy.

Ghulam Ishaq Khan's first preoccupation, therefore, was to protect the interests of the powerful military and civil bureaucracies, in particular, and that of the upper-middle classes, in general. At the same time, he had to ensure that he would not lose political credibility with the people. Soon after assuming the presidency, he announced that the elections scheduled by General Zia ul-Haq on November 17, 1988, would be held on that day, appointed a caretaker government to administer the country in the interim period, and invited General Aslam Beg and other service chiefs to attend the meetings of the caretaker administration. Ishaq Khan also confirmed the appointments of a number of judges of the Supreme and Provincial High Courts who had been kept in acting positions by General Zia. The judiciary returned the favor by helping the acting president distance himself from some of the policies of General Zia. In August the Supreme Court ordered that political parties did not have to be formally registered with the Election Commission in order to participate in elections. Had the court ruled otherwise, the Pakistan People's Party, having refused to comply with the requirements for obtaining formal registration, would have been barred from the polls of November 1988. In October 1988, the Lahore High Court declared the dissolution of the national and provincial assemblies by Zia ul-Haq as mala fide, illegal, and arbitrary. The court did not ask for the dismissed assemblies to be reconvened, arguing that such a step would have been too disruptive a move for the fragile political system to absorb. The judges ordered the elections to go forward as planned.

TABLE 2.4   Results of the National Assembly Elections of November 1988

	Punjab	Sindh	Frontier	Balochistan	Others	Total
Pakistan People's Party (PPP)	52	31	7	1	1ᵃ	92
Islami Jamhoori Itehaad	44	–	8	2	–	54
Minor parties	5	–	7	6	–	18
Independent	12	15	3	2	8ᵇ	40
Total seats	113	46	25	11	9	204ᶜ

ᵃThe PPP won the only seat in Islamabad, the federal capital.
ᵇAll the eight seats allocated to the Federally Administered Tribal Areas (FATA) went to independent candidates.
ᶜElections were held in 204 out of 207 constituencies. Elections were postponed in three constituencies because of the deaths of candidates.

Source: "PPP triumphs!" *Pakistan Times* (overseas weekly) (November 20, 1988), p. 1.

The pro-Zia forces, overwhelmed by the sudden death of the president, were in total disarray when the PPP began its electoral campaign. The PPP's public meetings drew large and enthusiastic crowds and its chairperson, Benazir Bhutto, was clearly the most popular political figure in the country at that time. None of the parties opposed to the PPP was confident of succeeding alone in the contest. Accordingly, they decided to shape an electoral alliance to face Benazir Bhutto. The alliance, the Islami Jamhoori Itehaad (IJI; Islamic Democratic Alliance), was formed quickly and without much preparation. Its name was to serve as a reminder to the electorate that its component parties stood for Islamic values rather than the socialism of the PPP, and that although appreciative of the contributions Zia made during his eleven years, they favored democracy over military rule. Several leaders who joined the IJI did not even have the time to register themselves as the alliance's candidates in the elections.

The elections, held on November 17, produced three surprises. One, Benazir Bhutto's Pakistan People's Party did less well than expected. It obtained 37.4 percent of the total vote cast and won 92 of the 204 seats contested. (See Table 2.4.) Two, a new party, the *Muhajir Quami Mahaz*, swept the polls in Karachi and parts of Hyderabad city. It captured eleven out of thirteen seats in Karachi and another two seats in Hyderabad. Three, the Islami Jamhoori Itehaad was unable to win any seat in Sindh. Some of its more prominent leaders, including former Prime Minister Muhammed Khan Junejo, were not able to withstand the PPP onslaught. Also defeated was Ghulam Mustafa Jatoi, a close associate of Zulfikar Ali Bhutto, who had left the PPP when Benazir Bhutto refused to give him a senior position in the party. Jatoi had formed his own splinter group, the National People's Party.

In the 1988 elections, voters showed considerable sophistication in sending astute messages to the politicians. Benazir Bhutto and her party had fought the election on one issue: the need to bring back democracy and repudiate eleven years of

TABLE 2.5   Results of the Provincial Assembly Elections of November 1988

	Punjab	Sindh	Northwest Frontier	Balochistan	Total
Pakistan People's Party	94	67	20	3	184
Islami Jamhoori Itehaad	108	1	28	8	145
Minor parties	6	1	17[a]	23[b]	47
Independent	32	31	15	6	84
Total seats	240	100	80	40	460

[a]Among the minor parties, the Awami National Party won 12 seats.
[b]Among the minor parties, the Jamiatul Ulemai Islam (Fazlur Rahman group) won eight seats, and the Balochistan National Alliance won another six.

Source: "PPP captures Sindh; good showing in Punjab," Pakistan Times (overseas weekly) (November 27, 1988), p. 1.

Zia ul-Haq. The electorate only accepted half of her message; it did not give her the mandate she had asked for but sent a sufficient number of PPP candidates to the National Assembly to give the PPP the majority. By making the Islami Jamhoori Itehaad the second largest party in the National Assembly, the electorate did not accept the PPP's argument that Zia was a total usurper who had governed for eleven years without regard to the people's will. Mian Nawaz Sharif, the president of Islami Jamhoori Itehaad, also sent one message to the electorate: Zia's political and social program had the support of the people and had to be carried forward. He was elected to both the National Assembly and the Punjab provincial assembly. Muhammed Khan Junejo, Zia's chosen prime minister, had distanced himself from the late president. He was defeated in what was considered a safe district.

The voters also acted with prudence in choosing their representatives to the provincial assembly. By making IJI the majority party in the Punjab legislature (see Table 2.5), they indicated their happiness with the economic and social policies pursued by Zia and Nawaz Sharif. They remembered with unease the tenure of the PPP under Zulfikar Ali Bhutto in the 1970s when Punjab, on the verge of an industrial revolution, suffered an economic recession instead. In Sindh, the electorate spoke with two different voices: The urban Sindhis, a majority of whom were the descendants of the refugees who had migrated from India at the time of independence, signaled their political maturation by electing MQM candidates as their principal representatives in both the national and provincial assemblies; the rural Sindhis, by voting overwhelmingly for the PPP, rejected both the radical Sindhi nationalists, who wanted at best a loose confederation with the rest of Pakistan, and the IJI that wanted to continue with a strong central government. The voters in the Northwest Frontier Province and Balochistan were also split: In the former, the strongly provincialist National Awami Party had to share the limelight with the PPP; in the latter, the winners were the Balochistan National Alliance, a party that advocated state rights, and Jamiatul Ulemai Islam that stood for the introduction of an Islamic system in Pakistan.

Acting President Ghulam Ishaq Khan chose to wait for a couple of weeks before calling upon Benazir Bhutto to form a government at the center. He spend this time conferring with a large number of political leaders and also with the senior officers of the army. When Bhutto finally received her call, it came with strings attached. She had to promise not to interfere in military matters, make a commitment to continue implementing the program of economic adjustment the caretaker government had agreed upon with the International Monetary Fund and the World Bank, and pledge that no fundamental changes would be made in the foreign policy put into place during the Zia period. A fourth promise could also have been extracted from her—to work in reasonable harmony with the government the IJI was being invited to form in Punjab under the chief ministership of Mian Nawaz Sharif—but was not.

The First Administration of Benazir Bhutto

Benazir Bhutto was sworn in as prime minister on December 2, 1988. The oath was administered by Acting President Ghulam Ishaq Khan in the presence of the entire military high command. Ten days later, Ishaq was elected president in a joint session of the national and provincial legislatures. The transition from military to civilian rule was thus effectively concluded three and a half months after the death of General Zia ul-Haq.

Benazir Bhutto was the twelfth person, the third Sindhi, but the first woman to serve as prime minister in Pakistan. Her appointment was greeted with great warmth and expectation both inside and outside Pakistan. Her assumption of office signaled not only the arrival of democracy to Pakistan after several decades of military rule but also the promise of modernization and Westernization. Pakistan's friends in the West, particularly those in the United States, drew comfort from the turn politics had taken in Pakistan after the death of Zia. For the West, Pakistan was still an important country, strategically located at the mouth of the Persian Gulf. Pakistan had also demonstrated an exceptional ability to withstand pressure from the Soviet Union, especially following the arrival of the Soviet troops in Afghanistan. For the West such a country was safer in the hands of a modern and Westernized leader such as Benazir Bhutto than any of the leaders who had opposed her in the elections of November 1988. Her opponents had identified themselves with the policies of Zia ul-Haq; they had promised further Islamization, firmer links with the Middle East, and continuing efforts to turn Pakistan into a nuclear power. None of these positions were attractive for the West, and under any of the leaders who espoused them, Pakistan would have found it difficult to remain closely associated with the United States and other industrialized countries. Pakistan, however, needed the support of the West more than ever before; by the time Bhutto took office, its economy was faced with a number of severe structural problems that could only be addressed if foreign assistance continued to flow (see Chapter 3).

The understanding Benazir Bhutto reached with the forces she was later to pillory as "the establishment" included some key appointments. Shahbzada Yaqub Khan was selected as foreign minister and Vaseem Jaffrey was appointed economic adviser to the prime minister.[34] Yaqub Khan had served both Zulfikar Ali Bhutto and General Zia ul-Haq—the former as Pakistan's ambassador to the United States and the latter as foreign minister. Jaffrey was a close associate of Ghulam Ishaq Khan; he had also held a number of important positions during the Zia period, including governor of the State Bank (Pakistan's central bank) and chairman of the Planning Commission. Yaqub Khan's appointment was to ensure that Pakistan's foreign policy—in particular its position on Afghanistan—would not undergo a dramatic change under Benazir Bhutto. By placing Vaseem Jaffrey in the prime minister's house, the establishment wanted to ensure that the bureaucratic model of decisionmaking that had served Pakistan for most of its history would not be abandoned in favor of the Fabian socialism introduced by Zulfikar Ali Bhutto in the 1970s.

Within a few days of assuming power in Islamabad, Benazir Bhutto established her first objective: freeing herself from the constraints that had been placed on her. Her strategy included a number of elements, all of them with a good deal of associated risk: She would improve on her domestic political position by dislodging Chief Minister Mian Nawaz Sharif from Punjab; she would cultivate a close relationship with the administration of President George Bush, which would help her to neutralize the influence of the army high command; she would gradually bring the armed forces under her control by making changes at the top of the command structure; and she would use the enormous discretionary economic and financial powers available to the prime minister to strengthen her domestic political constituency. She succeeded in only one of these four objectives: During her tenure Pakistan was drawn into a close relationship with the United States. She failed to achieve the other three objectives; her position remained weak.

The attempt to remove Nawaz Sharif started with the dispatch of Farooq Leghari to Lahore as the leader of the PPP's parliamentary group in the Punjab assembly. Leghari, the leader of a powerful Balochi tribe that straddles south Punjab and Balochistan, was a popular figure in the politics of Punjab. He was a former bureaucrat but had served the PPP with considerable devotion during the difficult days the party faced when Zia was in power. Leghari had been imprisoned several times during the martial law period and had consequently won the respect and admiration of the party's rank and file. However, he was not temperamentally suited to the task he was assigned; it would have involved a great deal of "horse trading," a term that was to become popular in Pakistan during Benazir Bhutto's waning days when party leaders sought to buy the support of legislators by offering them all sorts of financial inducements. When Leghari failed in his at-

tempt to form a PPP government in Lahore, Punjab, he was brought back to
Islamabad and assigned the portfolio of Water and Power in the central cabinet.
This early effort to remove an opposition leader from a province badly backfired,
and Nawaz Sharif became a sworn enemy, determined to embarrass Bhutto at
every possible occasion. It also signaled to other provincial leaders that Bhutto
was not prepared to work with them on terms other than her own.

Within a few months after becoming prime minister, Benazir Bhutto had lost
the support of some of the parties that had voted with the PPP during the early
days of her administration. These included the Muhajir Quami Mahaz in south
Sindh, the Awami National Party in the Northwest Frontier Province, and the
Balochistan National Front. The dispute with the administration in Punjab
proved to be very costly. It almost brought to a halt a number of development
schemes critical not only for the province but also for Pakistan. These included
the Kalabagh Dam on the Indus River that was necessary for Pakistan to meet its
energy needs. The rupture of the PPP's relations with the MQM sent the province
of Sindh into a paroxysm of ethnic violence involving indigenous Sindhis and
those who had moved into the province after independence. "According to [the]
statistics supplied by the Government's own agencies, during the period of only
seven months from January 1 to July 31 this year—after the elected government
had been in office for one full year—1187 persons were killed and 2491 injured in
various incidents in Sindh," President Ghulam Ishaq Khan told the nation in a
televised address following the dismissal of the Bhutto government. "Of these 635
were killed and 1433 injured in ethnic troubles."[35]

Benazir Bhutto opened another domestic front soon after taking office. She
made a number of efforts to subject the armed forces to her control. She began by
changing the leadership at the Interservices Intelligence; Major General Hamid
Gul was removed from the agency and replaced by Shamsur Rahman Kalu, a retired general. Bhutto started her campaign against the army with the ISI in the belief that a change in its command would be popular in Washington because the
agency's Afghan policy had been criticized by several people in the United States
(see Chapter 5). Besides, it was also well known that the ISI had developed a
strong interest in domestic intelligence and was instrumental in keeping Zia
ahead of the opposition during his eleven years in power. It made political sense
for Benazir Bhutto to dilute the power of the ISI or at least get it out of the business of domestic political intelligence. Only then could she be confident that the
armed forces would remain out of politics. President Ishaq Khan and the army
leadership reluctantly accepted the change in the ISI's command.

The establishment reacted less kindly to the prime minister's next attempt to
establish her control over the armed forces. In the summer of 1989, Bhutto sent a
proposal to President Ishaq Khan recommending the retirement of Admiral
Iftikhar Sirhoey, the chairman of the Joint Chiefs of Staff. The president refused
to sign the proposal, arguing that he was both the appointing and dismissing authority for the chiefs of staff and as such was not obliged to accept the prime min-

ister's advice. The "Sirhoey affair" was debated at length in the parliament, in the press, and in the living rooms of Islamabad. It was seen as the litmus test for the constitution of 1973, as amended in 1985. Did the constitution create a presidency that was largely ceremonial with all executive authority in the hands of the prime minister, or did it establish a quasi-presidential structure in which executive powers were to be shared between the president and the prime minister? Having attempted to take away the president's authority for the appointment of the chiefs of the armed services, Benazir Bhutto did not press her case further. The Sirhoey affair did not lead to a resolution of the constitutional issue on the division of power between the president and the prime minister. It only served to heighten the suspicion of the armed forces that the prime minister was not prepared to abide by the understanding that had led to her appointment in the first place.

By consolidating economic and financial powers in her hands, Benazir Bhutto further compounded her problem with the establishment. She retained the important portfolio of Finance; chose to chair the cabinet's Economic Coordination Committee (EEC), which was responsible for all important economic decisions; created a Board of Investment chaired by her that awarded licenses for the establishment of new, large industrial units; created a cell in the prime minister's office to oversee loans granted by commercial and development banks operating in the public sector; and established a Placement Bureau that reported to the prime minister and was assigned the task of finding jobs in the public sector for those who had suffered deprivation under Zia ul-Haq. The prime minister also revived the People's Work Program, initiated by the government of Zia ul-Haq, which provided large sums of money for the local councils for the implementation of small development schemes. The new program gave money directly to the members of the National Assembly, but some legislators were charged with misuse of funds. The basic purpose behind all these moves was to assist the people and the constituencies that had supported the prime minister and the PPP, but the changes created the impression that Benazir Bhutto was prepared to use the resources of the state in ways not entirely legitimate in order to advance her political objectives and to further the financial ambitions of her supporters. In his televised address to the nation following the dismissal of the Bhutto government, President Ishaq Khan had some hard words to say about official corruption: "The treatment of public exchequer like hereditary *jagirs* [estates] and the plunder of national wealth as booty were so widely reported that the word 'corruption' became the trade mark of policies in Pakistan."[36]

The establishment's disenchantment with Benazir Bhutto and her administration led to an unsuccessful attempt by the opposition to defeat her in the National Assembly. In November 1989, a vote of no confidence was moved by Ghulam Mustafa Jatoi, the leader of the Combined Opposition Party (COP) in the National Assembly. The press reported that both sides paid large sums of money to keep their supporters in line. The PPP, nervous about the outcome of the vote, sequestered its National Assembly members at Swat, a hill station some one hundred miles from Islamabad and brought them over to the assembly chambers shortly before the vote was taken. The opposition failed in its attempt—but narrowly—thereby compounding the uncertainties that continued to characterize Pakistan's political development. Following the vote in the National Assembly, the conflict between the center and the provinces escalated, affecting the government at all levels. Rumors about a military coup d'état began to circulate in the country, Pakistan's economy came under pressure as flight of capital increased, the country's credit rating was lowered by foreign lenders, and Pakistan found it difficult to borrow funds from abroad to pay for imports. On August 6, 1990, President Ghulam Ishaq Khan ended the period of uncertainty that surrounded the government of Benazir Bhutto by dismissing the prime minister and her cabinet, dissolving the national and provincial assemblies, and appointing caretaker administrations in Islamabad and the four provinces. The president also scheduled national and provincial elections for October 24 and 27, 1990, respectively.

The Second Ishaq Khan Interregnum

In less than two years after the death of Zia ul-Haq, President Ishaq Khan had put himself in the center of the political stage. His forty-minute address to the nation following Benazir Bhutto's dismissal listed in grim detail what he regarded as the wrongdoings of the PPP government. Although Ishaq Khan used the same constitutional provision for dismissing Bhutto that Zia employed in removing Junejo, a great deal of thought had gone into launching the process this time around. The president could not afford to make a mistake; he remembered that Zia's dismissal order had not withstood judicial challenge. If the judiciary once again passed the same verdict, Pakistan would be thrown into a constitutional crisis leading, perhaps, to military intervention. Accordingly, Ishaq and his associates prepared the presidential order for the dismissal of the prime minister very carefully. Predictably, the order was challenged in the high courts of Peshawar, Karachi, and Lahore and was upheld by the latter two.

The caretaker administrations that took office in August in Islamabad and the provincial capitals differed from those that supervised the elections of 1988. First, Ishaq Khan had chosen not to appoint a prime minister in 1988, assuming for himself the role of the chief executive. This time, he asked Ghulam Mustafa Jatoi, once an associate of Zulfikar Ali Bhutto and a founding member of the PPP, to be the caretaker prime minister. Second, the president launched an elaborate process for determining whether the members of the dismissed federal and provincial administrations would be held accountable for the misdeeds recounted in the presidential order. Eleven one-man courts were established to investigate the cases the president promised to refer to them. With these actions Ishaq Khan made clear that this time he would not stand by and let the electoral process simply take its course: He was determined to turn the elections into a vote of confidence over his decision to dismiss the PPP government.

The IJI had more time to prepare for the elections of 1990 than those held in 1988. Past electoral arithmetic suggested a simple strategy. Even when it was most popular, the PPP had failed to secure more than two-fifths of the votes actually cast. This time, its share was bound to be lower since its record in office was, at best, an indifferent one. If the IJI could reunite the opposition to the PPP more successfully than it was able to manage in 1988, it could sweep the polls. The president was prepared to lend the PPP opposition a helping hand. He persuaded Ghulam Mustafa Jatoi (the caretaker prime minister), Muhammed Khan Junejo (prime minister appointed and dismissed by Zia ul-Haq), and Mian Nawaz Sharif (the chief minister of Punjab while Benazir Bhutto was the prime minister) to work together within the framework offered by IJI. To maintain an understanding among these leaders was not an easy task; it was made even more difficult by the positions they occupied. Jatoi was not only the caretaker prime minister but also the president of the National People's Party, a splinter PPP group at the core of the opposition to Benazir Bhutto in her native Sindh. Junejo was the president of the Pakistan Muslim League, by far the largest party within IJI. Mian Nawaz Sharif was the president of IJI but did not hold an office in any of the parties that made up the alliance. On a number of occasions in the period leading up to the elections, it seemed that the unity among the political forces opposed to Bhutto would not remain. However, fear of the PPP kept the alliance together.

The PPP also undertook to reshape its image by inviting three small groups to form an electoral alliance. The result was the Pakistan Democratic Alliance that included Tehrik-e-Istiqlal of retired Air Marshal Asghar Khan, a splinter Muslim League group, and Tehrik-e-Nifaze Fiqh Jafreiya, a group that stood for the protection of the rights of the Shi'i.

"Taking place, as this election is, in the wake of the dissolution of the National Assembly by President Ghulam Ishaq Khan, the principal issue, if at all there is any before the electorate, is whether the PPP government was justly dismissed or not. It is around this that the battle lines have been drawn," reported the *Herald*, Karachi's influential news magazine.[37] The electorate vindicated the president by failing to give the PPP a majority in any of the five legislatures—the National Assembly and the four provincial legislatures. The PPP won only 45 out of the 206 seats contested at the national level and 61 out of the 460 contested in the provinces. (See Table 2.6 and Table 2.7.) The IJI's success went far beyond even its most optimistic projections. It secured 105 seats in the National Assembly and more than half of those in the provincial legislatures. The results were as lopsided as those of the elections of 1977, which led to a reaction against the government of Zulfikar Ali Bhutto and its eventual overthrow. Benazir Bhutto, hoping for a similar reaction this time, charged that the caretaker administrations at the center and in the provinces had indulged in widespread rigging to secure a victory for

Political Development

TABLE 2.6 Results of the National Assembly Elections of November 1990 (by party)

	Punjab	Sindh	Frontier	Balochistan	Others	Total
Islami Jamhoori Itehaad (IJI)	91	3	8	2	1	105
Pakistan Democratic Alliance (PDA)ᵃ	14	24	5	2	–	45
Muhajir Quami Mahaz (MQM)	–	15	–	–	–	15
Awami National Party (ANP)	–	–	6	–	–	6
Jamiatul Ulemai Islam Fazlur Rahman (JUIF)	–	–	4	2	–	6
Minor parties	3	–	–	5	–	8
Independent	6	4	3	–	8	21
Total seats	114	46	26	11	9	206ᵇ

[a]Pakistan People's Party (PPP) was the main component of this alliance. All the PDA seats were won by PPP candidates.

[b]Elections were not held in one Punjab district because of the death of the IJI candidate.

Source: Dawn (Karachi, October 25, 1990).

TABLE 2.7 Results of the Provincial Assembly Elections of 1990 (by party)

	Punjab	Sindh	Frontier	Balochistan	Total
Islami Jamhoori Itehaad (IJI)	208	5	32	7	252
Pakistan Democratic Alliance (PDA)	10	43	6	2	61
Muhajir Quami Mahaz (MQM)	–	27	–	–	27
Awami National Party (ANP)	–	–	15	–	15
Jamiatul Ulemai Islam Fazlur Rahman (JUIF)	–	–	15	10	25
Minor parties	2	11	–	13	26
Independent	20	14	12	8	54
Total seats	240	100	80	30	460

Source: "IJI wins majority seats in N.A.; Nawaz Sharif elected leader of house and prime minister," *Pakistan Affairs* (Washington, D.C., November 7, 1990), p. 3.

the IJI. Her charges were not supported by a group of foreign observers who had been invited to watch the elections.

The elections of October 1990 were full of surprises. There was a widely held view both inside and outside Pakistan that the highly charged atmosphere in which the polls were held would produce long-term political instability in the country. In the numerous analyses offered before the people went to the electoral booths to cast their votes, neither side was expected to come up with a firm mandate to rule. And another split verdict of the type given in 1988 was seen as too disruptive a development for Pakistan's fragile and fledgling political system to absorb. The electorate surprised the experts: It gave a strong mandate to IJI to govern, and it asked the PPP to act responsibly as the party in opposition. In making it possible for Mian Nawaz Sharif to take office as Pakistan's fourteenth prime minister, it signaled the arrival on the political scene of a politician not dependent on the landed aristocracy. Not only was Nawaz Sharif the first Punjabi to become prime minister in more than thirty-two years, he was also the first urban politician to take that office.

The 1990 elections also brought some of the provincial, regional, and ethnic parties into the mainstream of politics. At the same time, the electorate discarded those groups whose solutions to Pakistan's political problems would have seriously set back the process of nation building (in which the country was still engaged after more than forty years of existence). Thus the MQM, by siding with the IJI, became an integral part of the alliance that took office in November 1990. Similarly, the Awami National Party of Khan Abdul Wali Khan in the Northwest Frontier Province and the Jamhoori Wattan (Democratic Country) Party of Nawab Akbar Bugti in Balochistan gave up their separatist tendencies and resolved to work with the IJI to develop a Pakistani nation. The more extremist groups, mostly in the troubled province of Sindh did very poorly in the elections, indicating that the people of that province were still prepared to order their lives within the Pakistani federation.

Once again the 1990 elections confirmed that the Pakistani voters were not predisposed toward making religion the basis of statecraft. The Jamaat-i-Islami remained an important component within the IJI but won only four seats in the election. Although the voters put the IJI into office in Islamabad, they had not supported the formal Islamization of the Pakistani society, economy, and polity.

The First Nawaz Sharif Administration

In spite of the triumph of the IJI at the polls and the voters' expectations, the elections of 1990 did not bring political stability. The comfortable majority secured by the IJI should have provided greater security to its prime minister than was afforded to the minority government formed by Benazir Bhutto following the elections of 1988. The IJI ruled not only at Islamabad but also in Punjab and had a presence in all the other provinces. Mian Nawaz Sharif was more acceptable to the president, the armed forces, the civil bureaucracy, and the upper echelons of the society than was his predecessor, Benazir Bhutto. Between the IJI and the PPP, Pakistan had the making of a two-party political system. The conduct of Benazir Bhutto as the leader of the opposition in the National Assembly in the few weeks following the induction of the IJI government in Islamabad seemed to indicate that all major political forces were prepared to work within the system. Mian Nawaz Sharif's record as the "development-oriented" chief minister of Punjab gave some comfort to those who worried about the country's long-term economic prospects. The ingredients for stability seemed to be finally in place.

But stability did not come. Like his predecessor Benazir Bhutto, Nawaz Sharif wanted more power for himself than the political system, both in its formal and informal forms, was prepared to place at his disposal. As was the case with Benazir Bhutto, Nawaz Sharif felt particularly constrained by the troika arrangement. He was convinced that he would be able to do a great deal more for the country if he could free himself from the Islamabad establishment. Two deaths in early 1993—those of Mohammad Khan Junejo and General Asif Nawaz—seemed to offer Sharif the opportunity he was looking for. He made a bid for the chairmanship of the Pakistan Muslim League, a position held by Junejo until the time of his death. The PML was the largest party in the IJI alliance, and Sharif felt that in a parliamentary form of government it was necessary for the prime minister to control the party on which he relied for support in the national legislature. Sharif also believed that the military would not resist such a move, since an apolitical general, Abdul Waheed Kakar, had assumed command of the army under Nawaz's successor. If Sharif had convinced himself that the time had come to strike out on his own, that sentiment was not fully shared by the president. Ghulam Ishaq Khan was determined to apply the same degree of constraint on Sharif that was used earlier in the case of Benazir Bhutto. Consequently, the prime minister's effort to win greater freedom for himself met with the same treatment meted out in August 1990 to Benazir Bhutto—dismissal by the president under Article 58.2(b) of the constitution.

Sharif, like prime ministers Mohammad Khan Junejo and Benazir Bhutto before him, then appealed to the Supreme Court. Junejo and Bhutto had failed to convince the judges that the presidents—Zia ul-Haq and Ghulam Ishaq Khan, respectively—had acted unconstitutionally. Sharif was more successful; the Supreme Court, under the direction of Chief Justice Nasim Hasan Shah, ruled against the president and ordered the restoration of the National Assembly. Sharif was reinstalled as prime minister, but the president proved to be unforgiving and refused to cooperate. A constitutional crisis ensued. It was resolved by the army, working behind the scenes, forced both the president and the prime minister out of office. "For me it was an extraordinary spectacle to see two grown up men behave as if they were children," said Kakar later. "I had to intervene. I ordered both of them out of office."[38] In July 1997, Moeenuddin Qureshi, a retired senior official of the World Bank, was called back to Pakistan and became caretaker prime minister.

Qureshi headed the fourth caretaker government to take office in five years. It was a difficult time for Pakistan. The country was bankrupt, with foreign reserves adequate to pay for only a few days of imports. The people had begun to doubt whether democracy was a workable proposition for the country. The failure of elected officials to work together within the confines of the constitution had raised some serious questions about the long-term viability of the system in place.

TABLE 2.8 Results of the National Assembly Elections of October 1993 (by party)

	Punjab	Sindh	Frontier	Balochistan	Others	Total
Pakistan People's Party	47	33	5	1	–	86
Pakistan Muslim League (Nawaz)	52	10	9	–	1	72
Pakistan Muslim League (Chatta)	6	–	–	–	–	6
Islami Jamhuri Mahaz	–	–	2	2	–	4
Awami National Party	–	–	3	–	–	3
Pakistan Islami Front		1	2	–	–	3
Other	1		1	–	–	2
Independent	5	1	1	6	8	21
Total	111	45	23	9	9	197

Source: Yaseen Rizvi, Pakistan: Election 1993, Shirkat Printing, Islamabad, 1993.

TABLE 2.9 Results of the Provincial Assembly Elections of October 1993 (by party)

	Punjab	Sindh	Frontier	Balochistan	Total
Pakistan People's Party	94	56	24	3	177
Pakistan Muslim League (Nawaz)	106	8	15	6	135
Pakistan Muslim League (Chatta)	18	–	4	–	22
Muhajir Qaumi Mahz	–	27	–	–	27
Awami National Party	–		3	–	21
Pakistan Islami Front	2	–	4	–	6
Other	3	4	2	21	30
Independent	17	5	11	9	42
Total	240	100	80	40	460

Source: Yaseen Rizvi, Pakistan: Election 1993, Shirkat Printing, Islamabad, 1993.

But quickly and unexpectedly, Qureshi gained the confidence of the people. An August 1993 poll indicated that 85 percent of the population approved of his performance and wanted him to continue in office. Nevertheless, the caretaker prime minister focused a great deal of energy on ensuring that a free and fair election was held under his watch.

The Second Benazir Bhutto Administration

The elections of October 1993—the fourth to be held in eight years—produced a result not too dissimilar from that of October 1988. (See Tables 2.8 and 2.9.) Neither Bhutto's PPP nor Sharif's PML was able to secure a majority in the National Assembly. In fact, the PPP won six fewer seats than in 1988, whereas the

PML won eighteen more than the IJI won in 1988. Elections to the provincial assemblies produced the same results. In Punjab, the PML won twelve more seats than the PPP. It seemed that the voters, even if they wished to put Benazir Bhutto in power, wanted to constrain her. Perhaps they recalled the misuse of political authority that occurred during her father's tenure. Her first stint in office had not convinced the people that she and her associates could be trusted to provide clean and responsive government. Benazir Bhutto was sworn in as prime minister on October 17, 1993, for the second time in five years. Expectations were high that she, having learned some lessons from her first tenure, would preside over a more successful administration this time around.

Bhutto's initial conduct in office suggested that she had learned two lessons (not necessarily the right lessons) from her previous experience as prime minister. First, she wanted to ensure that this time the president would not mount an assault on her office. She could accomplish this either by changing the constitution to repeal Article 58.2(b) or by placing a trusted person in the presidency. The first possible course of action was not possible. Her party could not muster the two-thirds majority in the Senate and the National Assembly required to amend the constitution. Accordingly, she opted for the second course of action and persuaded a reluctant Farooq Ahmad Khan Leghari, her trusted lieutenant, to succeed Ghulam Ishaq Khan as president.

Leghari had been a loyal supporter of the PPP and the Bhutto family for seventeen years. He had left the Civil Service of Pakistan in 1969 soon after succeeding his father as the head of the powerful Legahri tribe that lived in several southern districts of Punjab. He won a seat in the National Assembly in the elections of 1977 and had served briefly as a member of the federal government before its removal by the military. After Pakistan went under martial law, and in spite of a number of overtures made by President Zia ul-Haq, Leghari remained with the PPP, agreeing to work under Benazir Bhutto, who had succeeded her father as PPP chairperson. He took an active part in the campaigns launched by the opposition against military rule and was arrested and imprisoned several times. He led the PPP battle against President Ghulam Ishaq Khan and Prime Minsiter Nawaz Sharif after the dismissal of the first Bhutto administration in August 1990. Given this resume, it is not surprising that Benazir Bhutto wanted to place him in the presidency. There was, however, another reason. She did not wish to give Leghari the portfolio of finance that he coveted; she wanted to be the finance minister herself in order to give a free rein to her husband, Asif Ali Zardari.

The second lesson Bhutto had learned from her first term in office was not to let Punjab, the country's largest province, fall into the hands of the opposition. Since Nawaz Sharif's Pakistan Muslim League had 106 seats in the Punjab assembly, compared to the ninety-four seats held by the PPP, she could only achieve this objective by forming a coalition government. This she did with the Pakistan Muslim League (Chatta group), a breakaway faction of the PML. The PML(C) demanded a price for joining the PPP: having one of its own members become the chief minister of the province. Bhutto granted that wish and Mian Manzoor Wattoo, once a close ally of Mian Nawaz Sharif, was elected the chief minister of Punjab.

The successful execution of these maneuvers was not enough to guarantee Bhutto political longevity or to assure the people that an administration had come to power that was interested in their welfare. Unfortunately for her own political career and also for Pakistan's political development, she did not learn the most important lesson from her earlier stay in office: The people desperately wanted good governance. Bhutto's second failure in office was even more spectacular than her first. (See Chapter 5 for a detailed discussion of governance, corruption, and development.) The prime minister concentrated her entire energy on consolidating her hold on the levers of power, while allowing an enormous amount of authority to accrue to Asif Ali Zardari, her husband. Zardari placed his friends and business associates in key economic positions (heads of public sector banks and public sector corporations) from which they were alleged to have embezzled large amounts of resources. By the summer of 1996, President Farooq Leghari had begun to show his impatience with the quality of governance provided by the Bhutto administration. It was Bhutto's quarrel with the judiciary that finally severed her longtime relationship with Leghari.

As a part of her effort to neutralize all opposition, Bhutto had begun to pack the provincial high courts and the Supreme Court with people beholden to her and her party. In early 1993, a lawyer from Islamabad filed a petition with the Supreme Court questioning the way these appointments were being made. On March 20, the Supreme Court issued its decision in what came to be known as the "judges case." The court told the administration that in appointing judges, the administration was required to obtain the consent of the chief justices of the superior courts. Since such consent had not been given in the case of several appointments made by the administration, the court asked for their review. The prime minister refused to follow the injunction of the court. The court asked the president to intervene and also hinted that under the constitution it could order the military to help implement its orders. Bhutto's position was weakened further on September 20, when Mir Murtaza Ali Bhutto, the prime minister's estranged brother, was gunned down, along with a number of his followers, outside his residence in Karachi. In a statement issued soon after this incident, President Leghari hinted at the possible involvement of the prime minister's husband in the murder of her brother. Once again, Pakistan seemed to be heading toward a major constitutional crisis. It was averted only when the president decided to act on his own and use the provision in the constitution authorizing him to dissolve the National Assembly and dismiss the prime minister.

President Farooq Leghari moved against Prime Minister Benazir Bhutto early on the morning of November 5. His order dissolving the National Assembly, dismissing the prime minister, and appointing a caretaker administration under Meraj Khalid was sent to the prime minister's residence while her husband was in

Lahore. A few hours after the prime minister had been dismissed, the caretaker administration ordered the arrest of Asif Ali Zaradari. The charges that President Leghari leveled against the prime minister in the dismissal order were very similar to those made three years earlier by President Ghulam Ishaq Khan. They included mismanagement of the economy, misuse of public authority for personal gain, and use of excessive force against the opposition in Karachi. In addition to being accused of corruption, Zardari was also charged with conspiring to murder Murtaza Bhutto.

The caretaker administration headed by Meraj Khalid, like the caretaker government of Moeen Qureshi, interpreted its mandate not only to organize another general election but to deal with the more serious problems confronting the country. The government chose to concentrate on two of them: improving the economic situation (see Chapter 3)and instituting a mechanism for holding public officials accountable for their actions (see Chapter 5). Khalid, prodded by President Farooq Leghari and impressed by the disgust of the people at the way Bhutto and her associates had enriched themselves, decided to set up a system to deal with the problem of corruption. The president promulgated the Ehtesab Ordinance and appointed the Ehtesab commissioner to take action against the officials whose cases were sent to him by a team of investigators working in the Ministry of Interior.

Ehtesab in Urdu means accountability; by taking these actions, the caretaker government introduced another term into Pakistan's political idiom. Many influential political observers advised Leghari and Khalid to do *ehtesab* first even if that meant postponing *intikhab* (Urdu for elections). Leghari rejected these *ehtesab* before *intikhab* arguments even though the caretaker administration had very little to show to the people in the area of accountability.

The Second Nawaz Sharif Administration

The people of Pakistan went back to the polls in February 1997 and gave an overwhelming mandate to Nawaz Sharif, the leader of the opposition and the president of the Muslim League. (See Tables 2.10 and 2.11.) The voters left the fold of the PPP with even greater exuberance than they had done in 1990 and seemed to be similarly ready to allow unconstrained political authority to the PML. The PML won 66 percent of the contested seats in the National Assembly and 58 percent of the 450 seats in the four provincial assemblies. The PPP secured only seventeen seats in the National Assembly and forty-one seats in the provincial assemblies. Bhutto's party failed to win a National Assembly seat in any province other than Sindh. In the provincial assemblies it had a marginal presence in all provinces other than Sindh. The PPP could have formed a government in Sindh, but Nawaz Sharif was able to woo the Muhajir Qaumi Mahaz and induct its own man as chief minister even in this province. The League governments took office with very comfortable majorities in the national and provincial assemblies. The

TABLE 2.10   Results of the National Assembly Elections of February 1997 (by party)

	Punjab	Sindh	Frontier	Balochistan	Others	Total
Pakistan Muslim League (Nawaz)	107	9	14	3	1	134
Pakistan People's Party	–	17	–	–	–	17
Mutahida Qaumi Mahaz	–	12	–	–	–	12
Awami National Party	–	–	9	3	–	9
Baluchistan National Party	–	–	–	3	–	3
Other	–	4	1	1	–	8
Independent	7	4	1	1	7	20
Total	114	46	25	10	8	203

Source: The Friday Times, Lahore, February 6–12, 1997.

TABLE 2.11   Results of the Provincial Assembly Elections of 1997 (by party)

	Punjab	Sindh	Frontier	Balochistan	Total
Pakistan Muslim League (Nawaz)	211	14	31	4	260
Pakistan People's Party	2	34	4	1	41
Awami National Party	–	–	28	–	28
Muhajir Qaumi Mahaz	–	29	–	–	29
Baluchistan National Party	–	–	–	10	10
Other	3	6	3	15	27
Independent	22	14	11	8	55
Total	238	97	77	38	450

Source: The Friday Times, Lahore, February 6–12, 1997.

party had received a clear mandate from the people to provide good governance and to restore health to the battered economy.

Nawaz Sharif and his associates took power at a time when the country faced serious political, social, and economic structural problems. There were a number of structural problems that had to be faced and corrected in the field of politics. Perhaps the most serious problem in the political structure was the unrepresentative nature of the system—a small number of landlords had been able to exert a great deal of influence in spite of the decline of the proportion of people living in the countryside and in spite of the reduced share of agriculture in national income. The only way of addressing this issue was to reapportion seats in the national and provincial legislatures, and for this the long postponed census had to be held. Landed interests had persuaded the government not to hold another count since the census of 1981, which had shown a significant decline in the share of the rural population. The decision by the Nawaz Sharif government to hold a population census in March 1998 may have set the stage to correct the imbalance in the political system.

The second political structural problem was connected with the confusion created by the informal troika system, in which responsibility for major decisions, and, therefore, accountability for them, was divided among three individuals—the president, the prime minister, and the army chief of staff. Nawaz Sharif dealt with this issue by using his comfortable position in the National Assembly to introduce some major changes in the constitution. The prime minister rushed two amendments into the constitution within six weeks of assuming power. The thirteenth amendment removed Article 58.2(b), which presidents had used with great frequency to dismiss prime ministers. The fourteenth amendment took away the right of the members of the assemblies to cross party lines, a practice that had introduced a great deal of political corruption. Both amendments further strengthened the prime minister.

The prime minister, still not satisfied with the amount of power he had accumulated, decided to move against the judiciary. By indicating that he wished to retain considerable control over judicial appointments, he adopted the position taken earlier by Benazir Bhutto. The result was another confrontation with the judiciary, and Pakistan again faced a constitutional breakdown. In the fall of 1997, Chief Justice Sajjad Ali Shah hit back at the prime minister on the contempt of court issue. Nawaz Sharif had spoken of the justices of the Supreme Court in unflattering terms, and the judges had responded by instituting contempt of court proceedings against the prime minister. President Leghari tried to persuade the prime minister to work within the system and turned down his request to remove the chief justice of the Supreme Court. The president declined, and the prime minister threatened him with impeachment. This crisis was only resolved with the resignation of President Farooq Leghari and the removal of Chief Justice Sajjad Ali Shah. The new president, Muhammad Rafiq Tarar, was a close friend of the Sharif family and the Supreme Court, under a new chief justice, was content to tread with caution.

Within one year of assuming office, Nawaz Sharif had accumulated as much power as Mohammad Ali Jinnah and Mohammad Ayub Khan had in their times. Instead of being dispersed among three officials, power had become concentrated in one office, that of the prime minister. Would this power be used to bring responsible governance? Or would it be deployed for personal gain, as in the past?

The first test for the new power structure came in May 1998, when India exploded five nuclear devices in an area close to its border with Pakistan. Pakistan responded with tests of its own two weeks later. The nuclear tests and the Western response to them plunged Pakistan into a deep economic crisis that it was structurally ill equipped to handle. (See Chapter 4.)

The fact that Pakistan had held five general elections in eight years; had six administrations take office, three of which were caretakers; witnessed the dismissal of three prime ministers on grounds of corruption and incompetence; and continued to turn to the military for resolving disputes among politicians are some of the many indicators of persistent political instability. Clearly, the country had failed to bridge the great divide that separated the structure of the society from the structure of the political system. The society had evolved rapidly since independence. A number of new socioeconomic groups had emerged that wanted a place for themselves in the political structure but were unable to find one because the political system remained dominated by one socioeconomic group: the landed aristocracy. This group, although powerful, was insecure about the future. It realized that if the political system were allowed to evolve as envisaged in the constitution, it would lose a great deal of power to the new groups. The constitution of 1973 had provided for the reapportionment of seats in the National Assembly on the basis of population distribution, which was to be determined by censuses held every ten years. This was not done; the landed interests were able to prevent a census from being held for seventeen years. Thus groups that lacked representation in this system had no choice but to resort to extraconstitutional means. The pressure that they exerted contributed to the periodic dismissals of prime ministers.

3

ECONOMIC DEVELOPMENT: CONTINUING POSTPONEMENT OF STRUCTURAL CHANGE

Pakistan was born with a number of serious disadvantages. In 1947, the year of its birth, it was not only politically, socially, and administratively backward compared to the rest of India but was, economically, also the poorest part of the British Indian Empire. The economy was basically rural: The bulk of its population lived in the countryside, and three-fourths of its GDP was contributed by the agricultural sector. Nearly four-fifths of the population depended on agriculture for their livelihood. There was little external trade; the few exchanges of goods and commodities that did take place involved the areas in India that were contiguous to Pakistan. The new country did not have a currency of its own. Its communications network—roads, railways, telephone, telegraph, and postal system—was an extension of the one centered in New Delhi, the capital of British India. The partition of the province of Punjab had split in two Pakistan's only economic asset—the large irrigation network that had been built by the British over a period of more than fifty years. Being basically agricultural, the areas that in 1947 were set apart to form the state of Pakistan did not possess the physical, human, or institutional infrastructure to support a modern economy. Given these handi-caps, then, it is not surprising that few people regarded Pakistan as economically viable.

Yet Pakistan survived economically; indeed, it was able to see its economy grow at an impressive rate, at least for four decades following independence. More than five decades after the country was born, the areas that now constitute Pakistan are among the most prosperous in all of South Asia. According to the World Bank, Pakistan's income per head of the population was estimated at $490 compared to $390 for India and $270 for Bangladesh. These estimates are for 1997, the last year for which the Bank had comparative data. The income gap between Pakistan and India is even larger if the gross domestic product is measured according to the purchasing power parity method, which estimates the real worth to the citizens of the income delivered to them by the national economy. According to this reckon-ing, income per head of the population in Pakistan was of the order of $2,230, compared to only $1,400 for India.[1] Most important among the striking charac-teristics of Pakistan's economy is the high rate of growth since 1947, the year the country was born. In the years since independence, the GDP has grown at an av-erage annual rate of more than 5 percent per annum. This rate of increase puts Pakistan among the fastest growing economies of the Third World. Growing at this rate, Pakistan was able to keep a significant number of its people out of poverty. In 1947, income per capita was on the order of $155 in 1996 prices. Fifty year later, although the population increased nearly fourfold, from 32 million to 127 million, per capita income increased by a factor of three, from $155 to $465 (in 1997). In fact, Pakistan could arguably have sustained an even larger rate of growth in its GDP. It could have built an even more robust record of growth based on its rich agricultural endowment, an exceptionally entrepreneurial human re-source, and easy access to large amounts of external savings for four decades fol-lowing independence. A rate of growth some 6 to 7 percent was not inconceiv-able. If that had happened, Pakistan's income per head of the population in 1997 could have touched $900. Had that happened, Pakistan would have entered the second half century of nationhood as a middle-income country. This could have occurred if political crises had not taken a heavy political toll at regular intervals in the country's history and if the external environment had not turned suddenly hostile.[2]

In fact, a closer look at the structure of the economy reveals features characteris-tic of middle-income nations. Even today, in the midst of a deep economic crisis, Pakistan has many attributes of a middle-income nation but its average per capita income places it among poor states. If this assessment is correct, the country should be able to achieve a rapid rate of growth; but, if that is to happen, the peo-ple of Pakistan will have to find workable solutions to the political problems they have been plagued with for so long. (See Chapter 2.) They will also need to resolve some of the deep-rooted structural problems that have contributed to their coun-try's relative underdevelopment. Finally, they will have to better accommodate their country to the rapidly changing external political and economic environments. In fact, an argument can be made that in the 1990s Pakistan left the path of high growth and is now moving along a path at which the structural rate of growth is not much more than the rate of increase in population. The big challenge for Pakistan today is returning to the high growth trajectory, an issue that we address in the final section of the chapter. First, however, we analyze the present structure of the economy, the country's recent economic history, the role of politics in shaping the economy, and, finally, some external influences that have operated on the economy. We then offer some insights into the development of three major sectors of the economy: agriculture, industry, and services. In the penultimate section of the chapter we look at the most difficult problem facing the country today: reducing the dependence on external resources and relying on domestic resource mobilization for financing both development and current expenditures.

The Current Structure of the Economy

Provided in Table 3.1 are statistics relating to the structure of the country's economy, as compared with India, all poor countries, and lower-middle-income countries. The purpose of these comparisons is to illustrate whether the structure of Pakistan's economy is in line with the level of its per capita income. Of the four areas chosen for comparison, three suggest that Pakistan is more developed than a typical low-income country; in fact, it is even more advanced than some of the lower-middle-income nations. The areas in which Pakistan displays a higher level of development compared to lower-income countries are (1) its contribution of agriculture to gross domestic product (GDP), (2) its share of labor force employed in industry, and (3) its level of urbanization. The process of development has moved resources out of agriculture and into industry, commerce, and services. In 1995, nearly one-quarter of Pakistan's total output was accounted for by the sector of industries and another one-quarter by agriculture; services contributed the remaining one-half. These sectoral shares give some indication of an economy having characteristics of a middle-income country.

Economic development has also resulted in the movement of labor from agriculture into nonagricultural pursuits, and from the countryside to towns and cities. By 1995, nearly one-third of Pakistan's population was living in the urban areas and over 40 percent of its labor force was engaged in nonagricultural pursuits. For low-income countries, the share of nonagricultural employment was much lower.

In the area of export diversification, Pakistan has not done as well: Agriculture still accounts for 30 percent of its total exports. But this seeming lack of progress is in part the consequence of the country's economic endowment. Even with a rapid growth in its economy, and even after the country has finally graduated into the ranks of middle-income nations, there are good reasons for which agriculture might continue to dominate the export sector. In fact, as will be seen in a later sec-

TABLE 3.1   Economic Statistics in a Comparative Framework

	Pakistan	India	Bangladesh	Low-income Countries
GNP ($ billions, 1997)	67.2	373.9	33.2	721.7
GNP per capita ($, 1997)	490	390	270	350
GNP per capita ($, 1997)[a]	1590	16500	1050	1400
Sectoral contributions to GDP (%, 1997)				
Agriculture	26	27	30	31
Industry	25	30	17	27
(Manufactures)	(16)	(19)	(9)	(16)
Services	50	43	53	42
Demographic Situation (1997)				
Population (million)	137	961	124	2048
Population Density (thousands per sq.km.)	169	313	920	65
Female % of Labor Force	27	21	42	27
Distribution of population (%, 1995)				
Rural	65	73	81	72
Urban	35	27	19	28
Central government expenditure (% of GDP)				
Current	19.1	14.5	Na	Na
Capital	4.1	−6.5	Na	Na
Military	6.1	2.4	1.7	Na
Trade as % of GDP	37	27	38	42

[a]These data refer to those generated by the United Nations Comparison Program (ICP). The ICP recasts traditional national accounts through special price collections and disaggregation of GDP by expenditure components.

Source: Computed from data in World Bank, World Development Report 1998–99: Knowledge for Development (Washington, D.C.: World Bank, September 1998); Tables 1, 2, 3, 12, 17 of World Development Indicators, pp. 214–247.

tion, if Pakistan is to make rapid progress, it must concentrate a good deal of its resources on developing its remarkable agricultural potential.

The data in Table 3.1 amply demonstrate that, as of the mid-1990s, Pakistan has many of the economic characteristics of middle-income countries. But the country's progress has not been uniform: In terms of social development, Pakistan has lagged behind a number of low-income countries—particularly the

TABLE 3.2   Pakistan's Growth Performance Compared with Other Countries (annual growth rates, in percentages)

	GDP		Population Increase	
	1980–90	*1990–97*	*1980–90*	*1990–97*
Low-income countries				
Pakistan	6.3	4.4	3.1	2.9
India	5.8	5.9	2.1	1.8
Bangladesh	4.5	4.5	2.4	1.6
Poor countries	4.3	4.2	2.4	2.1

Source: The World Bank, *World Development Report 1998–99* (Washington, D.C.: World Bank, 1985), various tables in the *World Development Indicators* section.

poor countries of South Asia. This subject is discussed at some length in Chapter 4; the main objective of this chapter is to find an explanation for the paradoxical situation in which Pakistan finds itself at the moment—a poor country with the structure of a middle-income economy.

Recent Economic History

One way of identifying the reasons for this divergence between the structure of the economy and the income that it produces is to analyze Pakistan's rather turbulent economic history. Over the last five decades, Pakistan has experienced wide fluctuations in the rate of growth of its national product. The 1950s were sluggish; the 1960s were exceptionally buoyant; the rate of growth slowed in the first seven years of the 1970s but picked up again in the last three years of the decade; the decade of the 1980s began, once again, on a buoyant note, but ran into serious problems by the close of the decade. Pakistan entered the 1990s faced with a serious economic crisis which has persisted to this day—early 1999. Table 3.2 indicates the growth rates of Pakistan's GNP by decades as well as a comparison of the country's performance with that of other countries. The table also underscores the important point that the country's economy has seldom moved in step with those of other developing countries. In the 1950s, the growth rate of Pakistan's national output was much lower than that of the average for other developing nations. The situation reversed itself in the 1960s, when Pakistan's economy outperformed that of most other developing countries. The aggregate growth rate during the 1970s remained high, but this figure was largely a statistical artifact: It reflected not so much the increases in the output of the productive sectors of the economy as the essentially nonproductive parts of the economy (e.g., commerce, defense, government, and various kinds of services). The growth rate in the 1980s dropped below the average of the poor countries but was high compared to the middle-income countries. The good performance shown by poor countries during the 1980s was because of the high rate of growth registered by the Chinese economy.

TABLE 3.3   Sectoral Growth in Pakistan, 1950–1990 (annual growth rates, in percentages)

	1950–1960	1960–1970	1970–1980	1980–1990
Agriculture	2.3	5.2	2.3	5.6
Industry	8.1	9.1	2.3	8.2
Other sectors	3.8	7.6	7.0	5.0
Growth in GNP	3.4	6.7	5.7	5.6

Source: Computed from data provided by the Government of Pakistan, *Pakistan Economic Survey 1984–1985* (Islamabad: Ministry of Finance, 1985), statistical annex; and Government of Pakistan, *Pakistan Economic Survey 1989–1990* (Islamabad: Ministry of Finance, 1990), statistical annex.

The fact that Pakistan has generally not been in step with the other economies of the Third World seems to suggest that, in spite of the deep dependence on foreign capital flows, domestic policy rather than external environment played a much more significant role in shaping the course of economic development. Successive governments seldom pursued the same set of objectives and seldom emphasized the same sectors of the economy. Consequently, there were sharp fluctuations in sectoral fortunes. For instance, manufacturing directed at the production of consumer goods was the sector favored by the governments of the early 1950s, to be replaced by agriculture in the 1960s. Throughout much of the 1970s, neither agriculture nor industry received much government attention; now social sectors were the clear favorites. In the concluding years of the 1970s and the early 1980s, the government turned its attention once again to the development of the agricultural sector. In the 1990s the government of Benazir Bhutto gave priority to investment in the electric power sector whereas her successor, Mian Nawaz Sharif, was keen on building roads and airports. These changes in government policies were reflected in the performance of the various sectors of the economy. As indicated in Table 3.3, the rate of growth of industry during the first postindependence decade was 2.5 times the rate of growth of the whole economy. In the 1960s, the rate of growth of the agricultural sector was 2.5 times the rate of increase in the previous decade. In the 1970s, agriculture as well as industry stagnated while the service sectors took the lead. In the 1980s, agricultural output has once again begun to increase rapidly, thus becoming (along with small-scale industry) the leading sector of the economy. In the 1990s, large-scale manufacturing as well as agriculture stagnated while expenditures on public management increased enormously.

The Role of Politics in Pakistan's Economy

To a considerable extent, politics was responsible for the wide fluctuations in the performance of the main sectors of the economy. Some reasons for these fluctuations can be discerned if sectoral performance is analyzed in the context of political periods. Pakistan's political history can be divided into six periods: The first lasted for just over eleven years (1947–1958) and was characterized by competitive parliamentary democracy. Governments changed rapidly during this period as the indigenous leaders of the areas that constituted Pakistan began the process of recapturing political power from the migrant community. The migrant community, having fought vigorously for the creation of Pakistan, took full advantage of the leadership role it had played by capturing the commanding heights of the administration set up in the country. This fact was resented by the leaders who were indigenous to the areas that were now part of Pakistan. What ensued was a bitter conflict for the control of instruments of power. The most vivid reflection of this conflict was the rapid change in prime ministers and governments in the nine years between independence in 1947 and the first military takeover in 1958. During this period Pakistan saw seven prime ministers in office.

The second period lasted for a little over thirteen years (1958–1971) and saw two military dictatorships—the first under General Ayub Khan (1958–1969) and the second under General Yahya Khan (1969–1971). This period started with the reappearance of indigenous leaders in the political system. Later, as they settled down to govern, the military and civilian bureaucracies forged a strong political alliance with a number of middle-class urban and rural groups. This was the one (and to date the only) time in the country's history when the political system represented the makeup of the society reasonably well. Later, however, the system created the impression that two groups—the people of East Pakistan and the refugee community—were being discriminated against. Once this impression was firmly established in the minds of those who thought they had lost their political voice, the political system lost its equilibrium. The result was the anti–Ayub Khan movement that led to his resignation in March 1969 and the civil war in East Pakistan that broke up Pakistan and created the independent state of Bangladesh.

The third period represented a brief interregnum in rule by the military; during these years (1972–1977), Zulfikar Ali Bhutto managed to retain political control with populist support. The initial enthusiasm about Bhutto resulted from his articulation of the wishes and aspirations of people who had begun to get uneasy in the latter part of the Ayub Khan period. An impression had been created, in part by Mahbubul Haq (the chief economist on the Planning Commission) that the rich and well-to-do were the real beneficiaries of Ayub Khan's economic reforms. Bhutto took up this theme and promised to reach the masses with an economic program that would ensure "*roti, kapra,* and *makan*" (bread, clothes, and shelter) to all citizens. The people believed him and the promise he had made; his remarkable success in the 1970 elections was due to the enormous support he received from a variety of urban-based social groups. Bhutto was widely expected to jettison the powerful landed community and mobilize state resources to deliver economic returns to the new social groups he had brought into the political system. Unfortunately for Bhutto, exactly the opposite happened. The landlords returned in big numbers to the electoral lists prepared by the Pakistan People's

Party for the 1977 elections. Bhutto was content to use the elections to give power back to the landlords. He used the power of state to make sure that the PPP candidates were elected. Another street agitation was the consequence of these maneuvers, which resulted in another period of martial law, the longest in history.

The fourth period began in 1977 with the establishment of Pakistan's third military dictatorship and lasted for a little over eleven years. The distinguishing feature of this martial law under General Ziaul-Haq was the use of the armed forces to reflect and convey the aspirations of lower and middle classes to the political system. Thus the army and other military services began to perform the role of political parties. They succeeded in part because under Zia the landed aristocracy was not able to dominate the political scene. However, Zia was unable (and perhaps unwilling) to institutionalize this change. This could have been done had Zia transferred power to a more broad-based political regime.

Although martial law was lifted on December 30, 1985, and a civilian government headed by Prime Minister Mohammad Khan Junejo was sworn into office the same day, General Zia ul-Haq did not allow political power to pass into civilian hands. He was prepared at best to share power with a group of politicians who did not question the military's continued presence in the political field. This partnership between the military and political establishments collapsed on May 29, 1988, when General Zia ul-Haq dismissed Prime Minister Mohammad Khan Junejo and his cabinet, dissolved the national and provincial assemblies, and ordered elections to take place in November. Zia was killed in an air crash on August 17, 1988, but the caretaker government he had appointed stayed in place to oversee the elections, which were held on November 17.

These elections ushered in the fifth period, a return to a parliamentary democracy under Benazir Bhutto. Under an arrangement termed the "troika," the Bhutto administration was forced to allow the military considerable authority in areas that included defense and foreign affairs. This arrangement worked for less than two years. On August 6, 1990, Ghulam Ishaq Khan, who succeeded Zia ul-Haq as president, dismissed Prime Minister Bhutto, dissolved the National Assembly and the provincial assemblies, and called for general elections on October 24.

Politics in Pakistan had come full circle: Ghulam Ishaq Khan's brief civilian interregnum had served to underscore once again the difficulty in achieving consensus among the country's important but diverse social and economic groups on a wide variety of issues. Shortly after dismissing Benazir Bhutto, in a television and radio address President Ghulam Ishaq Khan read a long list of charges against the PPP government, reflecting the disappointment of the civil and military establishment with the conduct of politicians in office. Most of these charges pertained to corruption and economic mismanagement by the Bhutto administration.

Mian Nawaz Sharif, Bhutto's successor as prime minister, shared Bhutto's fate, being dismissed on the grounds of incompetence and corruption. The 1993 general elections brought Bhutto back to power, but the quality of the governance she

TABLE 3.4   Economic Performance during Major Political Periods (average annual growth rates, in percentages)

	Competitive Parliamentary Democracy 1947–1958	First and Second Military Dictatorships (Ayub and Yahya) 1958–1971	Civilian Dictatorship (Bhutto) 1972–1977	Third Military Dictatorship 1977–1988	Return of Parliamentary Democracy 1988–1998
GDP	2.9	5.3	5.4	6.7	4.3
Agriculture	1.6	3.9	2.1	3.5	4.7
Manufacturing	8.7	8.1	5.2	8.9	4.4
Other sectors	6.1	6.0	7.8	6.1	3.2

Source: Computed from data provided by the Government of Pakistan, *Pakistan Economic Survey 1997–1998* (Islamabad: Ministry of Finance, 1998).

provided was even worse than it was during her first term as prime minister. Bhutto was dismissed in November 1996 by her protégé, President Farooq Leghari, who ordered another general election. The 1997 election brought Nawaz Sharif to power as prime minister for the second time in four years, but he came in with a majority in the National Assembly so large that he felt that he could ignore the opposition.

With the return of Sharif, Pakistan may well have begun the sixth period in its political history with a sense that the highly competitive democracy of the 1988–1996 period was in the process of being replaced by a move toward the reestablishment of an authoritarian state. There is belief that such a state would be more effective in overriding Pakistan's long-enduring establishment and would be able to broaden the political system.

These political developments are discussed in some detail in Chapter 2; the important point here is that over the last fifty years, Pakistan has watched many individuals try, in different ways, to take political power away from the established groups, particularly the powerful landed aristocracy, and broaden the political system by bringing in groups that had been excluded from it. If they succeeded, their success was transient.

Jinnah's appeal to the Indian Muslim masses put him at the head of a political movement with a vast following. However, the state created by the movement he led was dominated for a while by socioeconomic groups, most of whom had migrated from what was now the independent country of India. These *muhajirs*, by narrowing the political system, by keeping the old groups out of it, created a disequilibrium that could not endure. Ayub Khan used the army that he headed to intervene and broaden the system once again. He succeeded for a while with the help of a system based on what he called "basic democracies." The establishment struck back. Its efforts to remove Ayub Khan were successful because it was able to elicit help from those who felt that they had not benefited from the economic progress made by the country while Ayub Khan was in office. The next attempt at bringing in excluded groups was made by Zulfikar Ali Bhutto. He was successful in broadening the political base to the extent that his legacy survived for twenty years after he was physically removed from the scene. Bhutto came close to resolving Pakistan's basic dilemma—the existence of a great divide between the economic demands of a vast variety of social groups and the narrow interests of the political system dominated by a few interests. But Bhutto himself stepped back from the realization of the fruits of his initial success. He himself narrowed the system once again.

Zia, Bhutto's successor, instinctively understood the nature of the dilemma the country faced. His big mistake was to depend on the army and use the language of Islam, rather than the political system, to reach the people who remained outside. This approach could not work for very long; even Ayub Khan had realized that political institutions had to be put in place and nurtured to achieve the broadening of the system. The Zia system, therefore, came to be dominated by the bureaucracy, which also learned to use the Islamic political idiom in an effort to gain greater credibility for itself. Zia was succeeded by two politicians who concentrated their entire attention on obtaining and maintaining power instead of promoting political development. The result was intense political confrontation that brought the country to the brink of economic disaster at least three times. Neither Benazir Bhutto, Zulfikar Ali Bhutto's daughter, nor Mian Nawaz Sharif, who had been mentored by Zia ul-Haq, understood that heavy-handed management of the political system would not ensure their political longevity. Consequently, the period following the death of Zia in 1988 was as turbulent politically as the period that followed the death of Mohammad Ali Jinnah in 1948. In 1998, Nawaz Sharif, having gained full command over the national legislature and professing to be gravely troubled by the persistence of instability, began the process of putting himself at the center of the political system. The instruments that he used—ideology, domination of a political party, promise of economic improvement—had been used before. In 1999, the time of this writing, this approach does not seem any more likely to produce greater political participation than those that preceded it.

Pakistan's political history thus reflects a constant tussle among social groups for participation in or control of the political process. It is interesting to speculate as to how these conflicts may have affected economic decisionmaking and, consequently, economic performance. Such an analysis is best done in the context of the five periods identified in Table 3.4.

As indicated in Table 3.4, industry (especially large-scale manufacturing) led the economy during the period of competitive parliamentary democracy. That manufacturing rather than agriculture established the economic viability of Pakistan was a fact not many people had expected at the time of independence. In 1947, Pakistan's economy was primarily agricultural; agriculture was its principal asset, its output, and its only export. Instead of making use of this resource, however, policymakers turned to the industrial sector to lead the economy out of the difficulties created by the trauma of partition. There were essentially two reasons for this. First, in 1949 the informal customs union between India and Pakistan suddenly collapsed. This arrangement had allowed the free movement of goods, people, and currency between the two countries. With the cessation of trade, Pakistan was thrown on its own devices but had no industry to provide its people with even the most modest goods of everyday consumption. Accordingly, industries, especially consumer goods industries, had to be set up. To find resources for industrialization, the agriculture sector was taxed, albeit indirectly. The exchange rate was overvalued to depress the domestic prices of traded agricultural products. Cheap cotton and jute made a large textile industry quickly viable, but the low prices that farmers were paid depressed the rate of increase in agricultural productivity.

Internal politics was the second reason for the neglect of agriculture during this period. In the early 1950s, decisionmaking was in the hands of a few politicians and civil servants who had migrated from India. These migrants from the cities of India understandably displayed a strong urban bias: They had little knowledge of and little interest in agriculture. Accordingly, manufacturing rather than agriculture received most of the government's attention and the bulk of public development resources.

The political situation began to change in the mid-1950s. The return of the landlords to the political arena revived government interest in agriculture, and the assumption of political power by General Ayub Khan moved the focus of political power from Karachi, a city dominated by industry and commerce, to Lahore and Rawalpindi, two cities that were much more representative of indigenous and rural Pakistan.

These political changes had two important economic consequences: They made the "green revolution" possible, and they caused considerable dispersion of industrial capital. Because of the green revolution, the rate of increase in Pakistan's agricultural output during this period was among the highest in the world; in 1969, the last year of the Ayub regime, Pakistan produced 10 million tons of food grains, compared to 8 million tons in 1958. In the 1960s, therefore, agriculture as well as industry contributed to the country's remarkable performance. But the collapse of the Ayub regime was the consequence of a broad-based political movement that used the language of economics to get its point across to the people. Previously only the Pakistan Movement led by Mohammad Ali Jinnah in the 1940s had been able to focus the attention of the Muslim community on social and economic issues. Now as the opposition to President Ayub Khan intensified, it was talk of persistent poverty, economic deprivation, and income inequality that galvanized the people and persuaded them to even lay down their lives to remove the regime. The ensuing political chaos brought to the surface new forces that were to take Pakistan through a major structural change in the early 1970s. It resulted in the breakup of Pakistan and the emergence of Bangladesh as an independent state in the area that was once the eastern wing of the country founded by Jinnah. In the western wing, the agitation against Ayub Khan finally gave rise to populism.

Nationalization of a number of economic enterprises in the sectors of industry, finance, trade, and communication was one important manifestation of the structural change in what was left of Pakistan. The resulting expansion of the public sector was in line with Zulfikar Ali Bhutto's populist politics. In 1972, the public sector contributed only 3 percent to national output; by 1976, following implementation of the government's nationalization program, its contribution increased fourfold to more than 13 percent. The public sector's presence in the nonagricultural parts of the economy was even more pronounced in that it contributed more than 20 percent of the total output. For political reasons, the public sector received a much larger share of investment—more than 60 percent—and much greater attention from the policymakers.

Not unexpectedly, this sudden shift in priorities caused major disruptions. Hitherto, Pakistan had emphasized the development of the private sector, leaving to public management only those parts of the economy in which private entrepreneurs had little interest. Private capital moved out of industry and went into construction and commerce, two sectors in which returns were high; a great deal of private capital also left the country for the security offered in the Middle East, Europe, and the United States. If the rate of growth of GDP remained high during this period, it was not because of the value added in the productive sectors of the economy but because of the increase in such speculative sectors as trade and construction. Consequently, this was to be the only period in Pakistan's economic history in which the growth of output in both agriculture and industry was less than the rate of growth in GDP. A rate of economic growth lower than the rate of population increase could not be sustained for long, since it would result in massive pauperization of the population. What saved Bhutto was the large-scale migration of people from Pakistan to the Middle East and the remittances they sent to their families who stayed back. Although emigration may have prevented the emergence of mass poverty in the country, the vast amount of capital that flowed into the country by way of remittances produced a social change as profound as the one caused by the movement of 8 million Muslims into Pakistan from India. Once again, the political system proved unequal to the task of accommodating social change.

When the military forced Zulfikar Ali Bhutto out of office in July 1977, it also abandoned his populist economic policies. These policies had obviously alienated the social groups that were important for the military: the large landlords of Sindh; the middle-sized farmers of Punjab and the Northwest Frontier Province; the merchants and industrialists of Karachi, Lahore, and Multan; and urban professionals. All of these groups together made up the constituency that had supported Ayub Khan in the 1960s; under General Zia ul-Haq, the military instinctively went back for support to the same social groups. The further development of the public sector was constrained, and private entrepreneurs were invited back to invest in all sectors of the economy. Agriculture once again received a great deal of government attention and resources. Small industries—in particular, those that provided inputs for the agriculture sector and processed agricultural output—came to be especially favored. However, under Zia ul-Haq the economy did not return fully to the laissez-faire policies of General Ayub Khan. The powerful civil bureaucracy managed to retain control over the enterprises that had been brought under government control by the administration of Zulfikar Ali Bhutto.

Nevertheless, the economy responded quickly to the changes in policy introduced by the Zia government. From a rate of growth barely higher than 2 percent per year during the Bhutto period, the output of the agricultural sector increased to 4.6 percent. The rate of growth of manufacturing output nearly doubled, from 5.2 percent to 8.9 percent. The GDP increased at the annual rate of 6.7 percent, which was made possible not by the expansion of the nonproductive sectors of the economy, as had happened during the period of Zulfikar Ali Bhutto, but by the impressive increases in the output of the agricultural and industrial sectors.

It is one of the great ironies of history that Pakistan had to wait for Benazir Bhutto to come to power before the socialist orientation in economic management introduced by her father could be finally abandoned. Benazir Bhutto gave full rein to the private sector. A board of investment was set up in the prime minister's office to sanction the establishment of new industrial units in the private sector. Private entrepreneurs were also encouraged to take part in large-scale trading in commodities. Privately owned utility and construction companies were invited to invest in power generation, telecommunications, and highway construction. The private sector responded with predictable enthusiasm that could not be contained by the economy's weak institutional infrastructure. New and old entrepreneurs rushed in, prepared to offer financial incentives to all those willing to receive them in return for expediting the required bureaucratic clearances for establishing and managing their enterprises. The "free-for-all" environment created by a section of the private sector as it sought to exploit Benazir Bhutto's open approach to economic management raised some serious questions about the government's conduct in office. The presidential order dismissing the prime minister detailed some of the consequences of Bhutto's economic policies and her way of managing the economy. "Corruption and nepotism in the Federal Government, its functionaries and agencies, statutory and other corporations including banks working under its supervision has reached such proportions, that the orderly functioning of the government, including the requirements of the oaths prescribed therein, and the law does no longer carry public faith and credibility," read the order.[3] The president began judicial proceedings, charging Bhutto's administration with corruption. Eleven special courts were set up and dozens of cases implicating Bhutto and several members of her cabinet were brought to trial. Asif Ali Zardari, Benazir Bhutto's husband, was charged in a criminal court on numerous counts of corruption and extortion.[4]

Mian Nawaz Sharif became prime minister following the elections of November 1990 and continued most of the policies of his predecessor. The main difference between his approach and that of Benazir Bhutto was his emphasis on using public funds to provide employment for the educated unemployed in the urban areas and to build expensive infrastructure. The Sharif government launched two expensive schemes during its brief tenure. A "yellow cab" scheme provided thousands of persons highly subsidized credit to import cars for use as taxis. The scheme's two objectives were to improve transportation in the rapidly growing towns and cities and to provide employment opportunities to those who, because of the economic slowdown in the Middle East, could no longer move abroad in search of jobs. The most immediate impact of the yellow cab scheme was an enormous drain of foreign exchange as $600 million worth of cars were imported into the country. The other project—a motorway between Islamabad and Lahore—to be built with the help of the South Korean private sector was equally costly for the economy. It drained development resources from the public sector that should have gone into higher priority sectors. By the time President Ghulam Ishaq Khan moved once again to dismiss a prime minister on charges of corruption and incompetence, Pakistan was almost bankrupt, with foreign exchange reserves almost depleted and fiscal deficits at unsustainable levels.

Benazir Bhutto, back in power after the October 1993 elections, allowed her husband to use her power for personal gain, instead of focusing the government's attention on improving the health of the economy. Bhutto presided over the most corrupt government in Pakistan's history, a fact that was underscored by Transparency International in its annual report for 1996, which listed Pakistan as the second most corrupt country in the world (after Nigeria). As we shall discuss in Chapter 5, the misuse of public resources touched most state institutions, especially public sector banks and public corporations that were left bankrupt. Another prime minister was dismissed and another caretaker government stepped in to steady the economy.

The February 1997 elections gave Nawaz Sharif's Pakistan Muslim League an unprecedented victory. He commanded the support of three-fourths of the national legislature, which he used to consolidate power in his hands. (See Chapter 2.) However, the decision to follow India's example and test nuclear bombs in May 1998 invited international sanctions that brought Pakistan close to declaring a default on international obligations. In the winter of 1998–1999, Pakistan faced a deep economic crisis, perhaps the worst in its fifty-year history.

Political turbulence that followed Zia's death took a heavy economic toll. Since 1990–1991, Pakistan's GDP has increased at the rate of 4 percent a year, only marginally better than the population rate of increase. Has the structural growth rate declined to a level at which mass poverty would become the dominant feature of the Pakistani society and economy? This subject is discussed in the concluding section of this chapter.

External Influences on Pakistan's Economy

Domestic policies have been important in influencing the pace as well as the pattern of economic growth, but they cannot be held entirely responsible for the highly erratic performance of the economy. Other reasons were implicated, as well, including the economy's external environment. For Pakistan, external resource flows—through export earnings as well as capital transfers—have always been important in view of the country's very low domestic saving rate.

The rate of domestic saving in Pakistan is much lower than the average for developing countries. In 1960, Pakistan saved only 5 percent of its GDP. In the same year, India's saving rate was 14 percent and China's was 23 percent; the average for low-income countries was 16 percent. By the end of the 1970s, the savings rate had increased by only one percentage point, to 6 percent (India's increased to 20 percent, China's to 30 percent, and the average for the developing countries to 23 percent). In 1995, the most recent year for which such data are available, the average savings rate for all low-income countries was 30 percent. Within this group of countries, China saved 42 percent of its gross domestic product, India 22 percent, and Pakistan only 17 percent.[5] Despite a low rate of saving, however, gross investment remains high: It was 12 percent in 1960, 18 percent in 1979, and 19 percent in 1995. The gap between gross domestic saving and investment—the resource gap—was financed by highly concessional assistance in the 1960s, mostly from the World Bank and the United States. In the 1980s and 1990s, a fairly large part of the deficit was financed from short-term borrowings; at times, even high rates of interest did not inhibit Pakistan from going to the market. The result was that by the middle of the 1990s Pakistan carried a very large debt burden, estimated in 1995 at over $30 billion, or close to 50 percent of a GDP of some $60 billion. In that year, well over one-third of the total earnings from exports of goods and services was used up in servicing the external debt.

The country, therefore, must be mindful of the way it conducts foreign affairs; any major disruption in its relations with the outside world could produce serious economic consequences. Such disruptions have occurred many times in the past and have contributed to the wide swings that are so prominent in Pakistan's economic history. Accordingly, an analysis of Pakistan's relations with the world beyond its frontiers is important to an understanding of its economic history. There are ten developments worthy of note in this context—the trade war with India in 1949, the Korean War in the early 1950s, Pakistan's membership in a series of U.S.-sponsored pacts and agreements signed in the 1950s, the 1965 war with India, the migration of millions of Pakistanis to the Middle East in the 1970s, the invasion of Afghanistan by the Soviet Union in 1979, the Gulf War in 1990, the collapse of communism and the Soviet Union in 1991, conduct of nuclear tests in May, 1998, and the resurgence of radical Islam around Pakistan's borders in the 1980s and 1990s. All these developments had profound economic implications for Pakistan, but only three of these—the trade war with India, the war over Kashmir with India, and the testing of nuclear weapons—resulted from actions taken by Pakistan. The remaining developments were beyond Pakistan's control.

Pakistan began its existence within a large economic community made up of itself and India. For almost two years, the two countries maintained an open border between them, across which people, goods, and commodities were allowed to move freely. The western part of Pakistan, which still had a surplus of food, continued to send its surplus wheat and rice to the food-deficient areas in northern India. It also grew a large amount of cotton, which continued to go to the mills in Bombay and Ahmadabad to be processed into yarn and cloth. Pakistan's eastern part—present-day Bangladesh—was the world's largest producer of jute but had no jute-processing mills within its own borders. Accordingly, as had happened in the past, raw jute from East Bengal continued to feed mills in Calcutta. In exchange for these agricultural commodities, Pakistan received simple consumer goods from India—textiles, shoes, toiletries, electric fans, bicycles—as well as coal, cement, iron, steel, and electric power. Pakistan's administrative machinery was still not organized, and its central bankers were still learning their trade; consequently, much of this trade was undertaken by the private sector. In addition, the accounts between the two countries were settled privately without any substantial involvement of the central banks. There were no meaningful exchange controls. Although Pakistan had produced a currency of its own—the old Indian rupee with the word "Pakistan" imprinted on it—traders on both sides of the border continued to accept and exchange each other's currency. Pakistan did not seem to be in any great hurry to build an economic structure independent of India's. Its leaders, preoccupied with the gigantic task of organizing a new administrative and political structure and settling millions of refugees, were quite content to leave the economic side alone, letting it run much as it had done in the period before partition.

It is conceivable that the unofficial, informal India-Pakistan economic community would have persisted for many more years but for the devaluation of the British currency, the pound, in 1949 and the decision of India to follow suit. Much to the surprise of the government of India, Ghulam Muhammad, Pakistan's first finance minister, decided to retain the old value of the Pakistani rupee. This decision not to devalue meant that a new rate of exchange between the Indian and Pakistani rupees had to be fixed; but instead of the parity exchange that had existed before, India found that it had to pay 144 rupees for 100 Pakistani rupees. The Indian response to this sudden adjustment was a highly emotional one. It was seen as an act of defiance by Pakistan; New Delhi viewed it as a deliberate provocation aimed at giving the important message that Pakistan now regarded itself as economically independent of India. In today's world, exchange-rate fixing is considered to be the prerogative of sovereign states. The exchange-rate policies of countries may be influenced by such multilateral institutions as the International Monetary Fund (IMF) and the World Bank, but they are seldom the cause of grave tension between neighboring states. But Pakistan had emerged as an independent state in a world that had yet to become accustomed to the arrival of new nations with new names, new flags, and exotic currencies. Its effort to establish itself as an independent nation-state was accepted only grudgingly, particularly by its neighbor, India.

Pakistan's decision not to devalue its currency along with those of the United Kingdom and most other members of the British Commonwealth was to have consequences that the government in Karachi could not possibly have anticipated. In retrospect, it was a bold step—one that provoked a totally unexpected response from the Indian government. Declaring that it would not pay 144 of its rupees in exchange for 100 rupees from Pakistan, India put an embargo on all trade between the two countries. Suddenly, Pakistani consumers found themselves without a number of basic necessities, and, just as suddenly, the government of Pakistan found that it had to turn its attention to economic planning.

In refocusing its attention, the Pakistani government made two decisions with far-reaching consequences for the future of the country's economy. The first was the decision to industrialize quickly; the second was to turn to the influential merchant houses of Karachi to provide the lead in this effort. Pakistan's comparative advantage at that time did not lie in the industrial sector; given the absence of a mature industrial class, the government could have chosen a role different from the one it actually adopted. That is, it could have entrusted industrialization to the public sector. Later on, a number of other Third World countries, faced with a similar situation, invariably entrusted the public sector with the task of building an industrial infrastructure. Pakistan, at that time, took a different course.

The decision to go to the private sector was embodied in the Industrial Policy—the government's first significant statement on any aspect of economic policy. A few "commanding heights" were reserved for the public sector (such as the industries related to armaments production, iron and steel, heavy chemicals, and basic engineering goods), but all other industries were to be set up in the private sector. The size of the Pakistani economy at that time was very small, which meant that even if they had been allowed entry, private entrepreneurs would not have attempted to scale these "commanding heights." There was just not enough demand for the products such industries would have produced. The development of the industrial sector, for all intents and purposes, was therefore left in the hands of the private sector. Pakistan was ahead of its time.

Thus began a period of extraordinary industrialization in Pakistan—a period that was to last for two decades and one in which industrial output increased at the unprecedented rate of 11 percent per annum. In 1947, the contribution of manufacturing to the GNP was little more than 6 percent; it is now contributing four times as much to the national income.

The Industrial Policy would have remained a paper dream without the Korean War. That war rekindled the demand for Pakistan's agricultural exports—jute, cotton, leather, and wool. The market that had been lost in India for these commodities was found in North America and Western Europe. The West needed jute bags for hauling and transporting all manner of goods as well as commodities to supply its troops in Korea. Pakistan's coarse, short-staple cotton was ideal for making canvas, another item in heavy demand as war material. Coarse wool for gloves and socks and coarse leather for boots and straps also found a ready market. Commodities that Pakistan in ordinary circumstances would have found exceedingly difficult to market now fetched premium prices. The Korean commodity boom was heaven-sent for a country struggling to find resources for implementing an ambitious industrial development plan.

The unit value of Pakistan's exports increased by more than 80 percent between May 1951 and November 1952. Total export earnings came to $135 million in 1950–1951, nearly two and a half times the earnings of the previous year. Once again, the private traders—soon to become the private industrialists—reaped the bulk of the profit. These traders had built their businesses during World War II, supplying the same kinds of commodities for use by the British Indian army. That experience proved to be rewarding, and large profits flowed to the established trading houses. A high proportion of these profits was diverted into industry; according to one estimate, the marginal saving rate for these merchant-industrialists was around 80 to 90 percent.[6] Once the fighting men in Korea were well outfitted, the commodity boom burst. The unit price for Pakistan's exports fell as sharply as it had risen, and with it fell the country's export earnings and the traders' profits. In real terms, export earnings in 1953–1954 were lower than those in 1949–1950, the (fiscal) year before the Korean boom began. The traders, still at the early stages of their plans to industrialize Pakistan, sought and obtained all types of government help and protection. Beginning in 1954, the government put together an elaborate system of exchange controls to protect the country's infant industry from outside competition and to supply the budding industrialists with the capital, technology, and raw materials they needed at prices below world levels.

Hence, although the course of Pakistan's first large industrial effort was set by the Indian decision to embargo trade with its neighbor, it was given a massive push by the enormous profits that the war in Korea produced for a small number of trading houses. The government finally sustained the effort, however. As was to happen time and again throughout the country's economic history, the main impulse for change came from the outside. Once this impulse had produced movement, the government was pulled in to maintain the momentum.

The beginnings of economic planning in Pakistan followed the same pattern—an outside impulse that was later sustained by domestic effort. Economic planning came to the country largely as a consequence of the close relations forged in the 1950s and early 1960s between Pakistan and the United States.

A later chapter investigates the circumstances that turned Pakistan into a close ally of the United States in the 1950s. In this connection, it is sufficient to recall that, in 1954, Pakistan signed a Mutual Defense Agreement with the United States. The agreement brought numerous U.S. military advisers, a large quantity of military equipment, and an impressive amount of economic assistance to Pakistan. The close association that developed between the two countries also brought to Pakistan such U.S. nongovernmental organizations as the Ford Foundation and Harvard University's Development Advisory Service. One of the most ambitious tasks undertaken by Ford was establishment of the institutional capacity in Pakistan to undertake long-term economic planning. In India, planners followed the Soviet model, putting emphasis on the creation of a large industrial infrastructure for promoting development. As the U.S. advisers brought to Pakistan by Ford had no experience in national planning (other than what had been gained by a few professors of economics from such East Coast universities as Harvard, Columbia, and Princeton during World War II), what emerged was a long and sometimes painful process of learning by doing.[7]

The Ford Foundation and the Harvard advisers adopted two approaches. First, Pakistan could not go on managing its economy in the absence of a long-term framework; second, the economic planning involved had to be done by the Pakistanis with the assistance of foreign advisers. As it turned out, these approaches did not produce a long-lasting impact. The foreign advisers stayed for a long time (fifteen years) but were not able to get the Planning Commission to produce a development plan that could oversee the country's development over a long period of fifteen to twenty years. A twenty-year perspective plan covering the period 1960–1980 was prepared, but it was not really a planning document. It provided a broad framework for the preparation of five-year and annual development plans, but that framework was discarded when the Third Five-Year Plan (1965–1970) came into being.

This is not to say that the foreign involvement in building an economic planning infrastructure failed to bear fruit. During the decade and a half of foreign participation, the Planning Commission became an impressive institution. It not only wrote four plans—the first in 1955 and the last in 1970—but also oversaw their implementation. The First Five-Year Plan (1955–1960) was a highly pragmatic document, free from ideology and reflecting full cognizance of the constraints the country faced. But the plan was not implemented; the country was too preoccupied with unresolved political problems to give priority to economic planning. The Second Five-Year Plan (1960–1965) was written and launched in the euphoric martial law days. General Ayub Khan and his colleagues were by then well settled in positions of absolute power; they had declared economic development to be the raison d'être of their revolution; the economic planners, foreign as well as local, seemed glad that a group of people sure of their political objectives had taken over the reins of the government. Thus the second plan proved to be a remarkable success. In West Pakistan—the area that constitutes the present state of Pakistan—the growth of the national product averaged nearly 7 percent per annum during the plan period. The plan encouraged private entrepreneurs to participate in those activities in which a great deal of profit was to be made; the state was brought into those sectors of the economy in which the private entrepreneurs were reluctant to go. This judicious mix of private enterprise and social responsibility was hailed as a model that all other developing countries could follow with profit. This model was celebrated in two influential books written by two planners, one an American, the other a Pakistani. Gustav Papanek emphasized what he called the "social utility of greed"—the hope that pursuit of individual profit (which had been the basis of Pakistan's extraordinary performance) would ultimately provide the resources for alleviating poverty and improving the social situation. Mahbubul Haq was even more forthright in his book, arguing that an increase in income inequality was inevitable in the initial phase of development.[8] The Third Five-Year Plan (1965–1970) continued the approaches followed with such success during the second plan period and might also have produced an impressive rate of economic growth had not another external event—the 1965 war with India—intervened.

The second advantage of the U.S. connection was the large amount of concessional money that flowed into Pakistan to help the country in its development effort. The United States launched a large program of bilateral aid to help Pakistan meet its growing need for food imports and to provide cheap money to build the physical infrastructure.

In 1954, the year the Mutual Defense Agreement was signed with the United States, Pakistan became a net importer of food grains for the first time in its history. This was an extraordinarily unfortunate development for that part of old British India which, for more than a century, had provided its food surplus to feed the rest of the subcontinent. Now, largely because of rapid population growth and wanton neglect of the agricultural sector, Pakistan had to rely on food imports. The situation was met by the importation of large quantities of wheat under the U.S. PL-480 food aid program. After the collapse of the Korean boom, Pakistan had very small reserves of foreign exchange to spend on food imports. Without PL-480, it would have had to spend a sizable proportion of its foreign exchange earnings on food grain purchases, thus leaving very little over to meet the foreign cost of promoting domestic economic development. The PL-480 program was exactly what Pakistan needed. The rupees it paid for the American wheat went into a "counterpart fund," the resources of which were used to pay the local costs of numerous development projects.

In addition to the aid provided bilaterally by the United States, Pakistan, in the 1960s, became a recipient of highly concessional flows from the International Development Association (IDA), the soft-loan window of the World Bank. The IDA was set up in 1960, the year Pakistan launched its ambitious Second Five-Year Plan and two years after Ayub Khan's revolution. By that time, India had also run into severe balance-of-payments difficulties. The economic problems faced by the two South Asian giants were viewed with great sympathy in Washington; in time, Washington persuaded its European allies and Japan that a multilateral aid effort was needed to help South Asia through this period. Accordingly, the IDA was launched, and India and Pakistan became the two largest recipients of assistance from this new source of concessional funds. If the United States had not drawn close to South Asia by 1960, it is doubtful that the IDA would have become a reality. Pakistan's close ties with the United States were obviously very important

TABLE 3.5   Exports, Imports, and Foreign Assistance (yearly averages, in $ millions)

	1949–1950	1959–1960	1969–1970	1979–1980	1989–1990
Exports	171	160	338	2365	3486
Imports	276	379	690	4740	5101
Trade balance	–105	–219	–352	–2375	–1615
Foreign assistance	118	585	564	1470	2230
as % of GNP	9.0	20.0	5.3	4.6	6.0
Per capita (current $)	3.0	10.8	11.4	14.0	21.0

Source: Computed from data provided by the Government of Pakistan, *Pakistan Economic Survey 1989–1990* (Islamabad: Ministry of Finance, 1990), statistical annex.

for improving Washington's understanding not only of South Asia's economic problems but also of its geopolitical importance.[9]

Pakistan's foreign policy in the 1960s thus paid rich dividends in the form of large amounts of concessional resource flows. In terms of the proportion of GNP as well as real flows per capita of the population, foreign aid during this period was greater than it had been in the 1950s and greater than it was to be in the 1970s and 1980s (see Table 3.5). However, in per capita terms, foreign assistance continued to increase—to $21 in 1989–1990. In nominal dollars, that represented the highest level of foreign assistance per person in Pakistan's history.

But the large inflow of assistance had its adverse side, too: Although it certainly contributed to the remarkable growth in GNP during the 1960s, it also dampened the rate of domestic savings. Development planners have raised questions about the precise impact of aid on domestic savings without providing any unambiguous answers. Pakistan's low domestic savings rates suggest that the negative impact of easy access to foreign capital flows cannot be ruled out easily. There was some improvement in the 1970s, but the domestic savings rate remained very low when compared to that of other developing nations. Compared to India, to the average for all low-income countries, and to the average for middle-income countries, however, per capita aid received by Pakistan was much larger during the 1960s and 1970s.

The U.S. connection was suddenly severed in 1965, as the war with India over Kashmir—the fourth external event on the list of developments with serious economic consequences for Pakistan—had resulted in a considerable amount of rethinking in Washington and Islamabad about the usefulness of the close ties between the two countries. Islamabad felt let down by the lack of support from Washington; Washington found that the network of alliances—SEATO and CENTO—of which Pakistan was a part no longer had the relevance that John Foster Dulles, their architect, had ascribed to them during the Eisenhower years. After 1965, the United States not only stopped military assistance to Pakistan, it also cut down by a significant amount the level of economic assistance. The burden of providing resources for its development, therefore, began to shift onto Pakistan's shoulders. The impact of this sudden change in the external environment would have been even more severe had Bangladesh not opted out of the Pakistan Union.

There was a lively, often acrimonious, debate during the 1960s concerning the amount of resources the poorer East Pakistan had transferred to the relatively more prosperous West Pakistan.[10] The debate also touched on the mechanisms that made such a flow possible and on the question of how its direction could be reversed. For the purpose of this part of the story, however, it is not important to go into any great detail about the nature of the economic relations between East and West Pakistan from 1947 to 1971 or to determine with any precision the quantity of transfer of resources that took place between the two wings. What is important is to recognize that such a transfer did occur; it was probably much larger in the 1950s than in the 1960s and occurred mostly by way of foreign trade. During the first post-independence decade, East Pakistan, being a large exporter of raw jute, enjoyed a favorable external balance with the outside world. West Pakistan, in view of its massive imports of industrial capital, ran up large deficits. In other words, the external trade surpluses of East Pakistan financed the deficit of West Pakistan during the 1950s. In the 1960s, the situation began to change, but very slowly. The government of Ayub Khan initiated an ambitious development program for Bengal; consequently, East Pakistan's demand for imports increased substantially. At the same time, raw jute and jute textiles began to face stiff competition from a number of synthetic fibers and fabrics, with the result that, in real terms, East Pakistan's export earnings did not increase as rapidly as those of West Pakistan. By the end of the 1960s, the situation had reversed itself: In 1969–1970, the transfer of resources occurred, in net terms, from West to East Pakistan.

It is ironic, therefore, that the drive for the political emancipation of East Pakistan gained momentum precisely at the time when it needed resources from the western province. East Pakistan's separation and emergence as the independent state of Bangladesh was a net gain for West Pakistan. In less than two years, West Pakistan was able to divert to foreign channels practically all the goods and commodities it had previously exported to the eastern province. Largely as a consequence of this diversion, Pakistan in 1972–1973 ran a trade surplus of more than $15 million. This was the second time in its history that it had achieved a positive trade balance (the first occurred in the early years of the Korean War). At the same time, the emergence of Bangladesh meant that the most contentious issue surrounding the formulation of the Fourth Five-Year Plan (1970–1975)—the extent of resource transfer from West to East Pakistan—was finally resolved. West Pakistan could now retain its domestic savings.

The separation of East Pakistan had one other important consequence: It allowed West Pakistan to put more emphasis on cultivating a close relationship with its neighbors in the Middle East. Pakistan's geography from 1947 to 1971—

two wings separated by more than a thousand miles of Indian landmass—had generated a strong South Asian bias in the country's foreign policy. East Pakistan's emergence as Bangladesh changed that orientation. In the 1970s, Pakistan gradually moved away from being anchored to the politics of South Asia and began to play a much more important role in the Middle East.

The fifth development worth noting was the result of a number of events, but for Pakistan it culminated with the formation of a strong link with the countries of the Middle East. Pakistan developed its Middle Eastern connection at precisely the time when the countries of the Middle East were acquiring large capital surpluses as a result of the 1973 quadrupling in the price of exported oil. Almost overnight the oil-importing developed and developing countries found themselves faced with large current-account deficits. In 1973, the current-account deficits of oil-importing countries were equivalent to 1.1 percent of their GNP; by 1975, this figure had increased to 5.1 percent. A similar increase took place for the industrial countries. The sudden increase in the price of oil had the effect of a quick transfer of global incomes, however—from the industrial and oil-importing developing countries to the oil-exporting nations.

The poor countries were as severely affected as the middle-income countries. In the poor countries, current-account deficits as a proportion of GDP increased from 2.5 percent in 1970 to 5.3 percent in 1975; a corresponding increase was incurred by Pakistan, which saw its deficit surge from 2.9 percent of its GDP in 1970 to 5.0 percent in 1975. But there was an important difference between Pakistan and other low-income countries. Starting in 1974, hundreds of thousands of workers began to migrate from Pakistan to the oil-exporting countries of the Middle East. The number of Pakistanis going to the Middle East in search of job opportunities continued to increase until, by the middle of the 1980s, a pool of some 3 million workers had been formed. This pool was constantly replenished. The first wave of migrants was mostly composed of construction workers who were engaged by large Western construction companies building infrastructure projects. These workers were followed by semiskilled laborers who went over to maintain the physical infrastructure that was created in the 1970s. As the Middle Eastern economies became more sophisticated, they required people with modern skills, and once again Pakistan was one of the countries that provided them in large numbers. Economic recession in the Middle East in the middle and late 1980s reduced the demand for foreign workers; by 1987, Pakistan was no longer a net exporter of workers to these countries. However, Pakistan continued to receive large amounts of remittances from the workers in the gulf states. These remittances peaked in 1983–1984 when Pakistan received $2.9 billion through official channels alone. About the same amount came in through means such as the *hound* system, in which capital is transferred informally between private individuals.

In 1970–1971, a couple of years before the increase in oil prices, Pakistan had a trade balance of nearly $350 million as compared to remittances of only $60 million. In other words, remittances helped to pay for only a small proportion of the

TABLE 3.6   Trade Balance and Remittances (in $ millions)

	1970–1971	1977–1978	1980–1981	1982–1983
Exports	422	1287	2798	2430
Imports	−757	−2751	−4857	−5782
Trade balance	−337	−1464	−2765	−3352
Workers' remittances	60	1156	2097	2850
Remittances as % of trade balance	18	79	76	85

Source: Author's calculations, using World Bank data files.

differences between imports and exports. Following the increase in oil prices, the value of imports soared dramatically, in part because of the sharp increase in the price of oil. In 1977–1978, just before the second increase in the price of oil, the value of imports amounted to $2.8 billion, only half of which was paid from export earnings. A large trade balance therefore had to be financed. But it could not be financed entirely by aid because the flows of concessional assistance had declined precipitously since the late 1960s. The bulk of the trade imbalance was covered instead by workers' remittances. In 1977–1978, these remittances equaled 79 percent of the deficit-on-trade account—a proportion that had increased to 85 percent by 1982–1983. (See Table 3.6.)

Hence Pakistan never suffered the full consequences of the nearly sevenfold increase in the price of oil that occurred between 1973 and 1979. A large number of developing countries borrowed extensively in the international financial markets to pay for their imports; many others curtailed all but the most essential imports to keep the trade deficit within manageable proportions. Pakistan did neither; it did not have to restrict its imports and did not have to borrow heavily to finance its trade deficit. The remittances sent by its workers continued to increase rapidly and were used by the government to finance an increasing volume of imports. Consequently, unlike most other developing countries, Pakistan did not face a serious balance-of-payments problem during the global recession of 1980–1983. As had happened twice before—in the early 1950s because of the Korean War and a decade later because of the growing U.S. interest in South Asia—an external event came to Pakistan's rescue. The Middle East connection saved the country from having to restrict domestic consumption and investment.

The sixth event of economic consequence for Pakistan occurred in 1979, when Soviet troops entered Afghanistan, and for the United States Pakistan became a "front-line state," the new frontier between what seemed at that time as the expanding Soviet sphere of influence and the "free world." This new geopolitical situation once again revived U.S. interest in Pakistan. In the winter of 1980, President Jimmy Carter offered a few million dollars of American assistance to win Pakistan's support of Washington's efforts to win back Afghanistan from the Soviet Union. President Zia ul-Haq turned down the offer, calling it "peanuts." It

TABLE 3.7   Current Account Balance of Payments (before official transfers)

Year Ending June 30	US $ (billion)	As a Percent of GDP
1988	1.7	4.3
1989	1.9	4.7
1990	1.9	4.6
1991	2.0	4.3
1992	1.5	3.1
1993	3.7	7.1
1994	1.9	3.7
1995	2.5	3.6
1996	4.4	7.0

Source: Various issues of *Pakistan Economic Survey* (Islamabad: Government of Pakistan, Ministry of Finance).

was only with the victory of Ronald Reagan in 1980 that Washington began to treat Pakistan with renewed seriousness. The U.S. Agency for International Development, working with the Department of Defense, formulated a large program of aid that would cost the United States $3.2 billion over a six-year period (1981–1987). In 1982, but not without some resistance from a number of political lobbies hostile to Pakistan, this program won the approval of the U.S. Congress, and Pakistan became the third largest recipient of U.S. aid (after Israel and Egypt). The program even survived efforts led by Senator Larry Pressler, who proposed an amendment aimed specifically at punishing Pakistan for attempting to develop the capability to produce nuclear weapons. The amendment required the U.S. president to issue a waiver based on an understanding that Pakistan was not seriously engaged in developing nuclear capabilities. This certification was granted a number of times. In fact, in 1987, the U.S. Congress renewed the Pakistan assistance program for another six years. The new program was to cost the United States $4.02 billion and was to last from 1987 to 1993. That, as we shall explain later, did not happen.

The war in Afghanistan had other economic consequences as well. It brought 3.5 million Afghan refugees to Pakistan over a period of five years, from 1979 to 1984. It also brought traffic in guns and drugs to an inherently volatile society. Most of the refugees were accommodated in dozens of makeshift camps set up in Pakistan's border districts, but thousands of them took advantage of the tight labor market produced by the large-scale migration of workers to the Middle East. Large colonies of Afghan refugees, established on the fringes of such large cities as Karachi, Lahore, and Rawalpindi, contributed labor to the service sector starved by the migration of indigenous labor to the Middle East. Within a few years of their arrival in Pakistan, the Afghans also began to dominate the road transportation sector. A number of Afghan-owned firms began to operate efficient long-haul truck transport between Karachi, Pakistan's only port, and the rapidly industrializing areas in central and north Punjab and in the Northwest Frontier Province. The establishment of semipermanent Afghan colonies also increased the flow of remittances to Pakistan from the Middle East and the United States. Like Pakistan, Afghanistan had also provided workers to the Middle East, and the war with the Soviets had produced a steady stream of Afghan refugees in the United States. These Afghans began to remit large amounts of their savings to their families in Pakistan thus adding significantly to the flow of external funds to Pakistan. Finally, commerce in guns and drugs expanded Pakistan's already vibrant underground economy. This part of the economy had played an important part in providing capital for the resource-hungry small-scale industrial and commercial sectors; the enormous growth of the underground economy helped Pakistan nearly initiate its second industrial revolution in the second half of the 1980s. Had political instability not returned with Zia's death in August 1988, Pakistan may have experienced another period of rapid economic growth led by the industrial sector.

As Zia ul-Haq's rule was ending, Pakistan's economic future seemed particularly bright. This optimism was reflected in the Sixth Five-Year Plan (1983–1988) launched by the military government. The plan envisioned a rate of GDP growth of 6.5 percent a year. Even after an increase of 14.5 percent in the population during the five-year plan period, this rate of growth would have meant increasing per capita income to $460 in 1982 prices. At that level of income, Pakistan would have finally graduated from the category of low-income to that of middle-income countries.

That growth rate was not achieved. By the time of Zia's death in August 1988, Pakistan's external situation had begun to change and the country's failure to address its long-term structural problems had started to take its toll. While presenting the budget for 1988–1989, Mahbub Haq, finance minister in the caretaker government appointed by President Zia, called the economy "bankrupt." The caretaker government went on to negotiate an adjustment program with the International Monetary Fund that severely constrained Benazir Bhutto's administration when it took office in December 1988.

The seventh external influence on Pakistan's economy was the consequence of Iraq's invasion of Kuwait on August 2, 1990. The impact of this development on Pakistan's economy was almost immediate. It was hurt by the increase in the price of oil from 1989's OPEC average of $16.40 per barrel to around $30 in September 1990. Pakistan also suffered from the loss of remittances from the Middle East, in particular from Kuwait and Iraq, from the need to accommodate its citizens who lost jobs in the Middle East, and from the sharp decline in its exports to the gulf states. The World Bank identified a new group of countries adversely affected by the troubles in the Middle East and labeled them the "most immediately impacted countries," or the MIICs.[11]

Pakistan was one of the dozen or so countries placed in this category. For the first time, Pakistan had to share with other developing countries the consequences of an adverse turn in their external economic environment. A massive migration of its citizens to the Middle East saved it from the oil shocks of 1974 and 1979 when the price of a barrel of oil increased first from $4 to $12 and then to $30. No such comfort was available in 1990. Some modest amount of support was provided by Saudi Arabia in return for Pakistan's decision to send troops to the Arabian peninsula. Pakistan deployed 6,000 soldiers as part of Operation Desert Shield sponsored by the United States. The World Bank also provided $150 million worth of additional resources, but these were paltry sums compared to the amounts the country needed. Sartaj Aziz, finance minister in the government of Prime Minister Nawaz Sharif, estimated Pakistan's immediate need at $1 billion of external capital to deal with the problems created by the crisis in the Middle East.[12]

The eighth external development—in fact, a series of events—that produced important economic consequences for Pakistan was triggered by the withdrawal of Soviet troops from Afghanistan in 1989. A weakened Soviet Union watched helplessly as communism collapsed around its European border. In 1991, the Soviet Union itself crumbled and Russia and six independent states in Central Asia emerged out of the ruins of the once powerful Soviet empire, which had stretched across the European and Asian landmass. These rapid-fire developments changed the way the United States viewed Pakistan. Washington no longer needed Pakistan as an ally to stop the spread of communism. Pakistan was abandoned with almost indecent haste. In the fall of 1990, President George Bush refused to certify that Pakistan was not in violation of the Pressler amendment. This refusal meant the cessation of all U.S. assistance to Pakistan, economic as well as military. Washington stopped implementing the six-year program of assistance that had been agreed upon in 1987.

The ninth external event with grim economic consequences occurred in May 1998, when Pakistan decided to follow India and carried out a series of nuclear tests. The response of the industrial world to this development was instantaneous. Washington and Tokyo announced economic sanctions against both India and Pakistan. Two weeks after the Pakistani tests, the G-8 countries meeting in Birmingham (United Kingdom) announced that they would not support lending by the International Monetary Fund, the World Bank Group, or the Asian Development Bank to either India or Pakistan. These sanctions hurt Pakistan much more than India. The government in Pakistan, faced with the prospect of not being able to meet its external obligations, announced a series of steps that did little to stop the country's slide into economic chaos but did seriously weaken its creditworthiness. Measures adopted by the government included devaluation of the currency, imposition of controls on the movement of capital, and freezing foreign currency accounts maintained in the banks operating in the country. It was this last step that did the most damage, since it seriously hurt the expatriate community on which the country had relied for economic support ever since the mass out-migration of Pakistanis in the mid-1970s.

The tenth external development that needs to be noted is the rise of militant Islam and a number of spectacular acts of international terrorism associated with it. These include the bombing of the World Trade Center in New York in 1995 and the bombing of U.S. embassies in Kenya and Tanzania in the summer of 1998. These two acts were perpetrated by individuals with strong links to several Islamic movements in Pakistan. At the center of these activities was a Saudi national who had found his way into Afghanistan and had settled in Khost, a small town a few miles from the Pakistani border. Although the state of Pakistan was not involved in these acts, the fact that they were carried out by a number of individuals operating out of Pakistan or from the areas close to Pakistan was enough to discourage foreign private interest from investing in the country.

Although external influences affected Pakistan's economic development in many different ways—some positive and some negative—the real economy was shaped by a dynamic that was necessarily internal. Over a period of fifty years, Pakistan ceased being an agricultural economy and almost became an industrial state. Much of Pakistan's economic history can be written in terms of the developments that took place in three sectors—agriculture, industry, and services.

The Agricultural Sector

Despite some very significant changes in Pakistan's economy, agriculture remains the largest sector. It was proportionately much larger in 1947, when it accounted for 53 percent of the GDP, than it is today. Since 1947, other sectors of the economy—manufacturing in particular—have grown much more rapidly, with the result that agriculture today contributes only 25 percent to the domestic product. But even with this diminished position, the agricultural sector will set the pace of growth in the years ahead. The important question is the direction in which the sector must go, and in this connection there are differences among the experts.

Until now, food grain production was the most important activity in the agricultural sector, and its importance tended to increase over time. In 1947–1948, for instance, food grain crops were grown on 6.5 million out of the 9.3 million hectares of land under crop cultivation, a proportion of nearly 70 percent. Since that time, the area under crop cultivation has increased to nearly 23 million hectares while that devoted to food grains has increased to 12.6 million hectares. The implication is that, by the close of the 1990s, nearly 55 percent of the total cultivated land is planted with food crops.

Since the late 1960s, Pakistan has followed a simple strategy for increasing agricultural output. For reliable agriculture, the major sources of water are the rivers of the Indus system: the mighty Indus, with its right-bank tributary, the River Kabul; and the four rivers on the left—Jhelum, Chenab, Ravi, and Sutlej. The flows in these rivers are subject to great fluctuations. In the Jhelum, for instance, variation from its mean runoff is between 65 and 135 percent of the normal. To become reliable sources of irrigation water, these rivers had to be tamed—a process that began more than a hundred years ago but gained momentum as a result of the dispute with India over the division of the flow in the eastern rivers.[13] Accordingly, Pakistan's agricultural strategy included investment in such large-scale irrigation projects as the construction of the Tarbela and Mangla dams; construction of an intricate system of canals that, by linking the main rivers, transfer water from the western to the eastern rivers; and the sinking of large tube-wells to drain water from land that was rapidly becoming waterlogged and, therefore, saline. The strategy also acquainted all classes of farmers with the new high-yielding technology associated with the green revolution; provided generous subsidies on such inputs as irrigation water, fertilizer, and pesticides; and gave assurance of high government prices for wheat, rice, and sugarcane.

One important indicator of the modernization of agriculture in Pakistan is the rapid increase in the use of chemical fertilizer. The first recorded use of farm chemicals occurred in 1952. For the 1952–1953 crop year the farmers in Punjab used 1000 tons of chemical fertilizer, mostly for wheat and cotton. It was only with the advent of the green revolution in the late 1960s and the introduction of high-yielding, fertilizer-responsive wheat and rice varieties that the use of chemical fertilizer became common. In the 1979–1980 crop year, chemical fertilizer consumption reached 1 million tons; by 1989–1990, farmers were putting 1.9 million tons on the soil. By 1996–1997, 2.4 million tons of fertilizer were being used. The use of chemicals is no longer confined to food grains, however; the sharp increase in the output of cotton recorded in 1991–92, for instance, was largely the result of extensive use of pesticides. With an output of over 1.8 million tons of cotton, Pakistan is among the largest cotton producers in the world.

Pakistan's agricultural strategy produced remarkable results: The production of food grains increased nearly threefold in the fifteen-year period after the advent of the green revolution. In 1966–1967, the year before the introduction of high-yielding food technology, the total output of food grain was estimated at 7 million tons. By 1991–1992, grain output had increased threefold to 21 million tons, a growth rate of 4.5 percent per annum over a period of twenty-five years. The rate of increase for wheat, the main food crop, was even higher, at 5.3 percent per year. During this period the production of wheat increased from 4.3 million tons to 15.7 million tons. This was an impressive performance for an agricultural sector—perhaps the highest rate of growth anywhere in the world of a system as large as Pakistan's and over such a long period of time. The result was that Pakistan, by the early 1990s, had become a sizable exporter of rice—1.5 million tons a year in the late 1980s and early 1990s. It also exported wheat in 1983–1984, for the first time since the early 1950s. The question was asked whether this strategy should be continued into the future or whether Pakistan should seek to diversify its agriculture. There was a suggestion that if Pakistan did not abandon its food grain centered agricultural strategy, it could produce sizable surpluses of food grains that would be hard to market. A simple calculation done for the second edition of this book indicated that by 1995 Pakistan could be left "with a sur-

plus of 6 to 7 million tons of wheat and rice" . . . there is enough potential demand in the countries of the Middle East with which Pakistan has growing economic ties for it to be able to sell its entire projected surplus of 6–7 million tons.
At present prices, this would mean additional export earnings of some $1.5 bil-
lion by the year 1995.[14]

Arithmetic such as that tempted many people, including experts, to urge that
Pakistan should turn its agriculture into a granary for the Middle East. Extremely
impressed by the potential of Pakistan's agricultural sector, a Ford Foundation expert predicted in a paper appropriately entitled "Indus: The Great Grain
Machine" that it was not entirely inconceivable for Pakistan to export anywhere
between 20 and 30 million tons of food grain per annum before the end of the
1980s.[15] The paper was written in the early 1970s, when the price of grain had
soared to more than $400 per ton. If that price level could have been maintained
in real terms into the late 1980s, and if the Indus grain machine could have produced such surpluses, Pakistan could be earning $20–$25 billion from the sale of
food grains alone.

But before such calculations could seduce planners into abandoning the grain-
oriented strategy that had guided them for more than four decades, things turned
exceptionally sour. Before the country could become a granary for the Middle
East—even better, as was recommended by some, an orchard for the Middle
East—Pakistan's agriculture suffered a serious setback. From 1991–1992 to
1996–1997, the production of wheat increased from 15.68 million tons to 16.65
million tons, a rate of growth of only 1.3 percent a year. With the population
growing at a rate more than two times greater, Pakistan was back in the international market as a sizable importer of food grains. In the six-year period between
1991–1992 and 1996–1997, Pakistan imported, on average, 2.3 million tons of
wheat. The turn in the country's fortune could not have been more complete. In
less than half a decade, the planner's dream of making Pakistan a granary for the
Middle East had turned into a nightmare. By the winter of 1998, Pakistan was
desperately looking for foreign exchange to pay for more that 2 million tons of
wheat.

The failure of agriculture in the 1990s went beyond the food grain sector; in
fact, cash crops fared even worse than wheat and rice. Cotton, the backbone of the
economy, saw a sharp reduction in output. The story of cotton is in many ways
the story of Pakistan's agriculture. In the early 1960s, before the advent of the
green revolution, cotton production averaged around 300,000 tons a year. About
1.5 million hectares of land were devoted to the cultivation of this crop, mostly in
the southern districts of Punjab and in the province of Sindh. The green revolution had a less dramatic impact on cotton production than on wheat and rice; for
the food grains the availability of high yielding seeds produced sharp increases in
productivity. In the case of wheat, output per hectare of land increased from
about 800 kilograms in the early 1960s to over one ton in the late 1960s and the
early 1970s. The productivity increase in rice was even more spectacular. As

against an increase of 20 percent in the productivity of land devoted to wheat, rice growers were able to obtain yields that were nearly 60 percent greater, from 950 kilograms a hectare to 1.5 tons.

The increase in cotton yields came two decades later, in the late 1980s when average output increased to 500 kilograms per hectare compared to only 300 kilograms in the late 1960s. This increase of 67 percent did not result from the availability of improved varieties but from the application of large amounts of chemicals by cotton growers. They were able to do this because of the progressive commercialization of agriculture in Pakistan that began in the late 1960s. Farmers now had the income to spend on sophisticated inputs. For three reasons, all of them the consequence of government neglect, farmers were not able to sustain the increased productivity achieved in the two decades between the late 1960s and the late 1980s.

By far the most important reason for the loss of momentum in agriculture was the government's failure to maintain the rich irrigation network that supported the sector. The system was allowed to deteriorate to the extent that the availability of water to the farmers actually declined as a result of losses in the system. Second, the government failed to protect the farmers against the adulteration of the chemicals provided to them by both the public and the private sector. To the horror and despair of the farming community, the chemicals that they bought were highly adulterated and contaminated. Finally, the government did little to improve the agricultural research facilities on which the farmers depended for the supply of quality seeds, pesticides, and improved technology.

Cotton suffered the most because of these developments. The farmers who grew cotton depended on surface irrigation more than those who produced wheat and rice. They needed more sophisticated chemicals than other farmers, particularly to protect themselves against pest attacks. It was largely on account of pests that the output of cotton, following the record production of 2.2. million tons in 1991–1992, declined to the extent that lint had to be imported to keep the spinning mills open. The failure of the research establishment to keep the farmers supplied with disease resistant seeds added to the woes of the cotton growers. Corruption and poor governance—the subject of a later chapter—took a heavy toll on agriculture in Pakistan and reduced the sector's remarkable potential to the point that the country's dependence on foreign imports increased enormously.

The Industrial Sector

Against heavy odds and contrary to the expectation of many people who did not think that an independent Muslim state in British India would be a viable political and economic entity, Pakistan not only survived but also fared well economically at least during the first four decades after independence. Rapid industrialization soon after it achieved independence was one of the prime reasons for Pakistan's initial economic success. What are the reasons that led to Pakistan's rapid industrialization? What are the basic characteristics of the country's industrial sector? In what ways can industry contribute to Pakistan's future economic growth?

The First Industrial Revolution

Two industrial revolutions, one in the 1950s and the other in the 1980s—the second one launched but still not completed—helped Pakistan to industrialize. The impetus for the first came soon after Pakistan achieved independence. As discussed above, India's decision in 1949 to sever trade with Pakistan left the latter exceptionally vulnerable. The new country's leaders were already faced with a disgruntled population: One-quarter had migrated from India, leaving behind all their assets and most of their belongings, and the remaining three-fourths had run out of goodwill for the 8 million *muhajirs*, refugees who had arrived from India. The refugees had to be accommodated, sometimes in houses owned by the locals, and when they found jobs it was oftentimes at the expense of the host population. The collapse of the customs union with India and the consequent shortage of consumer goods added to the feeling of deprivation, which was already very high among all sectors of the population. It was in this environment that the leaders of Pakistan began their efforts to industrialize the country. They decided to concentrate their attention initially on the establishment of industries producing basic consumer goods. And because the state had neither the experience nor the resources to undertake industrialization itself and because Mohammad Ali Jinnah had wisely persuaded a number of rich Muslim business families to migrate from India to Pakistan, Pakistan turned to the private sector for laying its initial industrial base. The private entrepreneurs responded with enthusiasm to the government's invitation. The windfall profit from the increase in export earnings that followed the outbreak of hostilities in the Korean peninsula were reinvested in industry. The stage was thus set for Pakistan's first industrial revolution. It occurred in the private sector, its original focus was on the production of consumer goods, it looked only at internal markets, it was concentrated mostly in and around Karachi, and it reached maturity in about a decade. From 1950 to 1960, the output of the manufacturing sector increased at the rate of 18 percent a year, and by the time General Ayub Khan had consolidated his political hold over the country, Karachi, then the capital of Pakistan, had become a vibrant hub of industrial activity.

General Ayub Khan arrived on Pakistan's political scene promising to totally overhaul the economic system. He was troubled with the way his civilian predecessors had managed the economy. From a military perspective, the situation that Ayub Khan inherited at the time of his coup d'état seemed exceptionally chaotic. His administration's first objective was to clean up the mess it saw in the economic system. The military government started with some rather simpleminded notions about the role of the state in economic management. Its first impulse was to adopt a number of draconian measures aimed at curbing the private sector's free spirit. These included a series of martial law regulations designed to regulate consumer prices and curb excessive industrial profits. However, Ayub Khan and his military colleagues were quick learners; within a few months they had recognized that the economy could not be run by decrees, that the private sector should not be harassed into accepting policies that would seriously jeopardize its ability to make a profit, and that the government had an economic role to play but more in the area of providing direction to the private sector than in direct participation in economic management. In other words, once the military government had settled down it reverted to the industrial policy it had inherited: It continued to emphasize the development of the consumer goods industry, it continued to focus on import substitution rather than on the promotion of exports, and it continued to rely on the entrepreneurship of the private sector to lend dynamism to the industrial sector. The industrial revolution launched in the early 1950s developed and matured during this period of economic consolidation. However, this is not to say that Ayub Khan did not influence the direction of industrialization while he was in power. His policies changed the structure of the industrial sector in at least three ways.

First, Ayub Khan was not comfortable with the concentration of industrial capital in one city, Karachi. It did not suit his political purpose; Ayub knew that he would have to go to areas deeper in Pakistan if he were to cultivate a political constituency for himself, and he could not expect to get much help from the *muhajir*-dominated industry of Karachi. Also, Ayub Khan the soldier recognized that concentrating the bulk of the country's industrial wealth in Karachi, a port that could be easily reached by the Indian navy was not a good strategy. Accordingly, his government used a number of devices to diversify the geographical base of industry. By the time he relinquished political control, at least two other industrial bases had begun to take shape: one in and around Lahore, the other north of Rawalpindi. During the Ayub period, Lahore emerged as a major industrial base of Pakistan, second only to Karachi, while Taxila and Wah, two small towns north of Rawalpindi, developed into centers of heavy industry.

Second, Ayub Khan diversified the ownership of industry by inviting new entrepreneurs into the field. A number of the newcomers—including Gohar Ayub, the president's second son, who was an officer in the army when Ayub Khan assumed political power—were from the military and civil bureaucracies. The landed aristocracy was also encouraged to move their savings into industry. Those who did included the Noons, a landed family of Sargodah, the Hotis, landlords from Mardan, and the Qureshis who had large landholdings in Multan.

Third, by encouraging the rapid development of the financial sector, Ayub Khan made it possible for the newcomers to take part in industrialization. Pakistan's industrialization began with a number of private trading houses putting their savings into industry. There was little financial intermediation. During the Ayub period a number of private banks, including the Habib Bank,

the United Bank, and the Muslim Commercial Bank, expanded their business ag-
gressively, mobilized savings from the public, and made this money available to
private entrepreneurs for investment. The government also developed the capital
market; the number of companies listed on the Karachi stock exchange increased
as did the number of shares traded. Steps were also taken to organize a stock market in Lahore. Finally, the government encouraged public sector investment banks
to provide foreign capital to the entrepreneurs. During this period the Pakistan
Industrial and Credit Investment Corporation (PICIC) and the Industrial
Development Bank of Pakistan (IDBP) became major players in industrial development, providing large amounts of external resources for the establishment of
new industrial enterprises in the private sector. Both obtained large amounts of
capital from the World Bank, the former for investment in large industries, the
latter in relatively smaller enterprises.

The Second Industrial Revolution

Without the government's awareness, the seeds of Pakistan's second industrial
revolution were planted. The immediate reason for this development was the
green revolution. The introduction of high-yielding varieties of wheat and rice
sharply increased the agricultural sector's demand for water pumps, tractor im-
plements, cotton ginning machines, and oil expellers. The advent of the green revolution also increased the number of tractors in the countryside, thereby increasing the need for a service industry for their maintenance. All this led to significant
amounts of investment in simple manufacturing, most of which went into a
dozen or so small towns in Punjab and south Sindh. In addition, the government's tax policies that granted tax exemption to small cotton weaving enterprises resulted in expanding textile centers, such as those in Faisalabad, near
Lahore. But these were only the seeds of another revolution; the real beginning of
the second revolution was to occur later, during Zia ul-Haq's administration. But
before the second industrial revolution could take hold, the economy was delivered a severe shock by the policies adopted by Zulfikar Ali Bhutto, the immensely
popular populist leader with a very limited understanding of economics.[16]

Zulfikar Ali Bhutto became president in December 1971, a few days after the
Pakistan army surrendered to the Indian forces. In the three years since Bhutto had
resigned from his position as Ayub Khan's foreign minister in 1966, he had decided
that the course of industrialization pursued during the 1960s had not advanced
Pakistan economically. Instead, by concentrating on the private initiative, the government's program had generated enormous inequities, and by emphasizing the
development of consumer goods industries, Pakistan remained technologically
backward. Bhutto based these conclusions on three particular influences. One,
Fabian socialism was still popular when Bhutto was at Berkeley and Oxford. Two,
he found very persuasive the conclusions reached by Mahbubul Haq, chief economist of the Planning Commission during most of Ayub Khan's development

decade, about the distributional consequences of the economic model pursued by Ayub Khan. And finally, he was impressed by the socialist leanings of some of the cofounders of the Pakistan People's Party, in particular those of J. A. Rahim and Dr. Mubashir Hasan. The PPP's manifesto for the 1970 elections promised quick actions to correct the distributional problems resulting from Ayub Khan's economic policies. Although the party promised land reforms, it was clear that the emphasis was to be on assigning a more prominent economic role to the state. The promise to put the public sector in control of the economy was a throwback to the approach adopted by India, beginning with its first five-year plan (1950–1955). Bhutto and his colleagues were obviously unaware of the difficulties the Indians had encountered in adopting that strategy. Accordingly, once in power Bhutto and his administration moved quickly and impetuously. On January 2, 1972, only thirteen days after Bhutto assumed the presidency, the government nationalized thirty-one large industrial enterprises and commercial banks. Two weeks later, on January 16, the managing agency system was abolished and the management of the newly nationalized enterprises was put in the hands of the bureaucracy. On February 10, the government introduced labor reforms affecting not only the large manufacturing sector but also small industries that had begun to develop rapidly during the Ayub period. On March 19, the government nationalized life insurance companies. These decisions fundamentally restructured the industrial sector.

The decision to take over the management of large enterprises without providing compensation to their owners was a heavy financial blow aimed at the prominent industrial families who were instrumental in launching the first industrial revolution. The nationalization of commercial banks, which had supported Pakistan's initial industrialization, put all future entrepreneurs at the mercy of the state-controlled financial institutions. By nationalizing the banks, Bhutto wanted to break the "unholy alliance between big business and big money." Instead, he placed present and future industrialists in the tight grip of the state bureaucracy.

Zulfikar Ali Bhutto wanted to profoundly change the structure of Pakistan's industry. He succeeded in achieving this goal but did not realize all of the objectives he had in mind—or at least those he had proclaimed in the PPP's Foundation Papers and its election manifesto. Bhutto's industrial and labor policies did not improve income distribution in the urban areas; instead, by slowing down the rate of increase in industrial output, these policies increased urban unemployment and contributed to greater inequality between urban incomes. Further, his nationalization measures eroded the foundation from beneath Pakistan's private industry, the most dynamic part of the country's economy. And by following the nationalization of large-scale industry with that of small-scale agro-industries in August 1973, he put a stop to the fledging second industrial revolution. The overall ill effects of these measures are reflected in the poor performance of the industrial sector during the Bhutto period: Manufacturing output increased at the rate of only 5.2 percent a year compared to 8.1 percent during the Ayub and Yahya periods. (See Table 3.4.)

During the eleven years of Zia ul-Haq, Pakistan attempted to go back to the model of development adopted by Ayub Khan. It was only half successful. Zulfikar Ali Bhutto had changed the structure of the industrial sector so profoundly that the old model could not be fully adopted once again. Bhutto's policies had created strong vested interests that were not prepared to allow the government to loosen its control over the industrial sector. The bureaucracy was now comfortably settled as managers in the nationalized industries, workers in the nationalized banks were happy with the security offered by government employment, and industrial workers were content not to be subjected to the rigors of the marketplace. These were all powerful groups, and the government did not feel that it had the political strength to challenge them. Some attempts were made to denationalize the industries taken over by the Bhutto government, but with one notable exception they did not succeed. The exception was the Ittefaq Foundries near Lahore owned by the Sharif family that had migrated to the Middle East while Bhutto was in power but developed close relations with Zia ul-Haq. Nawaz Sharif, the oldest son of Mohammad Sharif, the doyen of the family, was picked by Zia and appointed finance minister of Punjab. The power of the vested interests was such that even with these connections, Nawaz Sharif had to surmount many difficulties before Ittefaq became a going concern again in the private sector.

In spite of the problems in returning the nationalized industries to the private sector, the Zia administration succeeded in reviving industrial growth. First, private entrepreneurs were invited back into the sector. The government's "major reliance is on liberation of the creative energies of the people," declared the authors of the Sixth Five-Year Plan (1983–1988). "The Plan is conceived within the framework of a significant deregulation of existing economic controls and regulations so as to free the energies of private individuals and organized sectors to participate fully in economic development." But this promise was not carried out fully. The energies of the people still remained tied to those of the government-controlled financial sector, and this control led to enormous corruption and misuse of public funds. Second, the administration adopted a number of measures designed to improve the functioning of state-owned enterprises. A new corporate structure evolved to manage them and an "expert cell" was set up in the Ministry of Production to oversee their performance. These measures paid handsome dividends: Not only did a number of state enterprises begin to make a profit, but their burden on the federal budget was also reduced significantly. Third, the government's promise not to interfere with the private sector once again encouraged small entrepreneurs to begin investment in the small towns of Punjab and the Northwest Frontier Province thus reviving the hope that Pakistan's second industrial revolution, initiated in the late 1960s, would finally begin to mature.

One other development helped the revival of industry in general and that of small-scale enterprises in particular: the rapid growth of the underground economy during the Zia period. This sector of the economy was helped by the exceptionally burdensome tax structure, a common feature in most developing countries. The marginal tax rate for the corporate sector as well as for high-income individuals had reached 85 percent in the 1970s. There was, therefore, a considerable incentive for many transactions to move off the books and into the black market economy. The return from these transactions fueled the underground economy, a fact that was recognized in the budget of 1985–1986 in which, apart from a significant reduction in the marginal income tax rate, the government also introduced "whitener bonds." These bearer bonds could be purchased by individuals without declaring the source of income; the government's aim was to invite capital to move from the underground economy into more legitimate activities. There were two other causes for the growth of the underground economy during the 1980s; in Pakistan, this sector benefited from illegal transactions in drugs and arms, contraband commodities made readily available by the war in Afghanistan.

The Afghan conflict produced almost unhindered traffic in drugs and arms across the border with Pakistan. The former came from poppy-growing farms in the tribal belt that straddles the Pakistan-Afghanistan border, the latter from the vast amount of armament that was put in the hands of the *mujahideen,* the Afghan freedom fighters, by the United States, China, and Saudi Arabia. The very high financial returns from this commerce could not go into formal sectors of the economy. They went, instead, into trade; small, unregulated industry; real estate, particularly in and around the major cities; and in domestic trade, particularly in luxury items. The development of the underground economy, therefore, gave fillip to the development of the small-scale industrial sector.

Industrial development slowed down during the twenty months of Benazir Bhutto's first administration for two reasons. Her government decided to reduce, but only very gradually, the profound presence of the public sector in the economy. Her approach to industrialization reflected in part the thinking of her times, which generally saw the government as being inefficient at best in directly managing economic enterprises. At worst, government ownership of economic assets encouraged corruption and serious misallocation of resources. The countries of Latin America had begun to dismantle the large public sector that had been created by populist leaders who were similar in many ways to Zulfikar Ali Bhutto, Benazir Bhutto's father.[17] The dismantling required extensive privatization, not only of industrial enterprises and public utilities owned and managed by the public sector. For dismantling to be completely successful, the government also had to place financial institutions in the hands of the private sector. Although Benazir Bhutto and her associates understood the new theory, they were reluctant to apply it fully to Pakistan. Doing so would mean the loss of power and patronage, something the prime minister was loath to do. She proceeded slowly with the implementation of the new economic model and thus lost precious time for Pakistan and an opportunity for herself.

Another reason for Bhutto's inability to create an environment that would speed the advent of the second industrial revolution was her desire to use public office for personal gain. She and Asif Ali Zardari, her husband, used the power of the state over financial institutions it owned and the public utilities it managed to create wealth for themselves and their close associates. This would not have been possible had the private sector been freed of government control and left to its own devices.

Bhutto, dismissed by President Ghulam Ishaq Khan on charges of corruption and mismanagement, was succeeded by Nawaz Sharif, a man of the private sector. People expected the new prime minister to quickly dismantle the large public sector built by Zulfikar Ali Bhutto and maintained by Zia ul-Haq and Benazir Bhutto. Nawaz Sharif made some promising moves. The Privatization Commission was placed under the direction of a retired military general well-known for his dynamism. Two public sector commercial banks were privatized, as were a number of large cement plants. Plans were formulated to reorganize and eventually privatize the Water and Power Development Authority, the largest public utility company in the country. Some industrial activity began to pick up, but soon Sharif was also tempted by the power he wielded. The Ittefaq group owned by his family obtained large amounts of capital from a number of cooperative banks in Punjab and then defaulted on these loans. It was also reported by the increasingly vigilant press that some of the industrial units privatized by the Sharif government had in fact been handed over to friends on very favorable terms. Again a Pakistani president had to step in and dismiss a prime minister on the grounds of corruption and mismanagement, this time Nawaz Sharif. Benazir Bhutto returned to power, but her performance the second time around was marked by even more controversies involving her husband. Finally, she was dismissed by the president on charges similar to those leveled against her in 1990 and against Nawaz Sharif three years later, in 1993. Pakistan seemed unable to find a prime minister who was prepared to work for the good of the country.

The Service Sector

Services include value added in branches of economic activity other than those covered by the sectors of agriculture and industry. The service sector includes wholesale and retail trade (including hotels and restaurants) and transportation, as well as government, financial, professional, and personal services such as education, health care, and real estate services. Also included are imputed bank service charges, import duties, and any statistical discrepancies noted by national compilers. This is a broad definition that aggregates a number of diverse activities into one category termed "services." Two points need to be underscored with reference to the development of the service sector in all economies. First, contrary to common belief, the share of services in gross domestic product increases with development. In 1995, value added in the service sector amounted to 35 percent of the gross domestic product in poor countries. The share for middle-income countries—those with per capita income between $750 and $4,000—was 49 percent, whereas for the higher-income countries it was on the order of 66 percent.

The fact that the share of services in Pakistan was 50 percent in 1995 is yet another indication of the relatively more developed structure of Pakistan's economy compared to other poor countries. Second, the service sector is generally more labor intensive than other sectors of the economy. In poor countries, Pakistan included, the service sector accommodates those who cannot find employment elsewhere. Street vendors are a common sight in developing countries. They also appear on the scene in relatively developed countries during periods of economic distress. Third, the structure of the service sector itself changes significantly as development occurs. The service sector in the United States and Western Europe looks very different from that in poor countries. In developed economies the average level of skill among people employed in the service sector is considerably higher than that of people employed in other sectors.

Pakistan's service sector has changed in many significant ways in the last fifty years. The most significant change occurred during the Ayub Khan (1959–1969) period, when the service sector began to modernize in an impressive way. Three activities benefited a great deal from the economic development occurring at this time. The financial sector not only grew rapidly but also modernized. A number of privately owned commercial banks, most notably United Bank and Habib Bank, penetrated deeply into the country with an extensive network of branches. These banks, along with the government-owned National Bank of Pakistan, also established themselves outside the country. The banks established training institutions that turned out a large number of graduates who found employment in the fast developing financial sector. Lahore, Pakistan's second largest city, acquired a stock exchange, adding another capital market to the one already existing in Karachi. Hundreds of new companies were listed on the Karachi and Lahore Stock Exchanges, deepening the reach of the capital markets. Two public sector institutions—the National Investment Trust and the Investment Corporation of Pakistan—made it possible for small savers to enter the capital markets and acquire shares in companies listed on the stock exchanges. The insurance industry began to pick up new business. Air transport developed rapidly. Pakistan International Airlines, the national carrier operating in the public sector, developed an extensive domestic and foreign network and acquired the reputation of being one of the more efficient international airlines. Urban and intercity transport companies operating in the public sector began to offer modern services to travelers. The country also began to invest in high-quality hotels catering to both domestic and foreign tourists.

The modernization of the public sector came to an abrupt halt when the administration of President Zulfikar Ali Bhutto nationalized large-scale industry in January 1972, and privately owned banks and insurance companies a little later. Bhutto did even greater damage when he politicized the management of such service sector firms as commercial and investment banks, public sector commercial concerns, Pakistan International Airlines, and urban and intercity transport companies.

Zulfikar Ali Bhutto fell in July 1977, but the government's attitude toward public firms operating in the service sector did not change. The administrations headed by President Zia ul-Haq and Prime Ministers Benazir Bhutto and Mian Nawaz Sharif continued to use firms operating in the public sector to accommodate friends and political associates as managers and then require these managers to find employment for political followers. This practice played havoc with the companies. By the time Benazir Bhutto's administration was dismissed from office in November 1996, most public firms in the service sector were either bankrupt or close to insolvency. The number of people they employed greatly exceeded their requirements. A significant number were "ghost workers" who collected paychecks but did not add any value to the work of the companies. The total amount of debt owned but not serviced by them amounted to some 12 percent of the GDP. The government had to commit a large amount of money from its already stretched budget to prevent these companies from defaulting on their debt. In the summer of 1998, Karachi Electric Supply Company (KESC), unable to service its debt and unable to pay for the fuel it needed to generate power from the plants it owned, was close to shutting down its operations. Before the administration of Zulfikar Ali Bhutto nationalized it, the KESC was reputed to be one of the finest power companies in Asia.

It was only in the late 1990s that policymakers in Pakistan woke up to the fact that their country had missed a great opportunity in not using its large human resources to develop an export-oriented service sector. The impressive performance of India's software industry drove this message home. But Pakistan lacked the educational resources that had turned Bangalore (India) into an Asian silicon valley. Nevertheless, President Farooq Leghari encouraged the Pakistani expatriate community to help its homeland develop a viable software industry. Slowly Pakistanis began to move into this area, and by the end of the 1990s software exports had begun to bring in some revenues.

Domestic Resource Mobilization

Pakistan faced deep economic trouble as it reached its fiftieth birthday. Its GDP growth rate had slowed dramatically, showing only a marginal increase in income per capita. Mass poverty was making a comeback, and the government was running large fiscal deficits. What revenues the government managed to raise did not even cover current expenditures. The entire development expenditure was being financed by external and internal borrowing. A large balance of payments deficit was also being financed through borrowing. By the end of the 1990s, Pakistan was one of the most indebted countries in the world. The total amount of debt, internal and external, exceeded the gross domestic product. Two-fifths of all export earnings went to service external debt, the stock of which was increasing rapidly because a great deal of government borrowing was short-term and thus obtained at high rates of interest. In the fall of 1998, after some Western countries imposed sanctions following its nuclear tests, Pakistan was on the verge of defaulting on its external obligations. The country clearly needed deep structural changes in order to deal with the crisis at hand. Without these changes Pakistan would have to be content with a very low rate of economic growth.

What brought the country to this situation? Excessive dependence on external capital flows—initially development assistance provided by friendly countries and friendly multilateral development banks and later by the millions of Pakistanis working in the Middle East, Europe, and North America. Policymakers became complacent and did not bother to raise domestic resources to meet government expenditures. For instance, as shown in Table 3.6, remittances sent by Pakistani expatriates in 1982–1983 were equivalent to 85 percent of the trade balance. By the end of the 1990s, the world was much less friendly to Pakistan than it had been in the first four decades after independence. Even the Pakistani diaspora, despite repeated appeals from leaders in the homeland, was reluctant to indulge the country by providing large sums of resources. A much publicized visit paid by Sartaj Aziz, the first finance minister in the second Nawaz Sharif administration, to the annual meeting of the Association of Pakistani Physicians in North America in the summer of 1998 resulted in great embarrassment for Islamabad. Aziz announced that the APPNA doctors had pledged a contribution of $300 million to the prime minister's "debt reduction fund." APPNA quickly issued a strongly worded denial.

In order to address the persistent resource problem, Pakistan needs to move on a number of different fronts simultaneously. First, it must bring the budget into reasonable balance so that government expenditures are not totally out of line with revenues. Authorities negotiating with the International Monetary Fund have repeatedly promised to do this. As part of an IMF program signed in October 1996, the government of Prime Minister Benazir Bhutto promised to reduce the budget deficit to 4 percent of GDP by the end of the 1996–1997 fiscal year. This program was reformulated by the caretaker administration that took office following Bhutto's dismissal in November 1996. In December 1996, Shahid Javed Burki, the caretaker finance minister, committed the government once again to the 4 percent target and revised the program with the IMF for the third time in six months. In March 1997, the IMF agreed to a more relaxed target of 5 percent. The 1996–1997 year ended with a deficit of well over 6 percent, however, in line with historical experience. (See Table 3.8.)

It is now recognized, both inside and outside the country, that Pakistan can no longer afford to run its customary budgetary deficits. The system of tax administration needs changes that will increase the number of taxpayers and reduce leakage from the system. In the late 1990s, only 1.1 million people, out of a total population of 138 million, were on the tax rolls. The constitution of 1973, bowing to the landed aristocracy, exempted agricultural income from being taxed. This anomaly needs to be removed. The government of Prime Minister Nawaz Sharif, by successfully moving two amendments through the parliament soon after tak-

TABLE 3.8   Fiscal Deficits (as percent of the gross domestic product—GDP)

Years	Annual Averages
1973–77	8.1
1978–83	6.6
1983–88	7.8
1988–91	7.5
1992–94	7.5
1995–96	7.1
1996–97	6.4
1997–98	5.5
1998–99	4.8 (projected)

Source: Author's estimate using data supplied by the Government of Pakistan and the International Monetary Fund.

ing office, had the votes to bring about this change. Some estimates suggest that over one-quarter of the revenue due to the government is not collected; most of the leakage occurs because of corruption in tax administration. The low tax base combined with losses stemming from corruption reduced the tax-to-GDP ratio to 13 percent in the late 1990s, well below the government's needs. Thus the government was forced to borrow large amounts from the private sector, adding to the burden of debt. The low tax rate also caused a serious decline in development outlay by the public sector. Some essential services that only the state can provide (e.g., primary education and basic health care) are suffering serious neglect.

Government expenditures must be curtailed. The country can do little to reduce the cost of servicing debt. This is an obligation that it simply has to meet. But expenditures on defense, another large item in the budget, have to be cut back significantly in spite of increasing tension with India since the May 1998 nuclear tests. There is considerable scope for reducing the size of the government, which grew following the nationalization carried out by the government of Zulfikar Ali Bhutto and the expansion of public sector employment that took place during the administrations of President Zia ul-Haq and Prime Ministers Benazir Bhutto and Mian Nawaz Sharif. The government needs to privatize public sector corporations that have begun to drain resources on a massive scale.

There is an urgent need to manage the federation in a responsible way from the perspective of state finances. The constitution obliges the government to issue a national finance award every five years, which apportions government revenues among the provinces and the central government. The fourth award, issued in 1991 by the administration of Prime Minister Nawaz Sharif, allowed the provinces to undertake expenditures expecting the federal authorities to cover whatever deficits they ran up. This compounded the budgetary problem and added to the fiscal deficit. Shahid Javed Burki led the effort to rationalize the system of distributing government revenues, and the fifth award was signed in

January 1997, a few days before the caretakers left office. In 1997 and 1998, the smaller provinces launched a campaign to reverse the award and go back to the formula adopted in 1991. Had that happened (or if it happens in the future)—it would have created a built-in propensity for the provinces to spend way beyond their means.

Finally, Pakistan must make a serious effort to close the balance of payments gap, the difference between total earnings and expenditure of foreign exchange. To do so, it must reverse its persistent policy bias against exports, for example, by emphasizing the production of high value added products by all sectors of the economy—fruits and vegetables by the agriculture sector, fashion garments by the large textile industry, computer software and data processing by the service sector. Some import liabilities could be reduced by an efficient management of the agriculture sector. I have already suggested that investments in maintenance of the irrigation network and in agricultural research should reduce the country's dependence on imports. There is no reason for the country not to gain self-sufficiency in food grains and vegetable oil, two large-ticket items in the import bill. The country also needs to reduce its debt load, which could be done by accelerating the privatization of public sector corporations and applying the receipts to the debt.

Pakistan's Economic Future

In the winter of 1998–1999, Pakistan's economy stands precariously at a crossroads. It can take one of two paths: restructure or maintain the status quo. Pakistani leaders could formulate policies and programs aimed at a deep restructuring of the economy. By doing so they might be able to set the stage for the revival of the economy and for achieving GDP growth rates that were common during the first four decades after independence. Or they could continue to bicker among themselves, putting off the structural change that is so desperately needed. The Pakistani economy produced by the latter scenario would grow at a rate not much higher than the rate of growth of its population.

The choices faced by the country are illustrated in Table 3.9. In the first scenario, the gross national product (GNP) increases by 4 percent a year, the rate achieved in the 1990s. This rate of growth is not much higher than the rate of population increase. A 4 percent growth in GNP would imply an increase of 1.2 percent a year in per capita income. Given the country's income distribution, the poor—the bottom 40 percent of the population—would realize very little. At this rate of growth the average income would increase to $569 by the year 2010, but there would nevertheless be a significant increase in the incidence of poverty. In 2010, some 82 million people, or 42 percent of the population, could be living in absolute poverty. In other words, at this rate of growth, Pakistan would have increased the number of people living in poverty by 35 million, from 47 million in 1997 to 82 million in 2010. Pakistan does not have the institutional strength to absorb a poverty shock of this magnitude without incurring major social and po-

TABLE 3.9   Two Scenarios about Pakistan's Economic Future

	1997	2000	2010(a)	2010(b)
Population (million)	137	149	196	196
GNP (billion)	67.2	75.4	111.6	141.5
GNP per capita	490	506	569	722
Poverty (% of population)	34	36	42	25
Poverty (millions of poor)	47	54	82	49

NOTES: The estimates for 2010(a) are based on the assumption that the population increases at the rate of 2.8 percent a year while the gross national product (GNP) increases at the rate of 4.0 percent a year between 2000 and 2010. For 2010, the rate of population increase is estimated at 2.8 percent while GNP increases at 6.5 percent.

SOURCE: Author's estimate using the population and GNP estimates in The World Bank's *World Development Report 1998–99*.

litical disturbances. Some of the law and order problems of recent years, usually attributed to ethnic, provincial, and sectarian rivalries, are also the consequence of the increase in poverty in recent years.

The second scenario illustrated in Table 3.9 projects the rate of GNP growth at 6.5 percent a year, more than twice the rate of increase in population and equal to the rates achieved in the 1960s and 1980s. As I have already indicated, this growth path can be realized only by a determined effort on the part of policymakers. If they are able to muster enough political will to overcome the opposition of the groups that would be initially hurt because of the needed structural changes, Pakistan could reach 2010 close to the threshold that separates poor from middle-income countries. Its gross domestic product could increase to $141.5 billion and income per capita to $722. At this rate of GNP growth, Pakistan would once again be able to make a dramatic difference in the level of absolute poverty. By 2010, the number of people living in absolute poverty could be 49 million, two million more than in 1997 but considerably lower in terms of the proportion of the total population. The proportion of the population living in poverty could decline from 34 percent, estimated for 1997, to 25 percent in 2010. An added benefit of this acceleration in the rate of growth would be to reduce the rate of fertility to manageable levels.

It should be clear by now that Pakistan's ability to overcome its many social and political problems depends on its ability to restore economic growth to levels achieved during the first four decades following independence. Restoring a high level of growth depends, in turn, on the ability of leadership groups to bring about deep structural changes. These changes were postponed for a long time because the country was able to secure sizable external flows. But that option is no longer available. Pakistan now faces an external environment that is only willing to support its development efforts if the country—its leaders and its people—are prepared to take some difficult decisions to set their house in order.[18]

4

████

SOCIAL DEVELOPMENT: MISSED OPPORTUNITIES

At one point in its history—in the late 1980s—Pakistan's average per capita income was very close to the line that, according to the World Bank's latest reckoning, separated the low-income and middle-income countries. At that time Pakistan should have achieved a relatively high level of social development. Instead, a number of indicators—the rates of infant and child mortality, the proportion of literate and educated people in the total population, enrollment ratios for male and female children, the rate of fertility, and the rate of population growth—suggest that successive governments in the past have paid insufficient attention to social development. As shown in Table 4.1, the situation in Pakistan is, in many respects, worse than that faced by countries with much lower per capita incomes. This situation needs to be rectified not only for humanitarian reasons but also because social development is one of the most important preconditions for sustained economic growth.

Economists now agree among themselves that, without social development, the cycles of poverty and economic backwardness cannot be broken. Indeed, an influential study of the development experience of more than eighty countries in the period between 1960 and 1980 has concluded that improvements in literacy and health contributed considerably to economic growth.[1] It is easy to understand how social development aids economic growth. Improved female literacy, for instance, enables mothers to become aware that hygiene and balanced nutrition are of great importance to their families—more specifically, that cleaner homes with better air circulation reduce the incidence of respiratory diseases, and that clean water and utensils prevent diarrhea and other intestinal diseases. Given that stomach and respiratory ailments now account for the majority of deaths among chil-

TABLE 4.1   Pakistan's Social Development Compared with Other Low-income Countries

	Pakistan		India		Sri Lanka		Other Low-Income Countries	
	1960	1996	1960	1996	1960	1996	1960	1996
Health								
Infant mortality rate (per 1,000)	162	88	165	65	71	15	163	80
Child (under 5) mortality rate (per 1,000)	25	123	26	11	7	2	30	18
Life expectancy at birth (males)	44	62	43	61	62	71	42	58
Life expectancy at birth (females)	42	65	43	63	65	75	43	60
Population per physician	5400	3300	4700	3600	4200	1200	3800	1500
Prevalence of child malnutrition (% of children under 5)		40		66		38		–
Education								
Primary school enrollment rate (%)[a]								
Total	30	62	61	90	95	104	37	78
Female	13	38	40	88	90	102	24	70
Male	46	67	80	97	100	106	50	82
Higher education enrollment rate(%)	1	7	3	10	1	8	1	6
Adult literacy rate (%)	15	38	75	85	28	91	23	50
Males (1995)		50		78		93		65
Females (1995)		24		38		87		41
Population								
Crude birth rate (per 1,000)	51	40	44	29	36	18	48	34
Crude death rate (per 1,000)	24	13	22	11	9	6	24	13
Total fertility rate	7.0	5.1	6.2	3.1	4.9	2.3	6.4	4.1
Contraception use (%)	–	11	–	35	–	62	–	–
Population growth[b]	3.0	2.7	2.3	1.8	1.7	1.2	2.6	2.1

[a]The enrollment rate is the ratio of the number of children in school to the number of children aged five to eleven. In the initial phases of a movement toward universal literacy, parents will often send children aged twelve to fourteen back to primary school. Thus, the percentage of children attending school may exceed those in the five-to-eleven age group.

[b]The data reflect growth in 1973–1980 and the projected growth for 1981–2000.

Sources: World Bank, *World Development Report 1984* (Washington, D.C.: World Bank, 1984), *World Development Report 1985,* and *World Development Report 1998–99* (Washington, D.C.: World Bank, 1998). Data for 1960 are from Tables 20, 23, and 24; education statistics, from Table 25; and population statistics, from Tables 19 and 20 of the annexes to the two reports.

dren (according to UNICEF, of the 15 million deaths of children every year in the developing countries, 5 million result from these diseases),[2] improvements in sanitation and nutrition should bring about a significant decline in infant and child morbidity and deaths. Reductions in the incidence of illness and in child and infant deaths are important for two reasons. Families tend to compensate with additional births for the children they lose in infancy; therefore, high rates of infant and child mortality are very closely linked with high fertility rates. In addition, the childhood diseases that are prevalent in the developing countries have long-term debilitating consequences. Poorly nourished and sick children are slow learners; second-degree malnourishment—not an uncommon occurrence among children who suffer repeatedly from stomach problems—seriously retards physical and mental development. Even if children escape death in early childhood, their ability to do sustained work during adulthood is seriously impaired, and the cost to society is enormous if such early malnourishment becomes widespread.

Education of women has other important consequences. There is an inverse relationship between the level of female education on the one hand and the age and incidence of marriage on the other. Better-educated women tend to delay marriage or not to marry at all. Those who do marry tend to have fewer children and are inclined to space births more widely. Literacy among women, therefore, has a direct impact on total fertility—the average number of children born per woman. Reduced fertility reduces the rate of population growth; reduction in the growth of population results in an increased rate of growth in per capita incomes.

There are other ways in which social development promotes economic growth. Literate farmers are more willing to adopt new technologies and are better able to use the inputs needed for increasing output; better-educated factory workers work more effectively with machines and are also less accident-prone; and better-educated office workers are less likely to follow precedent and, therefore, more apt to innovate. Education encourages the development of thrifty behavior as well as the habit of saving for the future; it also produces a higher sense of community belonging and, hence, generates social consciousness, and so on.

For underdeveloped societies, unplanned ad hoc social development is much more costly than planned and deliberate development. Now generally recognized is the fact that it is much less costly and much more productive to make a systematic effort to provide education, nutrition, health, sanitation, and shelter than to leave improvements in these basic needs to chance and individual taste. It is wasteful to sink drinking-water wells when those who use them do not fully appreciate the importance of handling water with clean hands and clean utensils; there is little need to stock dispensaries with medicines to cure stomach ailments when their incidence can be significantly reduced to begin with through hygiene and better nutrition; hygienic conditions do not improve when only individual households rather than communities as a whole undertake to provide sanitary facilities. In other words, important synergisms result from successful efforts to meet different basic needs, and an understanding of such synergism dramatically reduces the cost to the society.

Education and Development

The full impact of the statistics presented in Table 4.1 can now be fully appreciated. Educational statistics for Pakistan are revealing both in themselves and also when compared to those for other developing countries. For instance, the rate of adult literacy is low: At 38 percent, it does not compare very favorably with the rest of the developing world. The estimate just noted applies to Pakistan in 1995; during the same year, the average for all middle-income countries was 80 percent and that for all low-income countries was 40 percent. For South Asia, the average was more than 74 percent. It was argued in Chapter 3 that at one time in its history Pakistan shared many economic characteristics with middle-income countries. Viewed from that perspective, its adult literacy rate should be higher than that of the poor countries, if not as high as that of the middle-income nations. In terms of educational development, then, Pakistan obviously has not done very well.

The gap is even wider in the case of female literacy. The rate for Pakistan in 1995 was estimated at 24 percent, whereas that for the poor and middle-income countries was 77 percent and 55 percent, respectively. Pakistan's situation is more comparable to that of the countries of the Middle East than that of, say, South Asia. For instance, in the Gulf countries, female literacy is estimated at 12 percent while that of India is on the order of 38 percent.

Adult literacy rates tell only one part of the story. They result from efforts made over a period of time, not necessarily from the policies being pursued at this very moment. The adult literacy rates for Pakistan when compared with those of other countries are indicative of very little educational effort on the part of either the government or the people themselves. There are a number of reasons for these low levels of adult and general literacy, and it would be useful to analyze some of them.

The first reason, of course, is the low value placed on education among the people—particularly the people in the countryside. A wide gap exists between rural and urban literacy rates: 60 percent for towns and cities as against 20 percent for the villages. In the rural areas only 10 percent of the women are literate as compared to 16 percent of the men. The main reason for which the rural people place so little emphasis on education must be that they do not see much of an economic return from it. Indeed, the return from education would not seem great given the very few productive opportunities available for those who *do* receive education—a situation that characterizes predominantly agricultural societies in which agriculture produces little marketable surplus. From the time of independence to the late 1960s, Pakistan's agricultural sector remained economically stagnant. It did not innovate; its productivity did not increase; and its marketable surplus did not grow—all of which reflected a failure to commercialize. In other words, the environment in the countryside did not encourage rural parents to send their children to school because the economic rewards for the time spent in school could not be justified by the addition to income that education might eventually have brought.

If the literate or semiliterate people of Pakistan could not find productive opportunities in the countryside, they could always try their luck in the urban sector. In Pakistan, the urban economy was vibrant even during the economically stagnant 1940s and 1950s. Urban dynamism induced migration from the countryside, a great deal of which has occurred since independence. In the 1950s, urban population grew by 3.7 million, of which an estimated 2 million came from the villages. This rate of growth was maintained in the 1960s, when another 7.1 million were added to the urban population; during this period, 3 million came from the villages.

Such a high level of migration would indicate not only the existence of jobs in the urban areas but also a considerable awareness of these jobs among rural people. Thus the obvious question: Why was it that the availability of opportunities in towns and cities failed to create the need to improve human capital in the rural areas? Or, to put it differently, why didn't the growth of the urban economy persuade the rural people that high returns could be reaped from exporting a relatively literate labor force? Indeed, the rural people of Africa were so persuaded in the 1960s and 1970s. One reason for the high premium placed on education by families in rural Africa is the wide gap in earnings between labor on farms and wage employment in cities. Because of this gap, it made good sense to invest in education, not only in terms of the time spent by children in school but also in terms of the money many African parents were prepared to devote to education. But there was a difference in the nature of job opportunities available to African rural migrants as compared to their counterparts in Pakistan. In Africa, the explosion of the government sector, the Africanization of the government, and the expansion of the private sector combined to produce a tremendous demand for white-collar jobs. To fill these jobs, the migrants had to be educated up to the secondary level. Pakistan's urban development took a different form. The country had inherited a sufficient number of trained government workers from the British *raj,* but it did not have much of an industrial base at the time of independence. When that base was created, it produced a high level of demand not only for industrial workers but also for construction labor. Little or no education was required to fill these kinds of jobs. Accordingly, the dynamics of migration in Pakistan worked in a different direction than that taken in Africa: In the former case, migration failed to generate enough demand for education in the rural areas.

A combination of market forces on the one hand and social and cultural constraints on the other has contributed to a very low level of female literacy. It was only with the emigration of millions of young males from Pakistan to the Middle East and the large amount of earnings they remitted to their families that the social structure of Pakistan's countryside finally began to change. These remittances produced a small class of female entrepreneurs and, hence, some demand for female education. Up until the mid-1970s, when hundreds of thousands of rural Pakistanis began to migrate to the Middle East, economic benefits from educating women were very low—certainly, lower than those for male education. Culture played an important part as well. In all traditional societies, there is a lag between the time in which literacy spreads among men and the education of women. Social and cultural obstacles to female education can be overcome only after husbands and fathers have begun to shed their prejudices. As male literacy in Pakistan is still low, prejudice against female education, particularly in the rural areas, has not disappeared. This is one reason why—even under the Social Action Program (SAP)sponsored by the donor community including the World Bank, in which female education was given a high priority—expenditures in the sector remained far below projections. The SAP began to be implemented in the late 1980s and was renewed in the mid-1990s. Its main objective was to substantially increase government investment in education and to encourage parents to send their daughters to school.

With the market, society, and culture all working against increasing literacy, could government efforts have made a difference? The answer to this question is implicit in the analysis above: Direct intervention by the government would not have made much difference. It is always difficult to swim against the economic tide, but such an effort can be doubly perilous when a strong social and cultural undercurrent is also present. But governments can do more than intervene directly; they can improve the economic environment by altering the direction of the tide. Governments have indeed intervened directly in some cases—as, for instance, in India, where an activist policy was pursued in several states even when the underlying social and cultural forces would have kept the level of literacy low. Moreover, in the Indian Punjab the deliberate decision to commercialize agriculture resulted in increased government investment in rural infrastructure—that is, in the establishment of new market towns, village-to-market roads, reorientation of the railway system, village electrification, and agricultural research. What followed was a profound change in the structure of the agricultural sector. The sector made a quick transition from subsistence to export orientation, the management of which required the farmers to educate themselves and their families. Notwithstanding the greater emphasis placed by the Hindu and Sikh cultures on education, a good part of the large difference in literacy rates between the northern states of India and Pakistan can be attributed to government policy toward agricultural and rural development.

In the twenty-year period between independence in 1947 and the beginning of the green revolution in about 1967, the governments in Pakistan eschewed both courses. They did not intervene directly to improve the level of literacy, and they did very little to improve the economic environment in the countryside—an improvement that otherwise would have created incentives for the rural people to seek education. Instead, the governments put the bulk of the resources they wanted to commit to education into secondary and university education.

As with other sectors of the economy, Pakistan inherited a relatively underdeveloped educational system at the time of independence. The system was made up of three parts: public schools, run by the provincial governments or local bodies; private schools managed by charities; and colleges—both public and private—but all of them affiliated with one public institution, Punjab University. This university, founded in the nineteenth century, possessed a charter that gave it a great deal of autonomy. It set curricula that were followed by the colleges, conducted examinations at three levels (intermediate, bachelor's, and master's), and awarded degrees and diplomas. It was not until several years after independence that Pakistan's two other provinces were allowed to set up their own universities: Peshawar University for the Northwest Frontier Province (the main constituent of which was Islamia College) and the University of Karachi for the province of Sindh. As Balochistan did not acquire provincial status for some time after independence, its graduate teaching institutions remained affiliated with Punjab University. The number of universities operating in the public sector increased rapidly in the 1980s and 1990s. By the time Pakistan celebrated its fiftieth anniversary, some three dozen universities were working in the public sector.

The market produced one important but unexpected change in the structure of the educational system, a change that came in response to the demand of a social group relatively new to Pakistan. Independence brought into being almost overnight a class of urban professionals needed to man the new government and fledgling industrial and commercial enterprises. This class of people had existed before 1947, but its members were scattered all over India, mostly in Delhi and the large cities of the Indian states of Bihar, Maharashtra, and Uttar Pradesh. A small number resided in Lahore, the capital of Punjab, where they worked for the provincial government, managed a few modern commercial enterprises, practiced as lawyers in the High Court, and taught in the city's many colleges. Independence and partition brought to Karachi, Lahore, and Rawalpindi a very large number of Muslim professionals from the Indian cities of Delhi, Bombay, Luchow, and Allahabad. Now concentrated in only three Pakistani cities, they were able to exert a profound influence on the new country's social development.

The social, cultural, and political orientation of this class differed from that of the rest of Indian and Pakistani Muslim society: Its ethos and disposition were much more Western. The need of this class for education could not be met entirely by the existing schools and colleges, in which Urdu was the medium of instruction. Accordingly, within a few years after independence, the cities of Karachi, Lahore, and Rawalpindi witnessed the expansion of existing institutions of Western education as well as the establishment of new ones. The Grammar School and St. Joseph's in Karachi; Aitcheson, St. Anthony's, and Sacred Heart schools in Lahore; and Presentation Convent and St. Mary's schools in Rawalpindi began to meet the rapidly growing demand of this new social class of urban professionals for Western education. With the exception of Lahore's Aitcheson, these schools were managed by various orders of Christian missionaries. Aitcheson had been established by the British to provide the sons of Indian princes and landlords with Western education, in which particular attention was given to sports.

The new social class was also well represented in the armed forces. Consequently, in the mid-1950s, the army and the air force also established their own schools for boys, but in this case the institutions—Hasanabdal, Sargodah, and Pataro—were patterned after British public schools. When a large number of Americans arrived in Pakistan in the late 1950s and early 1960s to administer their economic and military aid programs, they set up their own schools in Karachi, Lahore, and Rawalpindi. The schools continued to operate even after the Americans had left, thus also continuing to meet the needs of the upper middle classes.

There was a similar concentration of private institutions at the secondary level, which, with one exception, were all managed by missionaries. Missionaries managed the Kinnaird and Forman Christian colleges in Lahore, Gordon College in Rawalpindi, and Edwardes College in Peshawar; these institutions catered to upper-middle class demands for higher education. The only nonmissionary institution that matched the quality of instruction provided by the missionaries was Government College in Lahore, which, largely because of its very influential alumni body, was able to maintain a standard much above that of other state-managed institutions.

Nothing existed in the country beyond four years of college education that would have satisfied the urban professional classes, however. They therefore turned first to the British universities—primarily Oxford, Cambridge, and London School of Economics—and later on to those in the United States—mostly the Ivy League colleges—for postgraduate instruction. A missionary school, an English medium college, and a British or American university was usually the path traveled by a very large number of children from Pakistan's growing and increasingly affluent upper middle class. This path was dictated by a combination of personal taste and the market's response. The government played mostly a passive role, its major contribution being to provide foreign exchange to those parents who wished to send their children to Europe and the United States for advanced education. As Pakistan maintained an overvalued rupee until the mid-1970s, provision of foreign exchange for education implied a fairly large state subsidy.

The government also played a passive role in the other and much larger aspect of the educational sector: mass literacy. In this area, owing to an absence of demand, the private sector did not help either. The consequence was that the system of education, as it developed in the period after 1947 to about 1972, basically reinforced social and economic differences in Pakistani society.

The first major state intervention in the education sector occurred in 1972 with the decision taken by the administration of Zulfikar Ali Bhutto to nationalize all colleges, including those run by the missionary community, and to ban the private sector from establishing new institutions.[3] For some unexplained reason, missionary schools were not brought under the control of the government. The declared purpose of this policy was to remove elitism from the system of education and to provide all citizens, irrespective of their economic and social status, equal access to institutions of advanced learning. The stated purpose of this reform may have been its real intention, but its effect was quite opposite from the one intended: The educational system was further fractured, and the private sector was no longer available to serve some segments of the market. The newly nationalized colleges lost a great deal of their prestige and were no longer regarded as institutions worthy of the upper classes. The exodus of students to foreign schools and colleges gathered momentum, and Pakistani boys and girls began to go abroad at an even earlier age. In the late 1980s, some 17,000 Pakistani youngsters were attending colleges and universities in Europe and the United States, spending an estimated $340 million every year. This amount was equivalent to 50 percent of the federal government's expenditure on education.

The government of President Zia ul-Haq reversed the policies adopted by the Bhutto administration. The private sector was permitted to establish educational institutions. In this respect, it went much farther than previous governments. The setting up of the Agha Khan Medical University in Karachi was one manifestation of this approach. This is a private university with its own charter; its main purpose is to train doctors and nurses for service in the country. The university has also set up its own curriculum and awards its own diplomas. This model was followed by other private institutions: The government, for instance, accepted the proposal of a group of private philanthropists to establish a school of business and policy sciences in Lahore—the Lahore University of Management Sciences (LUMS)—with its own charter and, therefore, with full authority to function independent of government-controlled universities.

The benign approach adopted by the Zia government toward the participation of the private sector in developing educational infrastructure had one other significant consequence: It resulted in the establishment of thousands of private schools in all major cities of the type that had been earlier operated by foreign Christian missionaries. These schools, established and managed mostly by women from the upper strata of Pakistani society, provided a Western education, using English as the medium of instruction. Most of these schools, by offering curricula developed in Britain for British schools and by allowing their students to take final examinations administered from Britain were able to insulate themselves from the indigenous educational system. This way they were able to avoid subjecting the upper-class children to the type of education that was decreed by Zia: Islamic in orientation and taught in Urdu, the national language. The new private schools charged tuition fees that only the affluent could afford. Because private funding through charitable and social foundations was virtually unavailable for this type of education and because the government was not prepared to provide scholarships to the poor to attend these schools, this type of education was available to almost none of the middle class and none of the poor.

The private sector also responded with some success to another kind of demand for training and education as Pakistanis increasingly began to look abroad for employment. Pakistan has seen three significant waves of out-migration since independence. The first wave occurred in the 1950s. Hundreds of thousands of people went to Great Britain to work in the factories that were being brought into production following the Second World War. Most of these workers came from the poor districts of north Punjab and Azad Kashmir. This wave of migration did not have any impact on the educational system. The second was different and had a significant impact on the educational system. It began in the mid-1970s following the quadrupling of oil prices that launched a massive program of economic reconstruction in the countries of the Middle East. The Middle Eastern countries needed workers, both skilled and semiskilled, to build physical infrastructure. They were happy to receive fellow Muslim workers from Pakistan, since they were less likely to create tension than workers from non-Muslim countries. At this time too Pakistan was completing its own ambitious program of construction—the Indus Waters Replacement Works. This program provided training to thousands of workers in all kinds of skills needed for such sophisticated construction activities as dams, barrages, weirs, canals, and power generating plants. Most of the training came from foreign construction companies that had come to Pakistan to participate in the Indus works or from privately run training institutions in large cities. The Middle Eastern demand for expatriate workers was met by the mid-1980s, and worker training institutions began to look for other countries in need of export labor. By the early 1990s, western Europe and North America had begun to recover from the deep economic recession induced by increased oil prices. These countries had declining populations and needed both semiskilled workers and highly trained professionals. Thus the third wave of migration included semiskilled workers who chose the path of illegal migration and professionals, who gained admission to Europe and North America legally. No firm estimates are available of the number of people involved in this third wave. According to some counts the Pakistani expatriate community in North America alone numbers more than half a million people. A significant number of these people are employed in the rapidly developing and changing service sector in Canada and the United States. They were trained initially in the medical and business schools and institutions of technology, many of which were established in the private sector precisely for this purpose.

Although the private sector was responding to changing needs of labor markets in the Middle East, Europe, and North America, the Pakistani government got involved in an educational activity that received little notice when it was launched. President Zia ul-Haq encouraged the establishment of *madrasas,* or religious schools, as a part of his program of Islamization. He allowed *zakat* (a tax on wealth introduced by the Zia government) funds to be used for this purpose. The religious community responded to this invitation with great fervor, and hundreds of *madrasas* were set up, most in areas in which the public sector had a weak presence. Accordingly, in the remote areas of Balochistan and the Northwestern Frontier Province, and in several small towns of Punjab and Sindh provinces, the *madrasas* began to fill the gap left by both the public sector and the private educational entrepreneurs who focused their attention on the more lucrative markets in large cities. The curriculum in the *madrasas* was heavily oriented toward religious studies. An unexpected development—the war in Afghanistan between occupying troops from the Soviet Union and *mujahideen* (freedom fighters)—turned the *madrasas* into training and recruitment centers for those who wished to participate in the *jihad* (holy war) in Afghanistan. Saudi Arabia encouraged the *madrasas* in their new role and poured funds into them. Iran, another Islamic power in Pakistan's neighborhood, encouraged the *madrasas* in order to teach its brand of Islam—Shi'ism—to those who followed it in Pakistan. It was the institution of the *madrasas* that spawned the Taleban movement in the late 1990s, which controlled most of Afghanistan by the winter of 1998–1999. The Shia and Sunni *madrasas*, sponsored respectively by Iran and Saudi Arabia, promoted sectarian violence that took thousands of lives in several large cities.

   Impressive private initiatives in the education sector and the Islamization of some parts of this sector notwithstanding, Pakistan continues to face a serious problem: the inability to provide basic education to a rapidly growing population, the majority of which continues to live in the countryside. For instance, the demand for education among the poor segments of the population may increase quickly as Pakistan begins to transform its agriculture from that of a subsistence sector to a sector producing large surpluses for the market. This transformation has begun to happen. The demand for basic education will also increase as the rural sector becomes better integrated with the rest of the economy. This, too, is happening as agriculture generates larger and larger amounts of surpluses to be processed for use in the urban sector of the economy. The rapidly growing urban sector, with some emphasis now being given to more sophisticated forms of industrialization, will also need a more literate labor force than the one available at present.

   Hence Pakistan's present educational problems result from a combination of social, economic, and political factors. Over the years the educational system evolved in a way that produced deep fissures in the society. The private sector produces well-trained, highly Westernized graduates who either find jobs in private businesses or go abroad. The public sector provides low-quality education to those who, upon completing their studies, find few opportunities outside the public sector available to them. They tend to use the political system to help them obtain employment in government departments or public sector corporations. *Madrasas* graduates, if not fighting in Afghanistan and numerous other conflicts inspired by Islamists around the globe, are entering the armed forces. These developments will affect Pakistan's political and social development in significant and mostly unpleasant ways.

   As further social and economic changes occur, the government must respond to them in ways that are productive and not destructive for the society.

Unfortunately, the government either has not responded to the challenges posed by the society or has not allowed the private sector to take the initiative. In the latter case, as happened with the development of *madrasas*, the results were often unproductive if not altogether dangerous.

The gap between supply and demand is likely to be even wider than that indicated by average enrollment rates (Table 4.1), inasmuch as the proportion of children in the upper years of primary school must be even smaller than that expected in a country with Pakistan's level of development. In a country with a poor literacy record, it is only when rates climb over 100 percent—as they have done in China and Sri Lanka—that the backlog begins to be cleared. Pakistan has a long way to go before it reaches that situation. Therefore, as primary-school graduates of today begin to seek employment over the next decade, they will not ensure a very well-educated workforce in the mid-1990s. Such situations have been known to persuade governments to launch mass literacy campaigns. The principal aim of these campaigns is to provide a basic form of education to those who were not able to attend school as children. Unfortunately, mass literacy campaigns have not been successful in the past. The reasons for failure are many and complex, the most serious being the inability of many adults to retain over a period of time a great deal of the knowledge that is typically imparted during intensive adult literacy drives. The planners in Pakistan, therefore, have decided not to take the mass-literacy route but, rather, have chosen to set up new primary schools and to expand the capacity of those that already exist.

In 1998 there were an estimated 22.5 million children between the ages of five and ten—11.5 million boys and 11 million girls. Of these, 15.8 million were attending school—10.6 million boys and 5.2 million girls. These statistics demonstrate a relatively low but increasing level of enrollment. For instance, in the second edition of this book, it was estimated that in 1990 only 51.7 percent of all children of primary-school age were formally enrolled in school; the proportion for boys was twice as high as that for girls: 62 percent for the former and 33.7 percent for the latter. Eight years later, in 1998, 70.2 percent of all school-aged children were enrolled in schools. The proportion of boys in classes had increased to 92 percent, whereas the proportion of girls was still low, only 47.3 percent. A vast number of children, 9.2 million in 1990, were not going to school. In 1998, the number of children out of school had declined to 6.7 million. In other words, Pakistan had managed to add 7.2 million new school spaces in eight years, an increase of 7.9 percent a year. The country was close to reaching universal enrollment rates for boys, but a major effort was still needed to reach the same stage for girls. The impressive performance of the past few years notwithstanding, reaching universal literacy any time in the future will still require a Herculean effort; even to get all children into school will be a task of monumental proportions. A few numbers may help in illustrating the enormity of the task faced by the planners in Pakistan. The current projection for Pakistan's population in 2000 is 138 million, which is 18 million fewer than the projection included in the second edition of this book. A population of that size in the year 2000 would imply 23.5 million children of school age: 12 million boys and 11.5 million girls. In order to get all children into classrooms by the end of this century would mean adding another 8 million more than tripling the number of school spaces over a period of two years. The increase for classrooms for girls would have to be even greater if all girls are to be put in schools by then. For a society still reluctant to place girls in coeducational institutions, increasing school spaces for girls means not only constructing new classrooms but also training a very large number of female schoolteachers. The latter poses an even more difficult challenge in view of the very low level of female literacy.

These numbers illustrate some of the reasons why even the rhetoric of the planners has softened over the years when it comes to improving the state of education in Pakistan. The framers of the Sixth Five-Year Plan were exceptionally brave with words when it came to setting the targets for primary education.

> The Sixth Plan approaches primary education with the earnestness and urgency that it has always deserved but never received. Universal compulsory education will be instituted within the Plan period. All boys of the relevant age group will be put into class I in the middle years of the Plan (1984–85) and all the girls by the terminal year (1987–88). A minimum of five years of schooling will be made obligatory to begin with and the tenure will gradually be raised to ten years. During the Sixth Plan, no student who is in school will be allowed to drop out before class V.[4]

As the statistics for the general enrollment rate and the enrollment rates for boys and girls show, the sixth plan's ambitious objectives were not achieved even by 1990, two years after the plan period. This lack of achievement was noted by the writers of the seventh plan. They toned down their rhetoric on social development and lowered the government's expectations with respect to universal primary education. The aim of the seventh plan was "to eradicate illiteracy among the youth by the end of the Eighth Plan (1993), through full enrollment of the primary age population."[5] Even this target was not realized; it required the commitment of financial and managerial resources of an order that Pakistan was not ready to put into education. The objective becomes even more difficult to achieve because, as discussed above, the more affluent segments of the society have been able to find ways to educate their young, but the poor have yet to recognize long-term benefits that would accrue from education. Even dedicating resources to education from special taxes has not solved the funding problem.

An attempt was made almost fifteen years ago, in the budget of 1985–1986, to raise additional resources to expand primary education—specifically by levying a new tax, called *iqra*—as there is said to be a precedent in early Islamic history for such a levy. By implementing this system, the government had hoped to serve two of its important objectives simultaneously: Islamization of the economy and improvement of the level of social development. But the *iqra* did not provide the required resources and education continued to be underfunded.In the summer of 1998, Prime Minister Nawaz Sharif turned to Mahbubul Haq, a former minister of finance who had gained international recognition for advocating rapid social development in poor countries.[6] Haq was appointed special adviser to the prime minister and was assigned the task of achieving universal literacy in the country in ten years. He planned to mount a national effort that included the use of most state employees, including half a million persons employed in the armed forces, as part-time teachers. However, Haq died in New York a couple of weeks after accepting this assignment.

Health and Development

Comparable efforts are also needed to improve health standards. As indicated in Table 4.1, Pakistan lags behind other low-income countries in this area as well. The reasons are similar to those that have contributed to the backwardness of the educational system: lack of demand on the part of the population for appropriate facilities and a pronounced urban bias on the part of the government. That is, as a result of low levels of rural literacy, especially among women, a demand for health facilities that would have elicited a suitable response from the government has not been forthcoming. In addition, the ruling elite have displayed a normal penchant for developing urban-based facilities. Consequently, the bias in favor of urban areas is exceptionally pronounced. For instance, 95 percent of the tuberculosis centers are located in cities despite the fact that 6 percent of all deaths in rural areas are caused by tuberculosis, as compared to only 3 percent in urban areas. The distribution of beds in institutions (hospitals, dispensaries, and various other types of health centers) is also highly skewed in favor of urban areas: 82.5 percent of all beds are in towns and cities, compared with only 17.5 percent in villages. In terms of the population served, there are twelve times as many institutional beds in urban areas as in rural ones. According to one analyst,

> Despite laments of "scarce resources," it is clear that the problem is not one of distribution of resources, but more importantly, of the distribution of resources between urban and rural areas—the government spends six times as much per person for operating and maintaining health services in urban as in rural areas. . . . Since 1972, eight new medical colleges have been set up in Pakistan. Had this option not been preferred, and instead a comprehensive Rural Health Programme been launched at an early date, nearly the entire population of Pakistan would have had access to some health facility by now.[7]

This maldistribution of health facilities did not go unnoticed by the government. According to the Fifth Five-Year Plan, "There are imbalances in the allocation of facilities between rural and urban areas," and "it is evident that the scale on which health services are available for the population of the rural areas is comparatively poorer than urban areas."[8] One of the plan's principal objectives was to restore some form of balance in health coverage between urban and rural areas. The objective was not realized, however. Accordingly, the Sixth Five-Year Plan promised a massive shift toward a Rural Health Programme, which was to receive 43 percent of the total outlay promised in the health sector. The sixth plan, like the fourth plan and fifth plan that preceded it, was unsuccessful.

There are three problems with the approach adopted hitherto. The first has been the failure to recognize that improvement in health is not entirely dependent on the provision of health facilities. For the reasons already discussed, health facilities—in the absence of improved literacy—are likely to remain underused or, at any rate, not used with a great deal of efficiency.

Second, in very backward societies such as rural Pakistan, initial improvements in health come not from the provision of additional hospital beds or even the stationing of doctors, paramedics, and nurses in large numbers. They proceed, instead, from the provision of better sanitation facilities. According to one group of health experts, "The most widespread diseases in developing countries are those transmitted by human faeces. . . . These diseases spread easily in areas without community water supply systems. . . . If water is not safe for drinking, or is insufficient for personal hygiene, diarrheal diseases will spread easily."[9] The predominance of intestinal diseases in registered cases of morbidity in Pakistan suggests that water-supply and sanitation facilities remain very backward. Their rural-urban distribution is even more skewed than that of hospital beds. Only 32 percent of the rural population has access to safe drinking water and to rudimentary forms of waste disposal. The entire urban population is accounted for, however, if access is defined in terms of residence. Therefore, the first step to be taken to improve the standard of health of the Pakistani population is to bring about a dramatic improvement in hygiene and sanitation.

The third reason for the backwardness of health in Pakistan is the emphasis on curative rather than preventive health. As the Planning Commission noted in the Fifth Five-Year Plan, "The current curriculum is heavily oriented towards curative medicine. The net result is such that in just a few years, there will be a large number of doctors who have been trained to practice only in hospital settings."[10] Yet this emphasis not only persisted but was being actively encouraged. For instance, in urging the Punjab government to expedite the construction of the "ultra-modern" Sheikh Zayed Hospital in Lahore, president Zia ul-Haq was reported to have remarked that "in terms of construction, machinery, and equipment he had not seen a hospital better than this hospital anywhere in the developing world."[11] Even the private sector was encouraged, perhaps unwittingly, to contribute to the pronounced urban bias in the health sector. Agha Khan Medical University's graduates did not find it easy to locate themselves in the countryside in spite of the links the new institution established with a number of rural health systems in the country. The university added to the surplus of doctors who were trained to work in a sophisticated environment and were therefore both unable and unwilling to serve in the countryside. It is not surprising that of the 48,000 registered doctors in Pakistan in 1998, only 30,000 were practicing in the country; the rest have either migrated or taken up nonmedical jobs in the country.

The implementation of the right approach toward health development—a recognition of the links between literacy and health, an emphasis on sanitation and hygiene, and a priority given to preventive rather than curative medicine—is possible only if significant additional resources can be raised and if a high proportion of these can be used in the countryside. As in the education sector, the government will have to find additional resources if major steps are to be taken.

The Population Problem

The claim on resources for social development will remain large for as long as the population continues to increase rapidly. In 1947, the year of independence, Pakistan had a population of 32 million; in 1985, it crossed the 100-million mark. In 1990, it was estimated to be 113 million. By the time Pakistan took its fifth population census in March 1998—seven years after its original schedule—the population had climbed to 131 million. Between 1947 and 1998, the average rate of growth was 2.8 percent per year. The 1998 census estimates seemed to indicate that the rate of fertility and the rate of increase in population had finally begun to decline; nevertheless, it is estimated that by the year 2000, Pakistan will have a population of 138 million. At 5.2, Pakistan's total fertility rate (the number of children born per woman) was considerably higher in 1995 than the rates for India (3.2) and Sri Lanka (2.2).

There are several reasons for which poor people, with little education, poor health and family-planning services, and low and insecure incomes, have many children. Where wages are low, the difference between the children's earnings and those of the mother will be small. Where women for social and cultural reasons are not encouraged to enter the labor force, a high value cannot be put on their time. In other words, the "opportunity cost" of their time is very low. Thus the time spent in pregnancy does not impose a serious economic burden on the family. This is the case in Pakistan's lower middle classes, in which, because of the rapid increase in family incomes, women are not called upon even to perform work in the home. Accordingly, this social class has a very high rate of fertility. Even in the poorer classes, in which women perform numerous household chores, income loss by mothers during pregnancy and the infancy of their children may be easily recouped by the children later on.

Lack of schooling opportunities, particularly from the age of twelve or so, also favors high fertility rates. Schooling, if it isn't free, not only adds to the parents' expenses but also removes the children from home, thus depriving the family of extra work hands. The education of women also tends to reduce birth rates, as educated women can grasp the disadvantage of frequent pregnancies and are more willing than illiterate women to accept family-planning advice.

High infant and child mortality rates constitute another reason for having many children. In Pakistan, one out of seven children dies before reaching the age of one; accordingly, Pakistani parents may feel the need to have many children to ensure that a few survive. Moreover, because boys are regarded as more important than girls (in Pakistan there is a strong preference for males), parents may need to have five or six children to be sure that two sons survive. The preference for sons is usually the result of the search for security in old age. A number of studies have confirmed that poor and uneducated parents in Pakistan are much more likely than well-to-do parents to expect to live with (and be supported by) their children. For many parents, the need for support in their old age outweighs the immediate cost of children. Despite a high rate of migration and increased incomes, this dependence on children has not declined. It remains at a high level because other institutions (banks, pension funds, government bonds, and insurance and mutual aid societies) have not developed.

In some developing countries, including Pakistan, family systems may also encourage high fertility. Early marriage and childbearing are easier if the new couple can begin married life in an extended household. In Pakistan, early marriage remains the norm, and the incidence of marriage (the proportion of women getting married) remains exceptionally high. The rate of household formation is relatively low. It appears, therefore, that marriage results not in the setting up of new households but in the enlargement of existing ones. The social environment is essentially pronatalist.

Still another reason for high fertility is limited information about, and access to, effective and safe means of contraception. In Pakistan, fewer than one-fifth of the couples of childbearing age exhibit some knowledge of birth-control practices. In addition, recognition that rapid population growth could seriously affect economic development has been slow in coming. These attitudes are not new; the Muslims in British India had a higher rate of fertility than other religious groups. British India's high-fertility population became concentrated in what is now Pakistan. The result was a sharp increase in population growth, which reached nearly 2 percent in the 1950s as compared to a little more than 1 percent in the 1930s. Significantly, it was a group of women who took the initiative to arouse public and private interest in population growth. Most of these women had done social work in the refugee communities that had formed in Pakistan after independence and had become aware of the problems created by high fertility rates. In 1952, this group established the Family Planning Association, which, in 1964, became affiliated with the International Planned Parenthood Federation. The association set up family-planning clinics in Karachi, Lahore, and Dhaka, but its first breakthrough came in 1959 when it organized an international seminar with the help of the United States. The seminar was supported and attended by Field Marshal Ayub Khan, who, having been persuaded to lend government support to family-planning activities, instructed the Planning Commission to develop an official program. The program, designed and incorporated in the Second Five-Year Plan (1960–1965), was limited in scope, although it did provide additional resources to the maternity and child health services in the form of counseling and conventional contraceptives.

The program gained momentum under the Third Five-Year Plan (1965–1970). A population policy was adopted with a number of specific demographic targets, the most important of which was a decline in the birthrate from 50 per 1,000 in 1965 to 25 per 1,000 in 1985. The program was innovative in three respects. Family planning as a government activity was separated from health, removed from the Health Division, and placed in a newly constituted Family Planning Division. Emphasis was put on the distribution of intrauterine devices (IUDs) rather than on conventional contraceptives. In addition, a cadre of *dais* (midwives) was recruited to motivate women to use IUDs. But the program failed to produce any of the promised dramatic results. According to the National Impact Survey carried out in 1968–1969, "Over 80 percent of women contacted by the surveyors were in favor of family planning but only 4 percent were found to be practicing any methods of birth control; 70 percent knew of at least four methods to delay pregnancy; 64 percent did not know anyone in the local area who was giving advice and service on family planning; and 6 percent reported they had contact with such persons or centers."[12] In other words, the program may have succeeded in motivating women to favor family planning, but it could not get them to practice it. There were two main reasons for the gap between interest and practice: the attitude of the families involved (husbands and mothers-in-law, in particular) and the lack of services.

The Fourth Five-Year Plan (1970–1975) continued to emphasize the need for population control but shifted its emphasis from IUDs to low-cost conventional contraception, particularly the condom. With the help of the Agency for International Development (AID), the government adopted a "mass inundation" scheme aimed at saturating villages with supplies of conventional contraceptives. The idea was to reach men rather than women. This approach was continued in the fifth plan (1978–1983) but was dropped in the sixth plan (1983–1988) in favor of the provision of services through clinics to those interested in controlling family size. The seventh plan's (1988–1993) "family welfare program" emphasized "better and wider birth control and delivery services and a more intensive and varied motivational"[13] approach.

The important conclusion that emerges from this overview is that successive governments found it difficult to settle on one approach, even one based on proven methods for controlling family size. A good deal of experimentation resulted in slowing progress toward reducing the rate of fertility. The 1965–1985 perspective plan had hoped to reduce the birthrate from 50 to 25 per 1,000; in 1998, the rate was still 27 per 1,000 and is likely to decline to about 25 per 1,000 in the year 2000, fifteen years after the target of the 1965–1985 perspective plan.

Table 4.2 provides one measure of the very slow rate at which fertility is declining in Pakistan. Today, in terms of population size, Pakistan is the seventh-largest country in the world. By 2040, it will have reached the stage of stationary population, but by then—with 380 million people—it would be the third-largest coun-

TABLE 4.2 Countries with the Largest Population in 1988 and Hypothetical Size of the Stationary Population

	1997 Population (in millions)	*Hypothetical Size of Stationary Population (in millions)*	*Assumed Year of Reaching Net Reproduction Rate of 1*
China	1227	1835	2000
India	916	1862	2015
United States	268	316	2000
Indonesia	200	370	2030
Brazil	164	303	2005
Russian Federation	147	na	2005
Pakistan	137	380	2030
Japan	126	121	2040
Bangladesh	124	246	2025
Nigeria	118	256	2040

Sources: World Bank, *World Development Report 1990* (Washington, D.C.: World Bank, 1990), Tables 1, 26, 27 of World Development Indicators; World Bank, *World Development Report, 1998–99,* Table 1, p. 190 (Washington, D.C.: 1998).

try after India and China. Pakistan's stationary population would be three times its size in 1998, whereas that of India would be twice as large. There is a built-in momentum associated with high birthrates, which would take a long time to dissipate unless the rate of decline in the fertility level could be sharply accelerated through a combination of efforts in education, health, and family planning.

Urbanization

Perhaps the most spectacular impact of a rapidly growing population is the growth of cities, including "megacities" with populations in excess of 10 million people (see Table 4.3). Pakistan could have two such cities by the year 2000: Karachi, with a population of 12 million, and the greater metropolitan area of Lahore-Gujranwala-Sheikhupura, with some 10 million people. In addition to these large cities, another six to eight—Faisalabad, Rawalpindi, Multan, Hyderabad, Gujranwala, Peshawar, and possibly Islamabad and Quetta—will have populations in excess of 1 million each. Together, these ten cities are likely to have a population of some 30 million people by the year 2000—about the size of Pakistan's total population at the time of independence. The demand placed on the nations' resources by such a large urban population will be enormous and, indeed, difficult to ignore. Urban populations are politically more articulate, cohesive, and organized than their rural counterparts and, consequently, wield much greater political force—hence the pronounced urban bias in the allocation of development and other resources. This bias is likely to be felt even more in Pakistan

TABLE 4.3   Growth of Pakistan's Urban Population (in millions)

	1960	1980	2000
Total population	45	92	138
Urban population	10	24	51
Population in cities of over 500,000 persons	3	12	25
Population in cities of over 1 million persons	2	9	21
Population in cities of over 10 million persons	–	–	18

Sources: Author's estimate, using data from Pakistan's population census of 1998.

than in other developing countries, because Pakistan lacks mature political institutions that could otherwise help to arbitrate between rural and urban interests. The pressure to commit a disproportionately large amount of development funds to urban improvement will come precisely at the time when Pakistan must not only bring about a profound change in the structure of its agricultural sector but also advance the social development of its large and rapidly growing population.

Although the type of urban development projected in Table 4.3 can no longer be avoided, what can be prevented is a further acceleration of this trend in the decades beyond the year 2000. Limiting population growth will require the commitment of considerable government resources as well as close attention to social development—in particular, primary education and the education of women.

Poverty

Pakistan is in the odd position of being a poor country with a low level of social development but without a great deal of poverty. Yet the Brandt Commission, in a report issued in 1980,[14] included Pakistan in the two poverty belts it identified. One of these runs north-south across the continent of Africa and includes all of the Sub-Saharan countries; the other begins with Yemen and Afghanistan, stretches across South Asia, and extends into Cambodia, Vietnam, Laos, and Indonesia.

These belts have a number of economic and social characteristics in common: More than one-half of the population of the countries included therein live in absolute poverty, and a very large number of the absolute poor are in the countryside earning meager incomes as small farmers or landless workers. By widespread agreement, a person is considered "absolutely poor" if and only if his or her resources are too meager to meet basic needs—and given that food is by far the most basic of these needs, the absolute poor in these countries are seriously undernourished. If the absolute poor do not have the resources to feed themselves adequately, they do not—and cannot—have access to such other essential needs as clothing, shelter, sanitation, and education. Hence the most frequent manifestations of poverty are sickness, disease, and premature mortality. According to the World Bank, people earning less than one dollar a day cannot meet their basic needs. There are more than a billion people in the world who are counted as absolutely poor by this criterion.

But absolute poverty in the poverty-belt areas is not confined to the countryside. Urban poverty is particularly prevalent in South Asia; the incidence of poverty is estimated to be higher in urban areas—particularly in the large cities—than in rural areas. The urban poor of Asia are also more visible: Tens of millions live in highly congested tenements in some dozen large cities or sleep in the open on street pavements. They seldom have regular jobs to go to during the day; the vast majority of them eke out a very meager living from self-employment in the informal sector of the economy. Although nearly a third of the population of the Asian cities is said to be absolutely poor compared to about one-half in the countryside, the cities continue to receive rural migrants. The rate of growth of Asian cities is twice as high as the rate of increase of the rural population.

Although the Asian poverty belt runs right through Pakistan, the above description of the characteristics of Asian poverty does not apply to Pakistan. If what is true for the rest of Asia were also true for Pakistan, then some 55 million of its people would be living in absolute poverty, with 20 million in the cities and 35 million in small towns and villages. To those familiar with the large cities of South Asia—Bombay, Calcutta, Delhi, Dhaka, Chittagong, even Colombo—pavement dwellers and transient people are a familiar sight. But such people do not dominate the Pakistani cityscape; a night census conducted in 1985 in Karachi counted only 18,000 pavement dwellers in the entire city (as compared to about 1.5 million in Bombay and 2 million in Calcutta). Other signs of Asian poverty are not easily visible in Pakistan, either. An anthropometric survey taken recently in South Asia suggests that more than one-half of the children have less than normal height and weight; but while similar surveys carried out in Pakistan also show some signs of malnutrition, potbellied children with large, prominent eyes are not a common sight in the country's cities and villages. Even to the casual observer, sensitive to the sights common in the poor countries of Asia and Africa, Pakistan for many years did not seem to be very poor. Illiteracy—in particular, the very low levels of school enrollment by females—is the only prominent social characteristic that Pakistan seems to share with the other countries of the Asian and African poverty belts.

How should one explain Pakistan's unique situation as a poor country with few visible signs of poverty? And if Pakistan has indeed succeeded in eliminating the worst forms of poverty, then where and how did this happen, and to what extent was this success the result of deliberate government policy?

For the present, little hard evidence exists with which to provide firm answers to these questions—but it is possible to speculate.[15] Two developments played a critical role in helping Pakistan deal with poverty—the sharp increase in agricultural productivity, especially in the late 1960s, and the migration of millions of Pakistanis to Great Britain, the Middle East, and North America. Both developments need a word of explanation.

Pakistan was perhaps as poor as the rest of poor Asia until the closing years of the 1960s. At that time, the green revolution began to take hold in the countryside, with benefits not only going to the large landlords (as is sometimes asserted) but distributed much more widely to all classes of people, including the landless poor. The economic boom in the Middle East began within a half a decade of the start of the green revolution, and its income distributive impact was equally pronounced. Consequently, and without much help from its own government, Pakistan succeeded significantly in reducing the incidence of absolute poverty. This is not to say that there were no Pakistani people living in absolute poverty, for there were—indeed, millions of such people. But their proportion was not as large as that in other poor countries of Asia and Africa. That is, the poor in Pakistan did not constitute as much as 40–50 percent of the population (as they did, perhaps, in the 1950s and 1960s); in the early 1990s, their proportion was no more than 10–20 percent. In any case, it is important that we understand how the incidence of poverty may have been reduced from about 40–50 percent to 10–20 percent in about two decades, and how Pakistan could avoid slipping back into the situation that prevailed in the 1950s and the early 1960s.

As noted, the first step toward progress came with the green revolution—particularly with the large-scale use of high-yielding wheat and rice seeds by the farmers of Asia and the Middle East. These seeds, developed in Mexico and the Philippines, produce considerably higher yields in the presence of a sufficient amount of fertilizer. But higher applications of fertilizer require an abundant and timely supply of irrigation water. Accordingly, green-revolution technology was adopted by farmers who had easy access not only to irrigation water but to chemical fertilizer as well—in other words, the larger farmers of the area. In the case of Pakistan, however, the first wave of entrepreneurs came from neither the large nor the small farmers; rather, the high-yielding seed technology was initially adopted by a new breed of middle-sized agricultural entrepreneurs who had exceptionally close relations with the government of Ayub Khan. Ayub Khan himself belonged to this social class, and his government did a great deal to help its members bring commercial farming to agriculture.

The leadership provided by middle-sized farmers was very important; had the technology been adopted initially by large landlords (and there were many at that time in Pakistan), it would not have spread as rapidly as it did. The very close economic relations between middle farmers and small cultivators helped. According to the agricultural census of 1972, by the start of the 1970s, more than one-half of the area under wheat in all farms was using the high-yielding varieties. The small farmers devoted less land to high-yielding rice (just over one-fifth as against just less than one-half by the large farmers), but in terms of income per acre of land, they were almost as well off in that they grew a great deal of high-value *basmati* rice.

Small farms are generally more productive than large farms; they use more labor per unit of land and are also more carefully managed. This productivity difference is evident in Pakistan and seems to have widened as a result of the green revolution. Just before the green revolution took hold, net income per acre for small farms was twice as high as that for large farms; by 1970–1971, this differential had widened to almost three times. In the five-year period preceding 1970–1975, the productivity of small farms increased at an annual rate of 17 percent, compared to 8 percent for large farms. But increases in productivity alone do not necessarily result in improved income distribution among different classes of farmers—particularly if, as is sometimes suggested for Pakistan, the introduction of new agricultural technologies leads to the concentration of land in the hands of large landowners. Once again, the available evidence suggests that what actually occurred was some redistribution of land in favor of the small and middle-sized owners. For instance, in 1960, the lowest 30 percent of the farmers tilled only 3 percent of the land, whereas the largest 30 percent farmed 75 percent. A structural change of significant proportions appears to have occurred between 1960 and 1972, when the share of the small farmers increased to 6 percent and that of the large farmers declined to 67 percent. The middle-sized farmers were the principal beneficiaries of this change, with the area they farmed increasing from 22 percent to 27 percent, which confirms that they were the ones who initially adopted the new agricultural technology. Their aggressive entrepreneurship produced a significant increase in the total area they farmed. Although a much-heralded land reform was undertaken by Ayub Khan in 1959, this redistribution was not so much the consequence of public policy as the result of land sales by large landlords.

Landless workers also appear to have benefited from the green revolution. Evidence suggests that labor shortages brought about a considerable improvement in rural wages. The feared displacement of workers produced by the mechanization of some agricultural activities did not occur; or, if it did occur, enough new job opportunities were created to absorb the workers made redundant by mechanization. The small-scale industrial sector working to produce inputs for the agricultural sector and also processing agricultural output was particularly important in absorbing the surplus farm labor. The green revolution therefore played an important role in improving the poverty situation, particularly in the irrigated districts of Punjab and Sindh, which constitute the agricultural heartland of Pakistan.

For the poorer districts—the districts that depend on *barani*, or rain-fed agriculture—help came from another source: the economic boom in Great Britain in the early 1950s, when it began to recover from the ravages of the Second World War, and the boom in the Middle East following the sharp increase in oil prices in the 1970s. As I have already mentioned, these booms generated two distinct waves of migration from Pakistan. The first created a pool of Pakistani-born people in Great Britain that now numbers about 750,000 people. The second wave produced a much bigger pool in the Middle East. As of 1990, more than 2.5 million

Pakistanis were working in the Middle East, this labor pool having been assembled over a period of fifteen years. Construction workers from the northern area of Pakistan—from the *barani* areas of the Punjab and the Northwest Frontier Province and from the Federally Administered Tribal Areas—constituted the first set of migrants, many of whom were recruited by U.S. and European construction firms. They had been employed on the massive irrigation works in Pakistan and were very familiar with this type of labor. The second set of migrants included people with somewhat greater skills. In 1979, at the time of the second sharp increase in the price of oil, the construction boom was over. The Middle Eastern economies, now much more mature, were in need of people with many different skills, including workers to maintain the large physical and economic infrastructure that had been built by then. Carpenters, plumbers, and electricians migrated in large numbers, as did doctors, engineers, accountants, bankers, nurses, teachers, office clerks, and typists. What the first set of migration to the Middle East accomplished for the rural economy was achieved by the second group for towns and cities. In both cases, the migrants sent back their savings, which were sizable, to help lift their families out of poverty or near-poverty into relative affluence.

In the absence of complete and reliable data, informed speculation must serve to gauge the impact of migration and the resultant remittances on poverty in Pakistan. The pool of migrants was built over a period of ten years (1974–1984), and people moved in and out of it; hence the total number involved substantially exceeded 2 million—the present size of the migrant population. Over time, it involved perhaps as many as 3.5 million people, or just over 3 million households, inasmuch as it has been common for one family to send more than one laborer to work. A very large proportion of these households—perhaps as many as two-thirds—came from the poorer segments of the society, and of the poorer families that exported labor, about three-fourths were from the less developed northern areas of Pakistan. These areas—the Northwest Frontier Province, the Federally Administered Tribal Areas, and the *barani* (unirrigated) parts of Punjab—had a total population of about 25 million in the mid-1980s divided into 4 million households. Of these, 2 million are relatively poor. If this arithmetic is correct, some 1.5 million of these 2 million families exported workers to the Middle East at one time or another.

Workers in the Middle East remitted some $30 billion during the fifteen-year period between 1975 and 1990; if only a fourth of these remittances were received by poor families, they would still amount to $3,200 per family—the equivalent of an increase of 75 percent in household income. An increase of this magnitude over such a short period of time must have had a significant impact on the economic well-being of the recipient families. An increase of the same magnitude occurred for the poor families in the cities that contributed workers to the two groups of migrants.

It appears, therefore, that without making a great deal of deliberate effort, Pakistan was able to significantly reduce the number of people living in absolute poverty. It is possible to speculate about the reasons that made this possible. The green revolution had a much more profound distributive impact than it is generally credited with. First, the rapid development of the small-scale industrial sector, which went unnoticed for a long time and was possibly aided by the growth of the agricultural sector, also helped the poor. Second, the very rapid rate of interprovincial migration, particularly migration from the crowded villages of Punjab and the Northwest Frontier Province to Sindh and Balochistan, must have reduced the pressure on land in the labor surplus provinces. And, finally, migration to the Middle East not only provided the poor who migrated with very high levels of income but also set in motion a process that, although not completely understood, came to the rescue of the poor who stayed behind. As a result, poverty in Pakistan for some time was less severe than it was in other South Asian countries. Of course, the circumstances behind that comparatively good fortune were not irreversible. Net migration to the Middle East has already stopped; the agricultural sector may have failed to attain the structural change that is needed in order to produce further increases in income; and interprovincial migration slowed down. Finally, high fertility rates may continue well into the future, adding millions more to the already large population. However, what mattered most was the sharp slowdown in the rate of economic growth in the 1990s. Pakistan is too large a country with too large a population to rely on migration to other parts of the world to solve the problem of poverty. The only viable solution for poverty is to rely on a robust economic growth coupled with public sector programs aimed at developing human resources.

The Status of Women

Some of the statistics already cited in this chapter on the rate of literacy, enrollment rates in schools and colleges, the rate of infant mortality, and the fertility rate all point vividly to the very low social status of Pakistani women, particularly among the poorer segments of the society. There is now persuasive evidence that, although human resource development does not by itself result in major economic transformation, the entire process of development can proceed only so far without developing human resources, especially if the benefits are to be distributed equitably. The relationship between improving the social and economic status of women on the one hand and sustaining long-term economic growth on the other is even stronger. However, the social status of women in Pakistan is even lower than in the countries at comparable levels of development. This leads to two obvious questions: Why have Pakistani women lagged so far behind women in other parts of the developing world? (See Table 4.4.) Are there policies and programs that the government could adopt to improve the status of Pakistani women?

Indicators of the social and economic status achieved by women fall into five main groups. The first indictors concern health: women's life expectancy at birth, causes of their mortality and morbidity, and the numbers of women living com-

TABLE 4.4   Indicators of Women's Status: Cross-Country Comparisons

	Year	Pakistan	India	Bangladesh	Low-income Countries
Sex ratio (females per	1965	93	94	93	96
100 males	1985	91	94	95	95
Female life expectancy	1965	45	44	44	50
at birth (years)	1996	60	63	59	60
Male life expectancy at	1965	47	46	45	48
birth (years)	1996	62	62	57	58
Total primary school	1965	40	74	49	73
enrollment ratio[a]	1985	42	98	59	104
Total primary school	1965	20	57	31	–
enrollment ratio[a]	1985	35	81	49	95
Total fertility rates	1965	7.0	6.2	6.8	6.3
(# children)[b]	1996	5.1	3.1	3.4	4.1
% fall in fertility		27%	50%	50%	35%
(1965–1995)					
Women of childbearing	1965	43	47	44	46
age as percentage	1985	46	49	46	50
of population					
% of women of childbearing	1986	11	35	25	n.a.
age using contraception					
Babies with low birth	1985	25	30	31	n.a.
weight (%)					
Maternal mortality (per	1990–	340	437	850	n.a.
100,000 live births)	1996				
Population growth rate	1980–	2.9	1.7	2.0	1.8
(% p.a.)	1998				
Female labor force	1981	6.0[d]	25.9	13.0	29.5[e]
participation rate (%)[c]					
GNP per capita	1997	490	390	270	350
% average annual growth	1965–	2.4	1.9	1.0	1.9
rates in GNP per capita	1998				

[a]Percentage of age group enrolled in the different levels of education.

[b]Represents the number of children that would be born to a woman if she were to live to the end of her childbearing years and bear children in accordance with prevailing age-specific fertility rates.

[c]Source: "Social Data," *World Tables, vol. II,* World Bank, 1983. The data reflect the "most recent estimate" at the time these tables were compiled, which probably referred to a point in the period 1979–1981.

[d]The 1981 Census shows 3.5%.

[e]Average for South Asia was 22.8%.

Sources: World Bank, *World Development Report 1990* (Washington, D.C.: World Bank, 1990), Tables 1, 26–29, 32; World Bank, *World Development Report 1998–99* (Washington, D.C.: World Bank, 1998), Tables 1, 6, 7.

pared to the numbers of men (the sex ratio). The second group relates to education and training of women: their enrollment rates in schools, colleges, and universities; and their access to vocational training. The third group concerns women's reproductive behavior: their fertility rate, incidence of marriage, age of marriage, and use of contraception. The fourth relates to women's economic behavior: their participation in the workforce, the contributions they make to household income, and the extent of control they exercise on household expenditures. The fifth relates to the overall control women have over their own lives and on those of their children.

The life expectancy at birth for Pakistani women in 1995 was sixty years—three years under the average for all poor countries. It was in 1988, for the first time ever, that life expectancy in Pakistan for men and women was reported to be equal. In developed and most developing countries, women tend to outlive men by about five years.

In 1995, Pakistan's female primary-school enrollment ratio, at 35 percent, was among the lowest in the world. Only eight countries had lower ratios; apart from Bhutan, all were in Africa. Enrollment rates are very low in the Northwest Frontier Province and Balochistan, where no more than one-sixth of primary-school-aged girls attend school. In the 1997–1998 school year, 5.7 million boys and 2.9 million girls were in primary school, a ratio of only 51 percent, one of the lowest in the world. That ratio improves to nearly 60 percent for colleges and universities in large cities (reasons for this are discussed below), but is only 16 percent for secondary vocational institutions.

The women of Pakistan carry a very heavy reproductive burden. Their average age at marriage is eighteen, and the incidence of marriage is 98 percent. Thus exposure to possible pregnancy, on average, is thirty-three years. Because only 14 percent of women of childbearing age use contraception, this long exposure results in a very high total fertility rate (TFR). TFR represents the number of children that would be born to a woman if she were to live to the end of her childbearing years and bear children in accordance with age-specific fertility rates. In Pakistan the TFR for 1995 was estimated at 5.2, one of the highest in the world and only 5.7 percent lower than in 1965. However, the census of 1998 suggests that the rate has declined somewhat in recent years. Such a high TFR and its very slow decline over time explains why the estimates of Pakistan's stationary population continue to be revised upward and why the country will have the third largest population in the world once the global population reaches stability. A high TFR also explains the high rate of maternal mortality in Pakistan and the high incidence of morbidity among women of childbearing age.

Women pass on their poor health to their babies. In 1995, 22 percent of the babies born in Pakistan weighed less than normal (Table 4.4). A low weight at birth contributes to high infant mortality, which for Pakistan is high at 90 for every 1,000 live births. There has been some improvement, with the rate of infant deaths declining by 20 percent in the last seven years. If a large number of children die, parents tend to compensate for this loss by producing more children than they need in order to achieve preferred family size. In Pakistan, as in most developing countries, there is a strong preference for boys; an average Pakistani family would like to have two boys survive to adulthood. Four births per woman would result in this objective, provided the infant mortality rate was not high; because Pakistan has a high rate, a total fertility rate of 5.2 is a form of insurance that parents take out. This type of calculation on the part of Pakistani parents has produced families larger than those desired and, consequently, a high rate of population growth.

Pakistan has one of the lowest sex ratios in the world, and it has declined over time. In 1995, there were only 95 women in Pakistan's population for every 100 men. This low and declining ratio is caused by two factors: high mortality rates for women and improving mortality rates for men. The high death rate for women is the result of three factors: a very high incidence of infant mortality for girls, which suggests fairly widespread practice of female infanticide, probably through parental neglect of young girls; a very high incidence of maternal deaths; and lack of adequate health care facilities for older women.

Pakistan has one of the lowest recorded worker participation rates for women. No firm estimates are available. According to the Population Census of 1981, the total female labor force participation rate (FLFPR)—rural and urban, formal and informal sectors—was only 3.5 percent. According to the Labor Force Survey of 1986–1987, the FLFPR was 11.9 percent. The agriculture census estimated the FLFPR was 20.3 percent, but the estimate included a large number of part-time workers. All estimates are much lower than the average for South Asia and for developing countries as a whole. Participation rates do not tell the entire story about women's economic situation, however. A very large number of working women are "crowded into low-return activities, which limit their income and act as a disincentive to their greater participation in economic activities."[16]

There is one sign of hope for Pakistani women. For various reasons, economic as well as social, the women belonging to the upper strata of society are acquiring education and skills that are comparable—in some cases even better—than those possessed by men. This accomplishment is a result of the rapid modernization and urbanization of the society since the mid-1970s that pulled men into the workforce prematurely. Modernization had a significant impact on the enrollment rates for women in colleges and universities. Because the society was not prepared to accept women into most workplaces, women stayed in colleges and universities. Upon graduation, a large number of them moved into professions, and their presence will have a profound impact on the country's social and political development. For instance, journalism (particularly English-language publications) and politics attract a number of talented women. The fact that Benazir Bhutto twice became Pakistan's prime minister, albeit for brief periods, and Abida Hussain played a prominent role as an opposition leader during Benazir Bhutto's tenure and later became Pakistan's ambassador to the United States to be succeeded by another woman, Maleeha Lodhi, is a good indication of the emancipation of the women belonging to the upper strata of the society.

The Islamization of the society ordered by Zia ul-Haq profoundly affected Pakistani women—producing a reaction with a depth and breadth that could not have been anticipated by the military president. According to a perceptive study on the social status of Pakistani women,

> it was only after the imposition of General Zia ul-Haq's martial law and the unexpected shift in policy at the top that women belonging to the upper and upper middle classes realized how fragile their hold on their rights was. With this came the realization that firstly, as one could not depend on the central government to guarantee women's rights, women themselves would have to be mobilized, and secondly, that until a greater number of women were made conscious of their lack of rights and were prepared to join forces to counter the prevailing trend, whatever rights were granted and enjoyed would remain insecure.[17]

Women's reactions to the policies adopted by Zia resulted in the establishment of scores of women's groups that adopted economic, social, and political objectives. The most important of these organizations was an umbrella group, Khawateen Mahaz-e-Amal (Women's Action Forum [WAF]), founded in Karachi in 1981. The WAF opened branches all over the country and within two years of its establishment boasted a membership of 15,000 women. The Zia government was obviously impressed by the reaction its policies elicited among women and the groups that represented them. It responded by recognizing the low social status of women as a development problem in the Seventh Five-Year Plan.

> The Sixth Plan recognized that women's development is a prerequisite for overall national development. The emphasis continues during the Seventh Plan as well. Concrete steps have been proposed whereby [women's] participation is ensured. Their training will receive high priority and infrastructure facilities such as hostels for working women and day care centers will be set up. To encourage self-employment they would be provided credit for small businesses. Non-Government Organizations engaged in welfare programmes for women will receive particular attention.[18]

Although the government can play a facilitating role, the status of women will improve only if society changes its attitude toward them. The first step toward such an attitudinal change may have been taken with the social and political mobilization of upper-class women as reflected by the formation of groups such as WAF.

Conclusion

A recurring theme in these pages is that Pakistan can no longer afford to postpone some of the deep structural changes needed in the economy. Among them is the need to improve social development, in particular, those segments of the society that have, for a variety of reasons, received insufficient attention from policymakers. Among the forgotten people are the women of Pakistan and the people living in more backward parts of the country. The problems faced by these underprivileged groups—poor access to education and health facilities—can only be addressed by the public sector. However, as I have already pointed out, that can happen only if the government is able to augment its resources, which would mean that the people who wield power would have to provide a greater share of their income to the government through taxation.

5

GOVERNANCE, CORRUPTION, AND DEVELOPMENT: SOME MAJOR OBSTACLES TO GROWTH AND MODERNIZATION

Poor governance and corruption, and their adverse impact on development, is a theme running through the three previous chapters. Whatever the issue was, poor governance and corruption took a very heavy toll. The pace of political development was affected when groups seeking to join politics on account of the social and economic power they had acquired were prevented from doing so. The establishment used all the devices at its disposal to keep the political system closed. The result was poor governance. In the area of economic development (the theme of Chapter 3) the establishment captured a significant share of increments to national wealth by virtue of its domination of the political system. The established groups that held sway over the formal political structure adopted a perverse set of policies that discriminated against less advantaged groups. This contributed to a serious slowdown in the delivery of social services such as basic education and primary heath care to a large number of people. Poor governance and corruption played an important role, whether it was Pakistan's failure to develop credible political institutions that gave a voice to important groups operating in the society or the country's inability to sustain high rates of economic growth over a long period of time, or, again, the country's failure to achieve a high rate of social development.

This chapter has four sections. The first traces a number of developments in Pakistan that brought poor governance and corruption to the center of the political stage in 1996–1997. The second section defines "governance" and "corruption" and provides some impressions of how they influence economic development. It uses examples from Pakistan's history to illustrate how poor governance and rampant corruption can inflict an enormous amount of damage on the economy and the society. The third section identifies the reasons for the corruption that has afflicted the Pakistani political and economic systems in the last several decades and for the people's vehement reaction to these developments in the fall and spring of 1996–1997. The fourth section provides an assessment of efforts being made by the government currently in power to deal with the twin problems of corruption and poor governance.

Poor Governance, Corruption, and the Fall of Benazir Bhutto's Second Government

In its annual report issued in the summer of 1996, Transparency International (TI), a Berlin-based nongovernmental organization that addresses the issue of corruption in both developed and developing countries, issued an assessment showing a very poor situation in Pakistan. The TI publishes a corruption-perception index every year in which a score of ten equals a country entirely free of corruption, whereas a score of zero equals a country in which all business transactions are governed by kickbacks, extortion, and so on. In 1996, Pakistan, with a reading of 1.00, was ranked fifty-fourth among the fifty-five countries for which measurements were provided. Nigeria was deemed to be the most corrupt and India, with a score of 2.63, was ranked forty-sixth.

Transparency International's 1996 report received a great deal of attention in Pakistan and provided the subject of corruption the salience it had not acquired before. There was a common perception that Pakistan's economic situation had deteriorated considerably in the course of the last year. A number of observers held that corruption in and poor management by the Bhutto administration were the main reasons for the rapid worsening of the economic situation. The Transparency International report confirmed what people had suspected. The first reaction of the administration of Prime Minister Benazir Bhutto to the finding presented by the Berlin-based organization was to dismiss it as propaganda inspired by some vested interests that wished to discredit her government. However, very quickly, the subject acquired a political significance that could not have been anticipated by the prime minister.

President Farooq Ahmad Khan Leghari had been watching the economic situation with concern for more than a year. In the summer of 1996 he issued several warnings to the prime minister advising her to take immediate steps to arrest the rapidly deteriorating situation, improve the quality of governance, and deal with the blatant resort to corruption on the part of several senior members of her government. The prime minister ignored the president's advice. She also paid little attention to concerns expressed by the International Monetary Fund, the World Bank, and the Asian Development Bank about poor governance. In November 1996, President Leghari came to the conclusion that the only option available to him was to invoke Section 58.2(b) of the constitution, inserted by President Zia ul-Haq as a condition for lifting martial law under which the country had been governed since July 1977. According to Article 58.2(b) of the amended constitution, "the President may . . . dissolve that national assembly in his discretion where in his opinion a situation has arisen in which the Government of the Federation cannot be carried on in accordance with the provision of the Constitution and an appeal to the electorate is necessary."[1]

On November 5, 1996, President Leghari determined that such a situation existed in the country. He issued an order detailing at considerable length the misdeeds of the government headed by Prime Minister Benazir Bhutto. The president charged that the prime minister had allowed widespread corruption to seriously damage important instruments of state. Poor governance and economic mismanagement had created a situation that could be remedied only by an appeal to the electorate. The caretaker administration installed following Bhutto's departure was instructed to take the steps needed to cleanse the economic and political systems. President Leghari believed that concern about mismanagement and corruption had so severely eroded the people's confidence in the leaders who governed Pakistan that the entire political system seemed close to a total collapse.

This was not the first time a president had invoked Article 58.2(b) of the constitution to dismiss the prime minister; President Zia ul-Haq used it in May 1988 to dismiss Prime Minister Muhammad Khan Junejo; President Ghulam Ishaq Khan, in August 1990 to remove the first administration headed by Benazir Bhutto; and President Ghulam Ishaq Khan, in April 1993 to dismiss Prime Minister Nawaz Sharif. The order issued by President Farooq Leghari borrowed a great deal from those promulgated by Ishaq Khan. In spite of repeated appeals to the electorate, Pakistan seemingly had not managed to cleanse its administrative and economic systems of corruption.

Although the country generally applauded Bhutto's dismissal, the people quickly became disenchanted with the failure of the caretakers to bring the people suspected of corrupt behavior to justice. President Leghari, working with Prime Minster Meraj Khalid, wrote a new piece of legislation into the law books. The legislation was promulgated as an Ehtesab (*ehtesab*, a Persian word, means accountability) Ordinance to cover all actions taken by government functionaries in the period since December 31, 1987. The decision to start the process with that date was taken after a good deal of debate within the caretaker administration. An earlier date would have applied the ordinance to the military government headed by General Zia ul-Haq. Since the military has its own laws and institutions to enforce accountability, the caretakers decided to use December 31, 1987 (the date martial law was lifted), and Pakistan began the slow process of returning to democracy. The ordinance defined corruption as a culpable offense and created a new set of institutions, including the Ehtesab Commissions, to process cases against public officials deemed to be corrupt. Under the leadership of an Ehtesab commissioner—the person appointed to head the Ehtesab Commission—the ordinance established a mechanism for holding public officials accountable for their actions while they held office. The commissioner was expected to function independently of the legislative and executive branches of the government, a job for which the caretaker administration tapped a retired judge of the Supreme Court. Cases against officials suspected of corruption were to be prepared by the Ministry of Interior with the help of intelligence agencies and then referred to the commissioner. It was only after the Ehtesab commissioner was convinced that the referred cases contained sufficient evidence that he was to refer a case to the three-member Ehtesab court established for trying officials accused of corruption.

The caretaker administration also made public disclosure of all assets owned by people wishing to contest in the elections a precondition for their participation. Detailed accounts were to be provided to the chief election commissioner, who was required to publish them for scrutiny by the people. Statements made by the candidates could be challenged before the election commissioner, who had the authority to keep people from contesting elections if he found that false returns had been filed.

The promulgation of the Ehtesab Ordinance and new electoral laws was not enough to satisfy popular demand for action against those who had forfeited people's trust. There was a strong sentiment in the country that President Leghari and the caretaker administration should devote their entire time to instituting accountability rather than hold another general election. People believed that past elections had done little to cleanse the Pakistani system and were not inclined to repeat the exercise once more. The elections planned for February 1997 would represent the fifth return to the electorate in less than twelve years. In the past—in 1985, 1988, 1990, and again in 1993—the voters had failed to elect the people who provided good governance (i.e., most of the people elected were not capable of providing good governance on account of their cultural background). If anything, each election had resulted in further corruption of the political system, along with a large number of economic institutions. *Ehtesab* (accountability) before *intikhab* (elections) became a popular slogan—initially raised by Ardeshir Cowasjee, a highly respected columnist.[2]

Although promulgation of the Ehtesab Ordinance and new electoral laws may not have satisfied the public demand for bringing corrupt officials to accountability, a number of other actions—many of them in the economic field (discussed in

Chapter 3)—taken by the caretaker administration laid the ground for the decisive defeat of Benazir Bhutto and her Pakistan People's Party in the elections of February 1997. The PPP won only seventeen seats in a house of two hundred, whereas the Muslim League returned 160 members to the national legislature. Candidate Nawaz Sharif's campaign against corruption played a significant part in bringing such a massive victory to his party, the Pakistan Muslim League. When Mian Nawaz Sharif returned to power as prime minister, it was clear to him that, in order to retain the confidence of the people, he had to move quickly to bring charges against public officials and to create a clean administrative environment. However, two actions taken by his administration in this area created the impression that he was more interested in punishing Bhutto and her associates than bringing structural changes aimed at reducing the incidence of corruption in the country. First, he introduced a bill aimed at giving the institutions created by the caretaker administration a longer lease on life. Under the constitution, all ordinances promulgated by the president lapse after ninety days unless they are ratified by the legislature. Nawaz Sharif could have submitted the Ehtesab Ordinance to the National Assembly for ratification in the form promulgated by the caretaker administration. Instead, he introduced a significant change in the legislation. He brought forward the date of its effectiveness to November 1990, thereby removing the provincial government he had headed in Punjab from October 1988 to August 1990 from its purview. Second, the prime minister created an Ehtesab cell in his secretariat to prepare cases for submission to the Ehtesab commissioner. Senator Saifur Rehman, a longtime political and business associate of the Sharif family, was appointed to head the cell. Rehman's appointment was not well received. There was a perception that he had been given instructions to focus his attention entirely on Benazir Bhutto, members of her family, and her close political associates. A number of developments since Sharif's accession to office seem to vindicate the critics of these moves.

The first big break for the new government came in September 1997, when it was announced that the government of Switzerland had agreed to freeze a number of accounts maintained in several Swiss banks by Benazir Bhutto; Asif Ali Ziradri, her husband; and Nusrat Bhutto, Benazir's mother.[3] It was also revealed that the Bhutto family was apparently associated with five offshore companies managed by a Swiss lawyer. The Pakistani press reported that documentation linking the Bhuttos to these accounts and offshore companies was provided by Jens Schlegelmilch, a Swiss lawyer and a long-term associate of the Bhutto family.[4] The government of Pakistan also moved British authorities to take actions similar to those taken by the Swiss officials against assets owned by the Bhuttos.[5] In late October, London sent a team of investigators to Islamabad to determine the seriousness of the case built by the Pakistanis before they could authorize the actions being requested by the Sharif administration. In a number of statements given to the press, both inside the country and outside, Benazir Bhutto admitted the existence of these accounts but vehemently denied that the amounts deposited in them were obtained illegally. She said that she did not have to resort to corruption to amass wealth, since she belonged to a wealthy family.[6] The admission that she had maintained accounts in foreign banks could result in her removal from the National Assembly because under the electoral law promulgated by the caretaker administration, all candidates who failed to make a full disclosure of their assets could lose their seats in the legislature. In the summer of 1998, a Swiss court indicted the Bhuttos, both Benazir and her husband, Asif Ali Zardari, on charges of money laundering and referred the case back to Pakistan for trial. And thus the matter stands as this chapter is being written.

The economic team in the caretaker administration that came to office following the dismissal of Prime Minister Benazir Bhutto began the difficult task of assessing the damage done to the economy as a result of corruption and mismanagement since the early 1990s. The economic team was headed by Shahid Javed Burki. He and cabinet colleague Hafiz Pasha developed a methodology for calculating the cost of poor governance and corruption incurred by the country during the three years the second Bhutto administration held office. They estimated the cost to the country at 20 to 25 percent of its 1996–1997 gross domestic product. Translated into an absolute amount, this was equivalent to some $15 billion.

The Burki-Pasha methodology for estimating the economic cost of corruption and bad governance was a simple one. It looked at the damage done to the more important sectors of the economy during Bhutto's tenure in office. The greatest amount of damage was done to financial institutions—commercial and investment banks owned and operated by the government, public sector insurance agencies, and investment institutions such as the National Investment Trust (NIT) and Investment Corporation of Pakistan (ICP). The two ministers had gathered a great deal of information on the value of nonperforming loans in the portfolio of public sector commercial banks, most of them the result of pressure on bank management to lend to friends of the regime. Most of the loans had been provided in the absence of suitable collateral. Burki and Pasha estimated that it would cost the government 10 to 15 percent of the 1996–1997 gross domestic product to deal with the banking crisis. They recognized that not all of the damage done to the banks occurred during the second Bhutto administration and that a large number of nonperforming banking assets had been accumulated over a long period of time. However, information collected by the two cabinet ministers indicated that the pace of this process had gathered considerable steam during the 1993–1996 period.

The National Investment Trust presented insight into the Bhutto administration's use of state-controlled financial institutions to benefit its friends and supporters. The institution was set up in the 1960s with two objectives in the mind of the government of President Ayub Khan: to provide a source of long-term finance for private industry and to broaden the base of industrial asset ownership. For two decades, the NIT was a well-run institution. It sold units to the public, took positions in new industrial ventures, and distributed respectable dividends to hundreds of thousands of shareholders. Most of the shareholders were small savers who were attracted to the institution by the security it offered and the returns it provided. However, during the Bhutto period, NIT was forced to lend for projects that were clearly not viable; the sole purpose of some of these projects was to siphon resources from such public sector institutions as NIT and ICP (Investment Corporation of Pakistan) and then liquidate. An oil refinery in Karachi and a cement plant in Chakwal, Punjab, were two examples of unworthy projects funded by the NIT at the insistence of the prime minister's secretariat. Both declared bankruptcy soon after receiving funds from the NIT.

By the summer of 1995, it was clear that the financial setback incurred by NIT from such transactions meant that its shareholders could not redeem their holdings without incurring major losses. This the government was not prepared to countenance, since it would have alienated a very large number of investors in NIT if it allowed the institution's shares to fall to their true value. Accordingly, in September 1995 the government took the decision of guaranteeing the redemption price of an NIT unit at Rs 13.8, some 25 to 30 percent more than the institution's net value. By issuing this guarantee, the government transferred the NIT losses to its books. When President Farooq Leghari moved against the government of Benazir Bhutto, the man who had presided over NIT during the Bhutto period fled the country, putting himself beyond the arm of the Ehtesab institutions that were to be set up by the caretaker government. The Burki-Pasha estimate of corruption included the amount of losses transferred to the national budget by the issuance of the guarantee in September 1995 as an item in the cost to the economy of corruption and poor governance.

The Burki-Pasha estimate also included the losses incurred by dozens of public sector corporations as a result of corruption and mismanagement in the 1990s. It looked carefully at institutions such as Pakistan International Airlines, Sui Southern Gas, Sui Northern Gas, Pakistan State Oil, Pakistan Steel, Heavy Mechanical Complex, the Water and Power Development Authority, and Karachi Electric Supply Cooperation. All public corporations had incurred heavy losses partly because of a large increase in the number of people employed by them, partly because of dozens of financially nonviable projects undertaken by them, and partly because of the large amounts that had leaked from the procurements made to execute projects. Increased employment expenditure, expenditure of vast amounts of money on unnecessary projects, and leakage from procurement were all the result of corruption at the very highest level of administration.

The Burki-Pasha estimate took other government actions into account as well in arriving at the estimate. For example, in 1994, the Bhutto government engaged two foreign firms–SGS and Cotecna of Switzerland–to undertake preshipment inspections of some categories of goods imported into the country. When the caretakers looked into the performance of the companies, they saw that, despite hundreds of millions of dollars paid to them, they had provided little benefit to the country in terms of an increase in customs receipts. The caretaker administration then canceled the contract under which the companies had been engaged by the Bhutto government. In September 1997, the government of Prime Minister Nawaz Sharif charged that the Swiss companies had paid a hefty commission to the Bhutto family in return for the contract awarded to them.[7]

Identifying all these losses and adding them together provided an estimate of the damage caused to the economy. The public discussion of corruption and Burki's public use of the Burki-Pasha estimate repeatedly drew two questions. How could a theft of such a magnitude occur? What happened to the amounts stolen and could they be recovered? The second question, for obvious reasons, is beyond the scope of this work.

The first question—how could such a situation develop in Pakistan when its chief executive could allegedly pilfer such a large amount?—needs a detailed answer to which this book can provide only a small contribution. A detailed answer to this question should explore a number of areas. It should include the culture of the Pakistani society that allowed its leaders to govern badly and to plunder state finances for such a long time. For want of a better term, the culture can be referred to as "feudal-tribal" in which relations between people are governed by custom rather than a system of codified rules and laws. The explanation should also include a number of developments occurring during Pakistan's fifty-year history that made it possible for those who wielded power to use it for their own benefit. Increasingly, several leadership groups in Pakistan were able to let personal greed override the public good and the citizens' welfare. Finally, the analysis must also deal with the set of circumstances that brought the issue of governance and corruption to center stage and led to the dismissal of the government of Benazir Bhutto, resulting in the massive defeat of the party in power in the elections held three months after its dismissal and in the adoption of a number of measures that may lead to the development of a legal framework within which this issue can be handled. At this point in the discussion, however, it is pertinent to deal with some general points pertaining to governance, corruption, and development.

Poor Governance, Corruption, and Its Impact on Development

Problems with governance are a major cause of corruption. Well-governed societies are able to protect their people from the ravages of corruption. Likewise, poorly governed people are more likely to encounter corruption. Causality, therefore, runs from governance to corruption rather than the other way around. Corruption has a negative impact on development. There is little substance to the popular belief that underdeveloped or developing societies are likely to have a greater incidence of corruption than those that are more developed. According to this interpretation, underdevelopment breeds corruption. It is legitimate to argue, however, that causality runs from corruption to underdevelopment rather than from underdevelopment to corruption. It should also be recognized that the cost of corruption falls very heavily on the poor. They have to pay the price for poor governance and official corruption, which is far more than their share in national product. Although the rich and the-well-to do can build defenses against poor governance, the poor do not have the resources to escape its consequences.

A definition of governance and corruption is useful at this point. The World Bank, in work done recently on these two issues, used a general definition of governance as the "exercise of authority, control, management, power of government."[8] The Bank emphasized that good governance is central to creating and sustaining an environment that fosters strong and equitable development, and is an essential complement to sound economic policies. Governments play a critical role in the provision of public goods. They establish the rules that make markets work efficiently and, more problematically, they correct for market failure. In order to play this role, they need revenues, and agents to collect revenues and produce the public goods. This in turn requires systems of accountability, adequate and reliable information, and efficiency in resource management and the delivery of public services.

The Pakistani state failed in all the areas associated with good governance, sometimes spectacularly. Successive governments failed to establish rules that make markets work efficiently. To this day the markets remain unclear as to their relationship with the government. In the years after the birth of Pakistan, the state chose to play a largely supportive role, leaving the generation and allocation of resources to the markets. Initially the Pakistani state was much too weak to interfere with the working of the markets. However, as the state gathered strength under the martial law administration of General Ayub Khan, it also became more intrusive. Policies such as a multiple exchange rate system introduced under the "bonus voucher scheme" and an import licensing mechanism that strictly controlled the establishment of new industries were adopted by the military government. These policies misallocated resources generally in favor of import substitution industries. At the same time a number of public sector corporations were created with the objective of dealing with perceived market failure. The state's intrusion into the markets took a giant step under the nationalization policies of the government of Prime Minister Zulfikar Ali Bhutto, adopted between 1972 and 1976. The Bhutto administration nationalized large-scale industries, private commercial banks, and private insurance companies. Public sector corporations were set up to manage the nationalized industries. A new financial institution—the National Finance Development Corporation—was established to channel resources into the public sector industrial corporations. The government also brought trade in such vital commodities as cotton, rice, and wheat under its control. Once again, new public sector corporations were given the task of managing nationalized commerce. Within two years, Zulfikar Ali Bhutto had put the state on the "commanding heights" of the economy. By the time he left office, the state's share in nonagricultural gross domestic product had been more than doubled from 24 percent to 51 percent. The ground was thus laid for the massive corruption of government that became a pronounced feature of the Pakistani economy in the early and middle 1990s.

The Pakistani state has also failed to generate an adequate amount of public resources to provide such public goods as primary education, basic health care, and internal security for its citizens. A recently published report offers a severe indictment of the state's performance in delivering basic services to the people:

> Pakistan's social and human indicators make dismal reading. Two thirds of its total adult population and 77 per cent of adult women are illiterate. Combined school enrollment is only 37 per cent. Basic health facilities are available to only half the population. The maternal mortality rate is very high at 340 per 100,000 [of live births]. One-fourth of newborn babies are under-weight and malnourished. Both the coverage and quality of basic services are extremely poor. Even these limited social services are coming under increasing strain every year because of a high population growth rate of around 3 per cent a year. Thus a low human development and a high population growth rate are locked together in a fatal unending embrace.[9]

The proportion of gross domestic product collected by the government as tax—not much more than 13 percent—is much lower than the potential because of the enormous leakage that occurs in the tax collection system. Tax administration, never very efficient or clean in the history of the country, has been increasingly corrupted during the years. According to one estimate the system leakage was of the order of 3 percent of the gross domestic product, twice the level ten years earlier.[10]

Finally, the systems to ensure accountability and provide reliable information on various aspects of governance became increasingly dysfunctional over time. The legislative system was either not allowed to develop or remained under the control of vested interests that did not have any stake in building its capacity to oversee the working of the executive. The judicial system became, for the most part, the handmaiden of the executive. Within the executive branch, general accounting and controls never acquired a sense of authority. In sum, poor governance has marked much of Pakistan's history. This in turn contributed to a massive and palpable increase in the incidence of corruption.

"The term corruption covers a broad range of human actions" according to a World Bank document issued in September 1997,[11] shortly before the annual meeting of the Bank and the International Monetary Fund held at Hong Kong. The Bank had begun to take a high-profile stance on this issue following the annual meeting speech given by James Wolfensohn, the Bank's president, in 1996. The document issued a year later sought to spell out the role the Bank could play in addressing the subject of corruption among its member countries. To help determine the effects of corruption on an economy or a political system, the Bank document suggested that "it helps to unbundle the term by identifying specific types of activities or transactions that might fall within it. In considering its strategy the Bank sought a usable definition of corruption and then developed a tax-

onomy of the different forms corruption could take consistent with that definition. We settled a straight forward definition—*the abuse of public office for private
gain.*"12

In regard to the relationship between corruption and economic development
(using the World Bank's broad definition of corrupt behavior), economists long
took a benign few of corruption. Some argued that corruption can increase economic efficiency. "Consider, for example, the allocation of import licenses. If officials were to sell these to the highest bidder, it is argued the outcome would be
more efficient than if they were merely given away, because that bidder would be
the only one who values imports most highly."13 That may be the case—as probably was the case during the Ayub Khan period in Pakistan—when corruption had
not become all-pervasive. There was anecdotal evidence during the Ayub period
that the recipients of import and industrial licenses either were close friends of
the regime or had greased the palms of people with the authority to grant them.
Nonetheless, most of the licensees made noticeable contributions to the rapid
modernization and industrialization of Pakistan during the Ayub Khan period. It
is now recognized that distinguishing between sporadic (as was the case under
Ayub Khan) and pervasive (as was the case in most of the 1990s) corruption is
imperative. Although the former may, under some circumstances, be beneficial,
the latter almost always is extremely destructive. Pervasive corruption can introduce serious distortions into the economy that bring more harm than good. Some
of these have been brought to light by recent economic work on the phenomenon
of corruption.14

Among the ill effects of corruption analysts underscore four in particular. First,
corrupt politicians and bureaucrats create opportunities for enrichment by resist-
ing liberalization, multiplying controls, following opaque procedures, and intro-
ducing unnecessary delays. This happened in Pakistan during the eleven years of
Zia ul-Haq's military rule. Zia and his associates wished to dismantle the elaborate structure of public sector management of the economy during the period of
Zulfikar Ali Bhutto (1971–1977), but by then strong vested interests had developed within the bureaucracy that fought against privatization of publicly held assets and liberalization of government controls on the economy.

Second, corruption unavoidably spills over into areas in which regulations
ought to be enforced, such as tax collection and control over environmental
degradation. Pakistan's tax collection system suffers from extreme corruption; it
suits those who pay taxes and those who collect them to work with one another
rather than for the benefit of the state. Corruption is the reason why the tax-to-
GDP ratio has remained so low—13.6 percent in 1995–1996—despite the high
incidence of taxes. Even a 50 percent reduction in the leakage that occurs through
corruption and mismanagement would increase the tax-to-GDP ratio to over 15
percent and pay for a significant improvement in the level of education provided
to the population. Environmental protection was targeted by corrupt officials
during the second Benazir Bhutto administration as a source of personal gain. It

is interesting that Asif Zardari, the prime minister's husband, chose the portfolio of environment in her administration before going on to become the minister in charge of investment. Control over environmental regulation seems to have provided him the opportunity to collect rents.

Third, markets for under-the-table transactions are, by definition, never open and transparent. Those who benefit from them are the least scrupulous and best connected, not the most efficient. There is a long tradition of this type of corruption in South Asia, including Pakistan. It is normally described as "petty corruption" and has involved such government functionaries as *patwaris* (clerks in the land administration system responsible for maintaining land records), *thanadars* (officials in charge of local police offices), and *chaprasis* (peons) who function as gatekeepers in the offices of tens of thousands of bureaucrats who interact with the public. These petty officials have always exacted a small price for serving the people; in fact, the very small amount of compensation received by them was predicated on the belief that such exactions were legitimate. However, when this form of corruption becomes endemic—when it begins to involve the people who read the meters maintained by public utility companies, teachers in schools and colleges, nurses in hospitals, clerks in post offices—as happened in Pakistan in the 1990s—the cost to the public becomes unbearable. It was the reaction to this type of corruption that brought down the government of Benazir Bhutto in November 1996 and led to her party's decisive defeat in the elections of February 1997. People seem to have been less concerned with the alleged exaction of large commissions on government procurement by senior officials of the government.

Fourth, a corrupt government disillusions the people and seriously undermines the legitimacy of government itself. This clearly happened during the second administration of Benazir Bhutto, as people began to question not only her legitimacy but the legitimacy of the system that had put her in power. Had she not been dismissed by President Farooq Leghari, there is good reason to believe that the people would have begun to question the viability of democracy in Pakistan.

Given the adverse consequences of corruption, why is it that the people of Pakistan tolerated its prevalence for such a long time but then suddenly reacted against it with unanticipated and unprecedented vehemence? An answer to this question is attempted in the following section.

Culture and the Culture of Corruption

The areas that now constitute Pakistan included two dominating social forces at the time of independence. Large landlords held sway over Punjab and Sindh, and tribal chiefs governed over much of Balochistan and the Northwest Frontier. As long as the dominant social groups paid taxes and did not disturb the peace, the British administration was content to let them manage their domains according to custom. If an effort was made to impose the rule of law, it was confined to the large cities in which the British resided or new social groups that had emerged as a result of British rule had gained some prominence. However, much of the countryside was left to be governed by *riwaj,* or custom and tradition. The landlord or the tribal chief could rule almost at will; according to long-established tradition, his only obligation was to create an environment that allowed his people to maintain themselves at a very basic level of existence so that they did not disturb the public peace. Those who worked on the landlord's fields were entitled to a share of the crop they helped produce. The share was determined by custom and could not be negotiated. Nonagricultural workers were also required to provide all manner of services to the landlord and the members of his family in return for payment in kind, the amount of which was also established by tradition. These arrangements could not be questioned; no recourse was available to the people in case they thought they had been wronged. There was no system of law, written or otherwise, that enforced *riwaj;* it was peer pressure that kept it in place.

The British successfully exploited this system for their purpose. They also brought another aspect of the culture of the northwestern areas of India—the areas that were to be partitioned from the rest of their domain to establish Pakistan. According to this, the ruler (the Mughul court from 1526 to the late 1700s and the Sikh rulers of Punjab after that) made large grants of land or provided jobs in the administration to subjects who had rendered exceptional service. The land grants were called *jagirs.* The British, having established their claim to vast areas that were not specifically owned by the landed community, used the "crown land" to endow *jagirs.* The *jagirdars,* as the recipients of these land grants came to be known, were to constitute an important part of the landed aristocracy that dominated Pakistani society over much of the first fifty years of the country's history. The British also used the opportunity provided by the expansion of the state to give jobs to those they wished to reward.

The grant of *jagirs* and the provision of a large number of jobs in government departments and agencies were not the only means the British used to develop a citizenry loyal to their rule. They also used extensive public works to create a class of people that would be beholden to them. This approach was used with great effect in the areas that now constitute Pakistan. The British brought large-scale irrigation to the fertile but thirsty lands of Punjab and Sindh. Water tapped from the Indus River system was deployed to bring millions of acres of virgin land under cultivation. The land that benefited from irrigation was either granted to the large landlords who were already present in these areas or was settled by people who were brought in from the more crowded areas of the eastern part of Punjab, the parts that now make up the Indian state of that name. These beneficiaries came to be among the most ardent, vocal, and reliable supporters of the British domain in India. They also provided the manpower for the large public sector assembled by the British in northwest India and also recruits to the British-Indian armed forces. The coalition of interests represented by the civil and military bureaucracies on the one hand and the landlord community on the other was fashioned during the first half of this century as the British consolidated their rule over the areas that constitute modern-day Pakistan. The British state exercised power by virtue of its close association with the landed interests. The landed interests in turn used custom and tradition—*riwaj*—rather than the rule of law to maintain their hold over common people.

Pakistan's founding fathers sought to establish a modern state in this cultural environment. That they succeeded initially was entirely the result of a fortuitous development—the arrival of 8 million refugees from India. The newcomers, whether they settled in the cities or went to live in the countryside, brought an entirely different culture with them. Refugees from India were generally more literate, more skilled, and more used to operating in an environment that was sanctioned by law than the indigenous people of the areas that became Pakistan. The landed community was too shell-shocked by the rapidly unfolding political events that led to the creation of Pakistan to resist the settlement of the refugees in the countryside. They were also unable to protect their political interests against encroachment by the leaders of the refugee community. The quick redrawing of the political map after the emergence of Pakistan was at the expense of the social groups that had dominated the provinces that now made up Pakistan. This sudden social transformation of Pakistan made it possible for the country to modernize politically and economically.

This situation (discussed in Chapter 2) could not last for long and it did not. It was inevitable that Pakistan's political and social systems would be *indigenized* and that the social groups, eclipsed by the trauma of the partition of British India and the creation of a Muslim state in the northwestern parts of the country, would reassert their authority.[15] It took them time to manage their reappearance, but halfway through the Ayub Khan period the landed community and the tribal *sirdars* returned in great force, and the old culture returned with them. In fact, it returned with a vengeance. The legal and judicial systems were compromised and the political elite began to exercise its authority without paying much attention to the legitimacy of the actions taken. In other words, the return of the old culture deteriorated the quality of governance. This brought corruption into the country. President Ayub Khan's willingness to let his sons take advantage of the economic power wielded by the state became a symbol of the perceived deterioration that had occurred in the quality of governance and the corruption of those in positions of power. The citizens reacted with disgust to these developments; the political movement against Ayub Khan succeeded in part because the people were not yet prepared to forgive those who had caused a rapid erosion in the quality of governance.

However, Ayub Khan's eclipse and the ascent of Zulfikar Ali Bhutto did not bring corruption to an end. If anything, traditional culture reasserted itself much more profoundly under Zulfikar Ali Bhutto. The quality of governance deteriorated under Pakistan's first elected prime minister and the incidence of corruption increased. Among the "reforms" introduced by Bhutto was the abolition of the Civil Service of Pakistan (CSP), the successor to the powerful and elitist Indian Civil Service (ICS) the British had used so effectively to maintain their hold over India. The ICS/CSP tradition put great store on paternalism—the *mai-bap* approach to dealing with people—in handling the affairs of government. Although this approach allowed the civil bureaucracy considerable latitude in exercising power, the use of authority was always constrained by the explicitly proclaimed or implicitly understood "rules of the game."[16] By eliminating the CSP, Bhutto removed an important check on politicians' use of discretion. This significant change in the country's institutional structure was accompanied by the transformation of the economy through a series of nationalizations. All this provided opportunities for the old establishment to practice the economics of *riwaj* on a grand and unprecedented scale. However, the widespread corruption of the economic system did not go unnoticed by the people. Like his predecessor, Bhutto also fell victim to a mass agitation launched against him by the opposition.

Zulfikar Ali Bhutto's successor, General Zia ul-Haq, could have turned the clock back to the early part of the Ayub period. He was not beholden to the landed community, nor did he need its support to keep himself in power. He could have bought political security for himself by cultivating modern elements in the country, mostly in the country's rapidly expanding towns and cities. These groups were hungry for the political participation that the landlord-dominated political system did not allow. Instead, Zia chose to govern much as the British had ruled. He used the assets available to the state to cultivate and retain support. Zia's eleven years in power were also marked by a further destruction of institutions (a process that Zulfikar Ali Bhutto began by abolishing the CSP) and by open resort to the use of personal power. It was during this period that the domination of the judiciary by the executive was completed. It took the superior judiciary ten years to recover the independence it lost during the Zia period.

There is a great deal the leaders of Pakistan can learn from an even casual study of their history. Three lessons stand out. First, regimes in Pakistan have fallen because of the public's perception about deteriorating governance and increasing corruption. It is no exaggeration to suggest that the people's reaction to pervasive corruption contributed significantly to the demise of several administrations in the past. In March 1969, Ayub Khan succumbed to a political agitation that demanded his ouster and the restoration of democracy. In July 1977, Zulfikar Ali Bhutto was removed from power by the military, largely in response to another political agitation that wanted the government to be subject to the will of the electorate. The people were not convinced that Bhutto's party, its claims notwithstanding, had won a majority in the national elections held in February 1970. In August 1990 President Ghulam Ishaq Khan dismissed Prime Minister Benazir Bhutto on charges of corruption. Three years later, in April 1993, he used the same power to send home the administration of Prime Minister Nawaz Sharif for the same reason. In November 1996, for the third time in six years, presidential power was deployed to remove a prime minister from office on charges of corruption. This time the action was taken by President Farooq Ahmad Khan Leghari against his erstwhile political associate, Benazir Bhutto.

Second, the people of Pakistan have demonstrated time and again that they are prepared to move against regimes that cross some vaguely defined threshold with respect to poor governance and corruption. All these actions and the political turbulence caused by them raise an important question: Given the poor performance of the government in recent years in terms of its ability to provide basic services to the citizens and the evident increase in corruption on the part of the functionaries of the state, why is it that people acquiesce for a long time to this kind of behavior but reject it thoroughly once some limits are crossed? Why, until recently, did they not seek protection from bad government and corruption? A way to solve the puzzle of voter tolerance toward underachieving state and ever increasing corruption is to assume that governments are made up of people who most of the time are guided by considerations of self-interest. In the absence of an institutional base that could protect people while providing them the security they expected from the state, most people took comfort from working within a traditional cultural environment. Transactions in this environment took the form of favors granted by those in power in return for gifts and favors. In such a situation, corruption became the norm. Although this method of governance was acceptable to the majority of the population, it was resented by the modernizing forces that gained some power as the economy developed. There was a reaction whenever the pendulum swung too far toward *riwaj* and norms of traditional culture. The reactions took place in 1969 (against Ayub Khan), in 1977 (against Zulfikar Ali Bhutto), in 1990 (against Benazir Bhutto), in 1993 (against Nawaz Sharif), and in 1996 (once again against Benazir Bhutto). It is too early to tell whether the decisive victory of Nawaz Sharif in the elections of 1997 has moved the pendulum away from the traditional culture of governance. It is also too early to tell whether the resignation of President Farooq Leghari on December 2, 1997, and the removal of Chief Justice Sajjad Ali Shah from office a few days later, and the resignation of General Jehangir Karamat, army chief of staff in October 1998, have once again produced a political situation so familiar in Pakistan—rule by one man, unconstrained by laws and rules of good governance. The departure of the president and the chief justice followed a long drawn out conflict between them and the prime minister. The departure of the army chief of staff followed his public criticism of the performance of the Sharif government. The seeming consolidation of power in the hands of one individual—this time Prime Minister Mian Nawaz Sharif—has already led some observers to conclude that "fascist politics" have returned to Pakistan.[17]

Third, even when leaders were made aware of the terrible consequences of bad governance and pervasive corruption and finally took steps to improve the situation, they responded with ad hoc measures that did not address the basic causes underlying these phenomena. The history of ad hoc measures runs way back into Pakistan's history. In the first decade following independence, legislation such as the Public and Representative Offices Disqualification Act of 1949 (PRODA) and the Elective Bodies Disqualification Order of 1959 (EBDO) were introduced. The second piece of legislation briefly introduced a new verb in Pakistani-English—those who were dealt with under its provisions were described as having been *eb-doed*—the overall consequence of these moves was, at best, minimal. Two later military rulers dismissed a large number of civil servants on the basis of indifferent performance or corruption. Ayub Khan removed 303 bureaucrats in 1962; Yahya Khan, his successor, followed with an even larger number in 1971. Once again, these measures only produced shock waves that had no lasting effect. The promulgation of the Ehtesab Ordinance by the caretaker government in 1996 and its variant by the administration of Prime Minister Nawaz Sharif fall into the same category. Short-lived campaigns and ad hoc measures of the type described above do not produce lasting impact. As emphasized in some of the recent literature on corruption—particularly in reference to intertemporal collective reputation model—public trust takes a long time to establish.[18]

A sustained and comprehensive program aimed at improving the quality of governance must have at least three components—macroeconomic policies that reduce the opportunities for rent seeking, a sharp reduction in the presence of the state in the economy, and the construction of a robust institutional base. Pakistan has to demonstrate credible performance in all three areas. The fact that it has failed to implement several IMF programs in the last several years indicates a lack of resolve to restore macro-economic balance on the part of the several administrations that were in office. The country's record of moving publicly controlled assets into private hands has been equally slow. It is, however, the last part that has proved to be the most difficult—establishing institutions whose functioning goes against the grain of established culture.

As discussed above, an important way of dealing with issues of poor governance and pervasive corruption is to change the culture that sanctions and supports these phenomena. To change the culture, the leaders must be prepared to reconstruct the institutions that were destroyed by successive governments in the country and to establish new ones needed by a modernizing economy. Institutional engineering needed to rectify the present situation must cover a wide front. It must deal with the reform of the civil service and the judicial system, institutionalize various kinds of accountability systems, strengthen electoral laws and put limits on campaign contributions, establish citizen organizations that can oversee the performance of public officeholders, and promote the independence of the press. In other words, the reform agenda in regard to governance and corruption is large and complicated. It can be implemented only if there is the political will to introduce lasting structural changes that would hurt (at least over the short term) a number of deeply entrenched vested interests. If a deep crisis provokes change, then the present appears to be the right moment in Pakistan's history to reform a system that has become progressively decayed and dysfunctional. Whether the government of Prime Minister Nawaz Sharif that took office in February 1997 is equal to this difficult task is hard to predict at the time of this writing (October 1998). Its record is mixed. Although it spent a great deal of time pursuing acts of corruption allegedly committed by the administration of Prime Minister Benazir Bhutto, it showed little interest in developing institutions that could be trusted to be evenhanded.

Conclusion

Widespread and pervasive corruption and poor-quality governance had become major issues by the time Pakistan celebrated its fiftieth birthday. The preceding analysis points to a number of conclusions about Pakistan's experience in these areas and what Pakistani rulers need to do to regain the confidence of those they govern. Although some serious efforts were made to structure a new system of accountability, the manner in which they were deployed created the impression of an intent to hurt opponents, not to build effective institutions. In this context it is appropriate to highlight eight conclusions.

First, corruption attracts enough public attention in developing countries to bring down governments. This has certainly happened in Pakistan where the fall of at least five administrations in the last thirty years could be attributed to the public's unhappiness with issues pertaining to governance and corruption. The military coups d'état against President Ayub Khan in March 1969 and against Prime Minister Zulfikar Ali Bhutto in July 1977 were provoked in part by a widespread perception of poor governance. Corruption was explicitly cited as the reason for the dismissal of the governments headed by Prime Ministers Benazir Bhutto (August 1990), Nawaz Sharif (April 1993), and Benazir Bhutto (November 1996).

Second, even though governments have been brought down by a strong perception of corruption, a government's fall did not necessarily bring improvement to the situation. Although time series on the incidence of corruption or perception about corruption are not available, few would argue that corruption in Pakistan reached a new peak in 1996. This perception was highlighted by the index published in the summer of 1996 by the Berlin-based organization Transparency International ranking Pakistan as the second most corrupt country in the world. The TI index for 1997, released along with its annual report in the summer of that year, suggests some improvement in the case of Pakistan. The country was now viewed as the fifth most corrupt in the world. This slight improvement in the perception of the people contacted by TI may have resulted from the attention devoted to corruption since the publication of the TI report in the summer of 1996.

Third, there is a high level of tolerance in the country for corruption. This is because of well-established cultural norms in which transactions between individuals are governed by mostly custom and tradition—*riwaj*—rather than by rules and regulations. These norms have been in place for a long time; in fact, they were strengthened by the actions of a series of administrations that have governed Pakistan—the grant of industrial licenses by the government of Ayub Khan; the distribution of route permits to road transporters by the West Pakistan administration of Governor Nawab of Kalabagh; the grant of urban land plots, in particular in Islamabad, by President Zia ul-Haq; and the use of public sector banks to provide loans to the friends of the regime by all administrations since the country achieved independence. All are examples of this kind of behavior.

Fourth, even though the public has displayed a great deal of tolerance for corruption and poor governance, they appear to identify a threshold that those who govern and rule must not cross. The threshold is, of course, not rigorously defined. But when it was crossed, governments were changed, either by military action or by presidential decree. The governments that took office, replacing those disgraced by charges of corruption, felt obliged to take ameliorative action. The actions taken were generally of an ad hoc character. No effort was ever made to introduce structural changes into the culture that supported corrupt behavior in the first place. The most recent examples of this approach are the promulgation of the Ehtesab Ordinance of the caretaker administration that held office from November 1996 to February 1997 and the establishment of the Ehtesab cell in the prime minister's secretariat by Mian Nawaz Sharif.

Fifth, ad hoc measures may produce results to satisfy public demand for accountability over the short term, but they do not change the culture that supports poor governance and a high incidence of corruption. The laws put into effect in the 1940s and 1950s—the Public and Representative Offices Disqualification Act (PRODA) and the Elective Bodies Disqualification Order (EBDO)—had little lasting effect. The large-scale dismissal of senior government officials by Presidents Ayub Khan and Yahya Khan did not produce a lasting effect and establish a clean administration. Without a deep structural change in the makeup of the society and its governing culture, the Ehtesab Ordinance of 1996 and the 1997 act of the same name may suffer the same fate.

Sixth, the stage may now have been set in Pakistan for finally addressing the problem of corruption. There are a number of reasons for this optimism. Among the more important are the following five. First, crises usually provide good opportunities for undertaking deep structural reforms. The well-known Indian reform effort began in 1991 when India was very close to bankruptcy. Some of the successful reform efforts undertaken in the countries of Latin America owed their origin to the severe debt crisis of the early 1980s. Today, Pakistan is faced with a serious economic and political crisis. The country's leaders could take advantage of this situation and institute long overdue structural reforms. Second, there is now a consensus in the country that the policies consistent with the "Washington consensus"—economic liberalization, opening to the outside world, creating a level playing field for all economic actors, reducing the state's ownership of economic assets—should also be adopted in Pakistan. Some of these approaches are being followed already. Deeper structural reforms can be built on them. Third, the role of the state as the owner of economic assets is being reviewed. There is now consensus in the country that the state must be brought down from the commanding heights of the economy it began to occupy starting with the nationalization undertaken by the government of Zulfikar Ali Bhutto. Fourth the elections of February 1977 have resulted in a palpable shift in the political landscape. The center of gravity seems to have moved away from the landed aristocracy and toward socioeconomic groups that draw their support from the urban areas, in particular the rapidly expanding cities. Fifth, the bureaucracy's stranglehold on the economy has been broken. Thanks in part to the changes introduced by Zulfikar Ali Bhutto, Pakistan is much less bureaucratic than, say, India. Diminution in the political authority of the landed classes and a sharp decline in the power wielded by the bureaucracy has finally loosened the grip of the landed-bureaucratic combine that has dominated the Pakistani culture for so long.

Seventh, it appeared that a number of political developments in 1997 had created conditions for evolving a more balanced system of governance in which the power of the executive was to be restrained by the judiciary. The removal of Chief Justice Sajjad Ali Shah by his fellow judges did not necessarily mean that the judicial system would become subject to executive control. It could be argued that the removal of the chief justice was an indication of the recognition by the higher judiciary that it must also be governed by rule of law and that judicial activism was not a license for abandoning all constraints. At the same time, those who wield executive authority may begin to recognize that it is in their interest to have in place some form of judicial overview of their actions. Such an overview would provide a way for those in power to keep the demands of their constituents in check. Unreasonable demands need not be met, on the grounds that they would invite judicial rebuke (if not punishment). This was more or less the explanation given by Prime Minister Nawaz Sharif when he introduced the fifteenth amendment to the constitution, which sought to put all exercise of authority in the hands of Allah with the executive only interpreting his will. In fact, in terms of erecting institutional checks on individual actions, this amendment may have exactly the opposite consequence by further strengthening the executive branch of the government.

Eighth, and finally, all these shifts in the structure of political power may have produced a more receptive ground for the introduction of a "second generation of reforms"—reforms that go far beyond those that fall under the category of the "Washington consensus."[19] These reforms cover a wide field. They include judicial reforms and reforms of the legal system. They must also include the reform of the civil service so that talent is once again attracted to public service. Included in these reforms is the establishment of institutions for ensuring accountability. The process begun with the promulgation of the Ehtesab Ordinance must be continued and deepened so that people develop a sense of confidence in a set of rules supported by a cluster of institutions that hold all public functionaries responsible for the exercise of power. Second-generation reforms also cover the straightening and establishment of regulatory institutions to promote competition, provide protection to consumers, and ensure prudent behavior on the part of the financial institutions to whom the people entrust their savings. This phase of the reform effort should also cover economic relations between the national and the subnational governments. The national finance award given by the caretaker government that held office in the fall and winter of 1996–1997 laid a foundation for the conduct of these relations on the basis of prudence and mutual interest. Whether this can be extended to other areas is a question that only time will answer.

6

FOREIGN RELATIONS: SEARCHING FOR A NEW IDENTITY

With one exception, Pakistan's foreign policy has been guided by a simple motive: to preserve its national integrity. The only exception occurred during the mid-1970s, when Prime Minister Zulfikar Ali Bhutto attempted with some success to play a prominent role in Third World and north-south politics. At that time, the Pakistan leadership, by moving into the front rank of the nonaligned movement, sought to lift the country above regional politics—even above the Muslim politics of the Middle East. With this one exception, Pakistan has conducted its foreign affairs in such a way as to neutralize what its leaders regard as the threat to its territorial integrity posed by its several neighbors.

The perception of this threat goes back to the Hindu-Muslim politics of the 1930s and 1940s. Chapter 1 noted the process by which the widening chasm between the Hindus and Muslims of British India led to the creation of Pakistan—a state founded essentially through the efforts of one part of the Indian Muslim community to provide a homeland for all the Muslims of British India. Chapters 2, 3, and 4 detailed the circumstances of Pakistan's birth and how they influenced its political, economic, and social development. This chapter explores the means by which the same set of circumstances shaped Pakistan's relations with other countries.

Initial Foreign Policy Tasks

Mohammad Ali Jinnah and his immediate successors saw the world into which they had brought Pakistan as inimically hostile. A number of prominent Indian leaders considered partition to be temporary; they were convinced that Pakistan, like the prodigal son, would return to the fold of Mother India. Clement Attlee's government in Britain had reluctantly acquiesced to the creation of Pakistan; as Attlee pointed out, "I earnestly hope that this severance may not endure, that the two new dominions we now propose to set up may come together again to form one great member of the Commonwealth."[1] This pronouncement did not, of course, reassure the Muslim leadership. Lord Louis Mountbatten, His Majesty's last viceroy in British India, was also openly hostile to Jinnah and his cause. The United States had supported independence for India but knew little about Pakistan and the reasons for which it had been created. The Indian leaders—particularly Mohandas K. Gandhi and Jawaharlal Nehru—were well-known in the United States, whereas Jinnah was a totally unfamiliar figure. The Soviet Union had long favored the anticolonial approach of Gandhi and his followers while covertly assisting the Indian Communist party in its efforts to dislodge the British. The religious foundations of the state of Pakistan could not have brought it into a close association with the Soviet Union, given the fact that the Soviet Union's own Muslim republics in Central Asia were at times openly resentful of Moscow's rule over them. Pakistan's religious foundation, however, could have been expected to win it friends among the Muslim nations. But in 1947, the year of Pakistan's birth, Islamic resurgence was still three decades into the future. Egypt, Turkey, and Indonesia all had their own problems. Afghanistan, the Muslim country with a long border with Pakistan, coveted some of its territory. Afghanistan refused to accept Pakistan as the successor to the British *raj* in Northwest India and was the only nation to vote against the admission of this new country to the United Nations. Jinnah and his colleagues looked around but did not find many friends that they could readily embrace. In the eyes of the world, not yet used to the emergence of new countries with unfamiliar names, Pakistan was clearly on probation. It had to pass the test of nationhood before it could be treated with any degree of seriousness.

India was different. It had been treated as a quasi state even when the British ruled it. India had fielded teams, under its own flag, at the Olympic games. The Indian army had fought in the various battles of World War II as a separate and distinct entity. In 1944, India had attended the Bretton Woods Conference, called to design an economic and financial system for the postwar world. Jinnah would have preferred that India adopt a different name such as Bharat or Hindustan— the names by which he continued to call India even after the country had decided to keep the old name—but the Indian leaders did not oblige.

In mid-August 1947, therefore, India had arrived on the international stage with a name that was well-known. Pakistan had to work hard to gain recognition.

It seems extraordinary now that Pakistan's early leadership had to try so hard to be recognized as a sovereign state. This was the first task in foreign affairs for Jinnah and his associates during the first year of Pakistan's independence.

The second task was to fix the physical boundaries of Pakistan and to have them accepted by the international community. In its attempt to accomplish this task, the country acquired two foreign policy problems that remain unresolved to this day: the problem of Kashmir and the problem of an undefined frontier with Afghanistan.

Relations with India

The departure of the British from India was a hasty affair. They left a number of loose strings; some of them, such as the problem of Kashmir, remain untied to this day. Jinnah, sensing the difficulties that might result after the British had left the scene, attempted to get them to assign the numerous princely states that made up more than a third of British India to the successor states of India and Pakistan. He wanted the principle that had been applied to partition India—the principle by which areas with a Muslim majority would be incorporated in the state of Pakistan—to be the basis of determining the political future of the princely states. The British, arguing that they did not have the constitutional authority to do this, demurred and left the question of accession to the princes. This action led to difficulties with the largest of the Indian states—Kashmir in the north and Hyderabad in the south. These two states were, in a way, mirror images of each other. Hyderabad had a large Hindu majority but was ruled by a Muslim family, the Nizams. Kashmir had a Muslim majority but the ruler, the maharaja, was a Hindu. Once the British had left, it became clear that the ruling Nizam of Hyderabad and the maharaja of Kashmir were not particularly anxious to see their states absorbed into the new countries; both flirted with the idea of independence. Although both would have been landlocked, an independent Kashmir might have made some sense. Kashmir bordered not only India and Pakistan but also China and Afghanistan; Hyderabad, on the other hand, was completely surrounded by India. China, with an undefined frontier with Kashmir, might have liked to see the state become independent; Russia might also have preferred that situation. Hyderabad's frontier was well defined, and even the leadership of Pakistan, though sympathetic toward the Nizam, saw that independence was not a viable option.

Intensely suspicious of each other's intentions, India and Pakistan resorted to the use of force; although Pakistan could not challenge India's march into Hyderabad, however, India was able to stop Pakistan from taking over the entire state of Kashmir. The Hyderabad problem was quickly settled by what India euphemistically called a "police action." The state was quickly run over by a well-equipped Indian force; the ruling Nizam was deposed; and the territory was eventually merged with some surrounding districts to form the state of Andhra

Pradesh. Those Hyderabadis who opposed the Indian move were allowed to emigrate to Pakistan.

The problem of Kashmir proved to be much more intractable. It was to sour the relations between India and Pakistan for decades to come and became the cause of open hostilities in 1965. In the summer of 1965, Pakistan made an attempt to settle the problem of Kashmir by force. This attempt took the form of infiltration into the Indian-held part of Kashmir of thousands of *mujahideen*—armed freedom fighters—with the expectation that they would be the catalysts of a popular and open uprising against India. But such an uprising did not happen, and the cover under which the *mujahideen* had been hiding was easily blown apart. Once it was established that the unrest in Kashmir had been engineered from the outside, India declared war, and its forces crossed the international frontier and entered Pakistan in three different places. Ayub Khan's government had proceeded under the naive assumption that India would somehow respect the difference between the cease-fire line in Kashmir and the international border between the two countries. Whereas the *mujahideen* could cross the cease-fire line, Indian armed forces were not expected to cross the international boundary. It was in a state of shock that Pakistan received the news of three sharp blows to its soft underbelly—blows to the frontier cities of Lahore and Sialkot and to the unprotected desert of Rajasthan. The all-out war between the two countries started on the morning of September 6, 1965, and lasted for seventeen days; then both sides, utterly exhausted from the effort they had expended, which had resulted in a total stalemate, agreed to yet another cease-fire. The first cease-fire had lasted nearly seventeen years, from January 1949 to September 1965; the second one remained in effect for just over six years. In December 1971, the two countries went to war again; this time the spark was ignited not in Kashmir but in distant East Pakistan. The main battleground on the western side, however, was once again the disputed territory of Kashmir. But this time the war, although it lasted, once again, for only seventeen days—from December 4 to 21—did not result in a standoff. After the third cease-fire, the advantage was clearly with India. India ended the war in possession of a large chunk of territory in the vicinity of Sialkot and of the more than 90,000 prisoners of war captured in East Pakistan. India might have continued to press its advantage had the United Nations Security Council, pushed by both the United States and China, not passed a firm resolution demanding the cessation of all hostilities.

The war in 1965 led to the signing of the Tashkent Declaration on January 10, 1966; the war in 1971 resulted in the Simla Agreement, which was signed by the two countries on July 2, 1972. The environments in which the two governments accepted the two documents were very different, as were the contents of these documents. The Tashkent Declaration was signed in a third country—namely, the Soviet Union—that acted as host and also helped to bring the two sides together. Indian and Pakistani leaders went to this ancient city in the south of the Soviet Union as equals, prepared to accept the mediating role of a superpower. The

Simla Agreement was signed in India, with the two sides conferring without the aid of a third party. By the time of this agreement, Pakistan had accepted India as the dominant power in South Asia, thereby abandoning its long-held policy of being treated as an equal.[2]

There were other differences as well. One of these was ironic in that the Simla Agreement was negotiated by Zulfikar Ali Bhutto, the man who had built his anti–Ayub Khan movement on the charge that the field marshal had sold Pakistan's interest to India at Tashkent. At Tashkent, the old cease-fire line in Kashmir had been restored to its status quo ante; at Simla the agreement reached was to demarcate a new "line of control" that took into account the oddities and incongruities of the old line. In effect, the two parties were now establishing a quasi-permanent frontier in the state of Kashmir. Finally, Tashkent, by an odd combination of circumstances, introduced the Soviet Union as an overseer of peace in South Asia. At Simla, the task of peacekeeping was recognized as some-thing that had to be achieved by the countries in the region without any assistance from the superpowers. In a sense, Simla represented a crucial stage in the process of South Asia's political maturation. Final touches were now being applied to the task left so utterly incomplete by the withdrawal of the British in 1947 and only partially finished with the 1971 breakup of Pakistan. The old British Indian Empire was now divided into three independent states—India, Pakistan, and Bangladesh—that, with a little bit of luck, could settle down to peaceful coexis-tence behind mutually agreed frontiers.

Once Pakistan had begun its proxy war in Afghanistan, it was anxious to keep peace with India. India, however, remained preoccupied with Pakistan, particu-larly after the secessionist movements in the Indian states of Punjab and Kashmir gathered momentum. Pakistan was accused of training freedom fighters in both states, a charge vehemently denied by the governments of Zia ul-Haq and the ad-ministrations of Prime Ministers Benazir Bhutto and Mian Nawaz Sharif. At least twice from 1985 to 1990, the two countries almost went to war.

According to an Indian defense analyst, the first of these two near wars was provoked on the Indian side by the convergence of four different interests. Prime Minister Rajiv Gandhi wanted an external diversion to help him handle V. P. Singh, his finance minister, who had proven to be a difficult subordinate. Singh had instituted corruption proceedings against a number of people close to the prime minister. A crisis with Pakistan would allow the opportunity to move Singh from finance to defense. The Research and Analysis Wing (RAW) of the Indian government, an intelligence agency, was disturbed about Pakistan's activities in the Indian Punjab and believed that the only solution to the problem was to strike back at Pakistan in the province of Sindh. General K. Sundarji, chief of staff of the Indian army had devised a plan to "reliberate" the areas of Kashmir under Pakistan's control by first throwing an Indian punch at Sindh and then moving into the Pakistani-held northern territories. Finally, Arun Singh, India's deputy defense minister, had developed a strategic vision about India that included the

incorporation of Pakistan once again into its territory. "At no point are we imply-
ing that some kind of plot was hatched or clear-cut decisive action was decided on
by the various actors. They appear to have been guided by their own compulsions,
taking advantage of each other when their interests diverged."[3]

According to this reading of India's intentions with respect to Pakistan, a plan
was put into operation in the fall of 1986 to intimidate and embarrass Pakistan on
the battlefield. Apparently, India planned to convert its triennial military exercise,
code-named Brass Tacks, into an actual military action against Pakistan's Sindh
and then follow it up with Trident, the operation to free Pakistani-held Kashmir.
As the Indian troops started to move toward Pakistan, Pakistan also began to mobilize troops on its side of the border. The crisis deepened quickly as each country
accused the other of bad intentions. However, on February 21, 1987, President Zia
ul-Haq, using a long-standing invitation by the cricket authorities of India to visit
their country, flew to New Delhi to watch a test match between the national teams
of the two countries. Once Zia was on Indian soil it was difficult for Indian Prime
Minister Rajiv Gandhi to ignore him. A meeting was held at which the two sides
agreed to pull back their troops from the border.

Pakistan had averted a serious crisis, but it remained wary of Indian intentions.
Its leaders concluded that a nuclear deterrent would be an effective check on
India. Accordingly, on March 1, 1987, an Indian journalist published an interview
with Abdul Qadeer Khan, head of Pakistan's nuclear research program. In the interview, Khan claimed that Pakistan had succeeded in enriching uranium to a
weapon-grade level and now possessed a nuclear bomb. Although Khan was
quick to deny having made any such claim, it was widely believed that the interview was given with the approval of Zia's government and was meant to serve notice on India.

The border between India and Pakistan remained quiet for three years after the
Brass Tacks episode, but tension returned in the spring of 1990. In the meantime,
the government had changed in Islamabad: President Zia was dead, and Benazir
Bhutto had assumed office as prime minister. The Indian leaders greeted this
change with enthusiasm, believing that it would be easier to work out an understanding with a democratic government than it had been with a military-led administration. There was a flurry of diplomatic activity soon after Bhutto took office. In late December 1988 Indian Prime Minister Rajiv Gandhi paid an official
visit to Islamabad to attend the summit of the South Asian Association of Regional
Cooperation (SAARC), and on December 31, he held private talks with Benazir
Bhutto. The talks resulted in three agreements between the two governments: on
cultural relations, taxation, and safeguarding the two countries' nuclear installa-
tions. However, this sudden warming of relations between the two countries was
viewed with some alarm by Bhutto's opponents. The word spread that the government of Pakistan People's Party was ready to sacrifice Pakistan's basic interests, including its long-held belief that Kashmir was not a legitimate part of India but a
disputed territory. Bhutto was put on the defensive and concluded that strengthening her position with respect to India would not be politically advantageous for her.

In the early months of 1990, Pakistan carried out is own military exercise. Named Zerb-e-Momin (the believers' counterpunch), its purpose was to deliver a clear message to India: If attacked, Pakistan still possessed the military strength to deliver a blow to India. The Indians were not impressed. As Pakistan had done in 1986–1987, India responded by massing its troops on the border. The movement of troops on the two sides of the border was accompanied by an escalation of violence in the Indian part of Kashmir. The situation deteriorated quickly and was viewed with sufficient seriousness by the United States to send a special emissary to Islamabad and New Delhi urging restraint on both sides. There was fear that an outbreak of hostilities could lead to a nuclear war. According to an American defense expert, writing in June 1990:

> If India and Pakistan, unable to resolve their differences in coming months, were to go to war over Kashmir, it would be the first major use of nuclear arms. Though neither state is thought to have deployed nuclear weapons as yet, both could do so quickly, perhaps within weeks. India's force could number 40 to 60 weapons, deliverable on any of the 200 advanced aircraft. That is enough to wipe out Pakistan's major cities several times over. Pakistan's nuclear force would be much smaller. It probably can make only 5 to 10 bombs and possesses only 40 to 50 first-class strike aircraft. Still this is more than enough to cause a million casualties in India.[4]

Once again war was averted but the two sides remained suspicious. India and Pakistan continued to coexist in an unstable environment in South Asia, with their leaders not beyond risking war for short-term political gains. Tension between the two countries increased in 1998 following their testing of nuclear devices in May of that year (see below).

Relations with Afghanistan

The Simla Agreement completed the task of drawing final international borders for India and Bangladesh, two of the three successor states of British India. For Pakistan, the third state, the job was only half done, since its border to the northwest—the frontier with Afghanistan—was still undefined. As with Kashmir, the Afghanistan problem was not one of Pakistan's making; it, too, had been inherited from the British.

As the British had extended their control over India and reached the Pathan areas in the northwest, their first impulse was to stop at the "scientific frontiers" following the line that ran between the cities of Kabul and Kandahar. Such a frontier would have brought the entire Pathan population under British sovereignty, but the Pathans were less inclined to favor such a final solution to British expansionism. What followed were the so-called Afghan wars, which convinced the British that what was possible and practical was considerably less than what was scientific and desirable. The Durand line was the solution, defined in principle within the Anglo-Afghan Agreement of November 1893 and signed by Sir Mortimer

Durand, the foreign secretary of India in the British government, and by Afghanistan's ruler, Amir Abdur Rahman. It ran a hundred miles south of the Kabul-Kandahar divide and cut the Pathan population into two—one Afghan and the other "tribal," with the latter only marginally integrated into British India.

Although the Durand line was confirmed by later *amirs* of Afghanistan—by Habibullah in 1905 and Amanullah in 1921—as well as by King Nadir Shah in 1930, it was not accepted by the government of King Zahir Shah after the British withdrew from India. Between 1947 and 1979, various Afghan governments consistently argued that the 1893 agreement was a treaty between two unequal powers. They sought a new frontier between the relatively more equal states of Pakistan and Afghanistan that would pay greater heed to the matter of ethnic purity within country boundaries. This was the reverse of the "scientific frontier" argument the British had advanced in the nineteenth century; although never explicitly stated, the scientific frontier Afghanistan sought with Pakistan ran along the Indus River. Such a frontier would have completed the ethnic purity of Afghanistan by giving it the vast majority of the Pathan population. The Afghanistan government was prepared to accept a second-best solution, which was also never very clearly defined but which hinted at the creation of Pakhtunistan, an autonomous province or independent country for the entire Pathan (Pakhtun) population.

It was through the exercise of this sort of logic that Afghanistan voted against the admission of Pakistan to the United Nations in 1947. Afghanistan was not prepared to accept the emergence of Pakistan as an independent state as long as the question of the location of the Pathan population was not resolved to its satisfaction.

This argument could not, of course, be accepted by Pakistan. Hence, for more than two decades, its relationship with Afghanistan was an uneasy one—a relationship exacerbated at times by domestic political problems. For instance in 1973, Zulfikar Ali Bhutto banned the National Awami Party—a political organization based in the Northwest Frontier Province with strong support among those segments of the population who wanted more political autonomy than successive federal governments were prepared to grant—on the grounds that it had covertly worked with the government of Afghanistan to undermine the authority of the federal administration. But the question of creating Pakhtunistan, either as an independent Pathan country or as an autonomous Pathan province within Pakistan and Afghanistan, lost its meaning after Soviet troops moved into Afghanistan. For ten years starting in December 1979, the Afghan *mujahideen* fought a bitter guerrilla war against the Soviets, using a number of refugee camps in Pakistan as sanctuaries. During this period some 3.5 million refugees moved into Pakistan and were accommodated in scores of camps established all along the long Afghanistan-Pakistan border. A number of Western powers, Japan, and the countries of the Middle East provided economic assistance to the refugees under the auspices of the United Nations High Commission for Refugees (UNHCR). In the late 1980s, the Afghan refugees constituted the largest group of displaced people in the world.

Soviet troops entered Afghanistan to support the faltering socialist revolution they had encouraged. Their entry completely altered Pakistan's relations with Afghanistan. To begin with, the Pakistani supporters of Pakhtunistan lost all credibility, thereby removing a major irritant from Pakistan's domestic politics.

A number of countries rushed in with assistance to Pakistan and the Afghan *mujahideen* (freedom fighters) who began to resist the Soviets. Weapons and money poured in from the United States, China, Saudi Arabia, and Egypt; in the decade following the Soviet invasion of Afghanistan the United States alone provided more than $2 billion worth of assistance to support the *mujahideen* effort. Some of the assistance provided by the United States went directly to the Afghan refugees who came to Pakistan and were accommodated in dozens of camps set up along the border between the two countries. Some of the money and military equipment was covertly given to the freedom fighters with the InterServices Intelligence (ISI) of Pakistan acting as the conduit.

While the war in Afghanistan picked up momentum, the ISI's role increased. It began to help the *mujahideen* with training and strategy. The ISI under Lt. General Akhtar Abdur Rahman, its director general, offered a great deal of assistance to one *mujahideen* group, the Hezb-e-Islami (Islamic party) led by Gulbuddin Hekmatyar. This policy had the support of President Zia ul-Haq and Saudi Arabia. Once the Soviet troops had left Afghanistan, Hekmatyar, by far the most religiously conservative of the Afghan *mujahideen* leaders, was expected to set up an Islamic state of the type favored by Saudi Arabia and Zia ul-Haq. The United States went along with this policy with some reluctance, fearing that the emergence of the Hezb-e-Islami as the most effective force among the seven groups would lead to the establishment of an Islamic government in Afghanistan. Washington was concerned that such a development would strengthen the forces of radical Islam in Central Asia. But policymakers in Washington had little choice, since Islamabad and the ISI clearly favored Hekmatyar. This preference became even more pronounced following the appointment of General Hamid Gul as the director general of ISI. Gul, a devout Muslim, had excellent relations with all Afghan groups, in particular with Hekmatyar. He was a strong exponent of bringing Islam not only to Afghanistan but to all of Central Asia. As will be discussed a little later, Gul's policies were to profoundly influence the eventual outcome of the struggle in Afghanistan.

The *mujahideen* forces succeeded beyond the expectations of their external supporters. The amount of material damage and casualties inflicted by them became a politically unacceptable burden for the Soviet Union. By 1987, Soviet President Mikhail Gorabachev had begun to indicate that a socialist Afghanistan was no longer an objective that his country wanted to pursue. A solution in which all Afghan parties, including the Soviet-supported regime in Kabul and the *mujahideen* based in Pakistan, were allowed participation would be acceptable to him. This change in the Soviet position led to the initiation of "proximity talks" (so named because of Pakistan's refusal to meet the Afghan delegation face-to-face, which would have implied recognition of the Communist regime in Kabul) between Pakistan and Afghanistan under the aegis of the United Nations. Finally in April 1987, the two countries met in Geneva and signed an agreement that laid the groundwork for the withdrawal of the Soviet troops from Afghanistan. The United States and the Soviet Union put their signatures on the accord as its guarantors. Although the level of conflict did not immediately subside following the Geneva agreement, the Soviets kept to the schedule they had accepted for the troop withdrawal. Their departure did not immediately cause the collapse of the Communist regime in Kabul, headed by President Najibullah.

In the spring of 1989 within a couple of months of the departure of the Soviet troops, the *mujahideen* launched an offensive on the city of Jalalabad but were beaten back by the government troops. Benazir Bhutto, the new prime minister, neither shared ISI's Afghan strategy nor its support for Hekmatyar. She held the ISI responsible for the Jalalabad fiasco, transferred its director general, and sought to take command of the Afghan policy. However, her twenty months in office did not change the situation in Afghanistan. Hekmatyar celebrated her dismissal by launching another major attack, this time on Kabul. According to a Western observer, writing in October 1990:

> During the twenty months since the Soviet troop withdrawal, the *mujahideen* have been unable to build a broad political coalition or unified military force—partly because of ISI's insistence on a leading role for Hekmatyar and other [Islamic] fundamentalist groups. As U.S. frustration with the continued stalemate has grown, Washington has reduced its military aid to the guerrillas and has sought a political solution to the conflict in talks with Moscow.[5]

In the winter of 1990, the U.S. Congress signaled its unhappiness with the situation in Afghanistan by reducing its assistance by one-half. A year later the United States withdrew all support from Afghanistan, which, in retrospect, was a grave mistake. In 1995, a new force suddenly emerged on the political scene of Afghanistan. Calling themselves the Taleban (students) and led by people who were not identified with any of the *mujahideen* groups, this force advanced from the borders of Pakistan toward the main urban centers of Afghanistan. Jalalabad, Kandahar, and Herat fell quickly, but Kabul was able to resist the Taleban advance for sometime. However, in late 1995, Kabul was also conquered. Najibullah was arrested and hanged along with a number of his close associates. The Taleban went on to establish an extremely conservative Islamic regime in the areas under their control. Women were ordered to cover themselves completely when they ventured outside. They were excluded from the schools and were not allowed to work outside the home. Music and television were banned. As the world watched these developments in horror, the Taleban continued their march. By the summer of 1998, with the capture of the northeastern city of Mazar-e-Sharif, their control over the country was virtually complete. When moving into Mazar-e-Sharif, Taleban forces captured a number of Iranian diplomats and executed them. This action was a signal to Iran, led by Shia clergy, that the fiercely Sunni Muslim Taleban would brook no interference in Afghanistan. Iran responded by amassing troops and equipment on the border with Afghanistan and threatening invasion. At this point the Western countries, in particular the United States, began to take note of the developments in this remote region of the world. A meeting was organized in New York attended by the United States, Iran, and other regional powers to diffuse the situation. This was the first occasion since the 1979 Islamic revolution in Iran that the diplomats from that country worked on the same side of an issue with the United States. According to a Western observer: "To the outsider the differences between the two groups seem minor but the same could be said about the Christians who fought pitiless religious wars in medieval Europe and until recently in Ireland. The Taleban Sunnis so loathe the Shias that when they took Mazar-e-Sharif, a Shia town, in August, they went from house to house cutting the throats of civilians."[6]

What is clear from all these developments is that the situation in Afghanistan developed in ways that could not have been foreseen in December 1979, when the troops from the Soviet Union moved into Kabul. The Soviet incursion was meant to help the Communist regime established a few years earlier in Afghanistan to consolidate its hold over the country. Instead, the Soviet Union suffered a humiliating defeat at the hands of a group of essentially primitive warriors who quickly learned to use the sophisticated equipment generously supplied to them by the United States. At the same time, developments in Pakistan led to the establishment of religious schools called *madrasas* that provided education to those ignored by the state. (See Chapter 3.) The *madrasas* operating in Pakistan's northwestern regions—in the provinces of Balochistan and the Northwest Frontier—produced the Taleban (students) who organized themselves quickly into a formidable force that overran all of Afghanistan in less than three years. Many in Pakistan cheered these developments and hoped that the Islamization of Afghanistan would send their country in that direction. The Soviet invasion of Afghanistan in 1979 may have solved Pakistan's Pathan problem, but it created another dynamic that may have serious consequences for the country. Would Pakistan succeed in limiting the influence of the Taleban to Afghanistan, especially when their emergence was the consequence of developments inside its own borders? This question may be difficult to answer at this time.

Relations with the United States

The grave doubts expressed about the legitimacy of Pakistan's birth and the fact that some of its borders are contested by its neighbors are the reasons for which Pakistan since 1947 has sought a sense of security through outside alliances. Its foreign policy—regardless of the government in power—was dictated by this single concern. Whereas India under Jawaharlal Nehru introduced nonalignment as the guiding principle for all Third World relations with the First or Second World, Pakistan adopted a very different approach. It painstakingly worked on building a relationship with the United States in which the obligations of the partners were clearly spelled out. The Mutual Defense Agreement signed with Washington in 1954 was based on an unabashed declaration by Pakistan that it opposed Communist expansionism in return for a somewhat less ambiguous promise by the United States to underwrite Pakistan's integrity as a nation-state. The signing of this agreement was followed by Pakistan's entry into CENTO—the Central Treaty Organization, with Turkey being the other regional member—and SEATO—the South East Asian Treaty Organization. The three alliances—NATO, CENTO, and SEATO—threw a chain of defense around the periphery of Communist Europe and Asia; Turkey with membership in NATO and CENTO and Pakistan with membership in CENTO and SEATO formed the two critical links in this chain.

These formal alliances with the United States not only kept Pakistan out of the Nonaligned Movement but also caused the United States to become intensely suspicious when Zulfikar Ali Bhutto, first as minister of fuel and power and later as foreign minister in the administration of Ayub Khan, sought to bring Pakistan into close relations with China and the Soviet Union. Bhutto's approach toward international relations was totally different from that of Field Marshal Ayub Khan and his military associates. The military's interest in maintaining close relations with the United States was based on the recognition that in any prolonged conflict with India or Afghanistan, Pakistan would need to maintain access to a source of arms and equipment. The military believed that the agreement of 1954 and membership in regional defense pacts ensured such access. Bhutto disagreed. He was of the view that in any regional conflict in which Pakistan was involved, the support from the United States would not come automatically but, instead, would be contingent on an assessment of the advantages or disadvantages connected with providing such support. If this reasoning was correct, he believed that it was in Pakistan's best interest not to depend on one superpower but to be close to all the powers with interests in South and West Asia. This reinterpretation of Pakistan's best interest led to the diversification of its external relations. Under his prodding, Pakistan concluded a number of economic cooperation arrangements with China and the Soviet Union.[7]

Pakistan's friendship with the United States was put to the test in September 1965, at the time of the first war with India. Washington adopted a neutral position between the two combatants—an attitude that Pakistan, particularly in view of the 1954 Mutual Defense Agreement, found extremely distasteful. Bhutto was vindicated, and the prestige of the United States suffered a serious blow. In a survey of public opinion conducted in October 1979 by the Pakistan Institute of Strategic Studies in 175 locations throughout the country, less than 8 percent of those questioned said that they "liked the United States more than any other country in the world." By comparison, China was chosen by 36 percent, whereas 43 percent said that they had no clear preference. The survey was conducted shortly before the Soviet Union sent its troops into Afghanistan, and Pakistan once again found itself drawing close to the United States.

On December 27, 1979, Soviet troops entered Afghanistan and Pakistan was designated the "front line" state by the foreign-policymakers in Washington. The first offer of economic and military assistance from President Jimmy Carter was spurned by Pakistan—General Zia ul-Haq described the amount of assistance promised as peanuts. After President Ronald Reagan came to Washington, contacts between the two countries were renewed and an elaborate program of aid to Pakistan was worked out. The program included the sale of forty F-16 planes to Pakistan, considered one of the most sophisticated fighting machines in the arsenal of the United States at that time. It also included ships, tanks, and artillery pieces. On the economic side, the United States offered help for developing Balochistan, Pakistan's most backward province, as well as assistance in building institutions for rural development throughout the country. In the fall of 1983, the U.S. Congress approved an aid package for Pakistan valued at some $3.2 billion, to be made available over a period of five years.

Although the crisis in Afghanistan once again brought Pakistan into close relations with the United States, neither country made an attempt to formalize the new arrangement by signing new treaties or arrangements. In the meantime, having been invited to join the Nonaligned Movement, Pakistan's leadership was anxious to keep itself at some distance from Washington. Domestic opinion must also have been a factor in this decision; after all, the survey by the Institute of Strategic Studies was conducted a few weeks before a large crowd had set fire to the U.S. Embassy in Islamabad. The situation in the Middle East—further complicated by the Iranian revolution, the war between Iran and Iraq, and the very close ties that the United States maintained with Israel—meant that Pakistan, anxious to be identified as a friend of the Islamic states in the area, could not afford to be seen as getting very close to Washington.

In the fall of 1990, Pakistan entered into another uneasy relationship with the United States. Washington delivered a series of rebuffs to the caretaker government that took office after the administration of Benazir Bhutto was dismissed in August by President Ghulam Ishaq Khan. The first shot was fired by Robert Oakley, the U.S. ambassador to Pakistan. In a speech given in Washington in middle September, Ambassador Oakley suggested that the accountability process begun by the caretaker government was aimed at discrediting Benazir Bhutto. He asked for a more evenhanded approach that would include in the accountability process the regimes that came before Benazir Bhutto's. Ambassador Oakley's suggestion was not well received in Pakistan's official circles but struck a sympathetic chord among those in the United States interested in Pakistan affairs. "If Pakistan's generals are now tempted to traduce those ground rules [elections in which all political figures can participate on an equal basis], as they have done in the past, they need to know that Washington is paying close and worried attention. Ambassador Oakley was right to register that," an editorial in the *New York Times* noted.[8]

The second shot also came from Washington and took the form of the failure by President George Bush to issue necessary certification to the U.S. Congress about Pakistan's nuclear program. Before Congress could authorize aid to Islamabad, the Symington and Pressler amendments obliged the president to certify that Pakistan's nuclear program was peaceful. Certification was held back for a few months in 1988 and 1989 as well but on both occasions, the strategic importance Pakistan had acquired because of the war in Afghanistan helped to change the president's mind in Pakistan's favor. The situation in 1990 was different; Washington had lost interest in the Afghan conflict following its rapprochement with Moscow, and the dismissal of the government of Benazir Bhutto had activated a number of lobbyists in the corridors of the U.S. Congress who were inclined to teach Pakistan a lesson. President Bush's failure to certify had the effect of a cutting off all military assistance from October 1, 1990, and of limiting economic aid to disbursements from the projects already in the pipeline. Pakistan was set to lose more than $500 million worth of capital flows from the United States in 1990–1991.

These developments came at an unfortunate time, when considered from the perspective of Washington's long-term interest in Pakistan. In October, the people of Pakistan were engaged in a bitter political fight between the supporters of Benazir Bhutto and those she described as "the establishment." The tough U.S. stance was seen as partisan in Pakistan and difficult to comprehend because the caretaker government of Ghulam Mustafa Jatoi had taken considerable political risk by dispatching a contingent of Pakistani troops to Saudi Arabia in support of the U.S. position in the Middle East. "In Pakistan where feelings are quickly hurt when Americans say anything about this country's shortcomings, the suspension of military aid draws outrage that cuts across all regions and classes, reinforcing a range of anti-American constituencies, including Islamic militants," wrote an American journalist.[9] It was obvious in the fall of 1990 that a great deal of delicate repair work would have to be done by the United States before the relationship between the two countries could be normalized.

The United States was too preoccupied with the problems in other parts of the world to be much concerned with South Asia. However, India and Pakistan reappeared on Washington's radar screen in May 1998 in a way policymakers had not anticipated. The Bhartaiya Janata Party (BJP), a Hindu fundamentalist organization, came to power in Delhi in March 1998 at the head of a coalition government. The BJP's electoral program had promised Indian voters that BJP would make India a nuclear power if put into power. The promise was kept, and India tested five nuclear devices on May 11 and 13. Pakistan followed with its own nuclear tests on May 28 and 30. The United States responded with economic sanctions on both countries, the effect of which was much more severe on Pakistan, given its precarious economic situation. Washington let it be known that it was prepared to relax the sanctions if the two countries signed the Comprehensive Test Ban Treaty (CTBT). For a few weeks it seemed that both India and Pakistan would agree to U.S. demands, but by the fall of 1998 not much progress had been made. It was uncertain as to how this matter would be resolved.

Relations with the Third World

The Myth of Independence, a book written by Zulfikar Ali Bhutto upon leaving the administration of Field Marshal Ayub Khan, contains a recipe that Third World countries should follow in conducting their external relations. Bhutto asked his readers, "Should the smaller nations therefore obediently follow the dictates of Global Powers and exchange their independence for material gains and promises of economic activity?" He then went on to answer the question himself:

> Caught in the nutcracker of the global conflict, the underdeveloped nations might in despair conclude that they can only marginally influence the *status quo,* that in reality they have no independent choice but to trim their policies to the requirements of one Global Power or another. This is an unnecessarily pessimistic view, a negation of the struggle of man, expressed through the nation-state, to be free. It is still possible for the smaller nations, with adroit handling of their affairs, to maintain their independence and retain flexibility of action in their relationship with [the] Global Powers.[10]

With these words Bhutto provided an entirely new basis for the conduct of Pakistan's foreign policy. Hitherto, Pakistani leadership had sought security by aligning the country closely with one global power; now Bhutto argued for an approach that would keep the country equidistant from all major powers. Such a policy could be pursued only if Pakistan joined with other small nations to protect their common interests. It was basically this approach to foreign relations that Bhutto began to practice when he returned to power in December 1971 first as president at the head of a martial law government and later as prime minister.

But the translation of theory into practice proved to be difficult for a country in Pakistan's position. In 1971, Pakistan had suffered a military defeat at the hands of the Indian army; it had lost a large chunk of territory to India, and India had taken more than 90,000 of Pakistan's soldiers as prisoners of war. A policy of scrupulous nonalignment would not have delivered Pakistan out of this uncomfortable situation. It is to Bhutto's credit that he did not seek overt support from any of the global powers to reach agreement with India at Simla. When the agreement was finally concluded on July 2, 1972, Pakistan had demonstrated for the first time its ability to look after its interests without any outside assistance. The Kashmir cease-fires of 1949 and 1965 were negotiated with the help of the United Nations; the World Bank acted as the arbitrator for the Indus Water Treaty of 1960; and the Tashkent Agreement of 1966 was concluded with the help of the Soviet Union. The Simla Agreement demonstrated to the world—or at any rate to the Indian leadership—that Pakistan was now mature and confident enough to be able to venture into international politics without being chaperoned by global powers.

Indeed, this demonstration of maturity was necessary if Pakistan was to be brought into Third World politics and admitted into the Nonaligned Movement. After all, Jawaharlal Nehru was one of the founders of the movement and, for as long as Pakistan continued to be closely aligned with the United States, India exercised the right to veto its entry as a formal member. After the Simla Agreement was signed, India no longer had any objection to Pakistan joining in. Bhutto took full advantage of the opportunity now available to play a role in the arena of international politics. Nkrumah, Nasser, and Sukarno—the Third World leaders Bhutto most admired—had been prominent international statesmen, and he wished to join their ranks.

Once Pakistan had been accepted as a full member of the Nonaligned Movement, it was called upon to play an important part in the Third World's political and economic affairs. For instance, Pakistan was one of the nineteen Third World countries invited to participate in the Conference on International Economic Cooperation, which met for over a year in Paris in 1975–1976 to arrive at an understanding between the north (the industrial countries) and the south (the developing countries) on the question of reforming the international economic structure. Pakistan also played an active role in the fifth session of the United Nations Conference on Trade and Development (UNCTAD), held in Manila in 1979, and in the Special Session of the United Nations General Assembly that was convened in 1980 in New York to launch a round of north–south economic negotiations.

The nonaligned approach to international politics also helped Pakistan develop close relations with the Islamic countries of West Asia and North Africa. Some earlier attempts to forge such relations with these countries were rebuffed, most noticeably by Gamal Nasser of Egypt, who considered Jawaharlal Nehru's India to be a much more congenial companion than Ayub Khan's Pakistan, which had allowed itself to be incorporated into a number of defense alliances and treaties. But the new, unaligned Pakistan was found to be acceptable by a variety of different political interests in the Middle East. Some of these countries—especially Saudi Arabia and the ministates of the Gulf region—actively sought a close relationship with Pakistan.

Relations with the Muslim World

It has been suggested that the Muslims of South Asia have always displayed an extraterritorial loyalty and have instinctively identified with religious causes that more often than not were more imaginary than real. The reference here is to the Khilafat movement of the 1920s, during which time the Muslim community of British India sought to preserve the integrity of the Ottoman Empire. The rise of

Kemal Ataturk and the secularization of Turkey caught the Indian *khilafat* move-ment on the wrong foot. A number of frustrated leaders from this movement joined Mohammad Ali Jinnah's Muslim League, and, once Pakistan came into be-ing, the same group attempted again to work toward some form of pan-Islamism. It was only after the severance of Bangladesh that some progress was made in this direction. Bhutto recognized very early the opportunity that was now provided to him:

> The severance of our eastern wing by force has significantly altered our geographic focus. This will naturally affect our geo-political perspective. The geographical dis-tance between us and the nations of South-East Asia has grown. . . . At the moment, as we stand, it is within the ambit of South and Western Asia. It is here that our pri-mary concern must henceforth lie.[11]

This reorientation in Pakistan's geopolitical situation occurred at a time when the Middle East was going through a profound political transformation, which, in turn, was hastened by the tremendous increase in national incomes that occurred with the explosion in the price of oil. Suddenly the new leaders, intellectuals, and policymakers of the region began to think of their own political, economic, and social situation. Their dialogue was no longer with the West, as it had been during the days of Nasser, but with their own people; and, in many different ways, the leaders of Libya, Iran, and Saudi Arabia were involved in this process of redefini-tion. So was Zulfikar Ali Bhutto in his own country: His Islamic socialism was much more than the political cynicism many then believed it to be; indeed, it rep-resented an attempt to achieve a harmonious balance between the social concerns of two different philosophies, Islam and socialism. Bhutto seems genuinely to have believed that such a synthesis was especially pertinent for addressing the many political, social, and economic problems faced by Pakistan. It is not surpris-ing, therefore, that Bhutto drew very close during his years in office to Muammar Qaddafi of Libya, King Faisal of Saudi Arabia, and King Reza Shah of Iran. All three leaders appealed to Bhutto in different ways: Qaddafi's popular appeal and parallel progress along Islamic and socialist paths fascinated the Pakistani leader, as did King Reza Shah's ability to modernize Iran while keeping the *mullahs* in check. King Faisal, in part because of the extraordinary wealth of his kingdom but also because of his immense piety and sagacity, was able to command the respect of practically all the Muslim leaders, including Bhutto. Bhutto was receptive to their advice; it was these leaders who persuaded him to recognize Bangladesh and to negotiate a settlement with India on the exchange of prisoners of war.

The only factor in common between the policies pursued by the Bhutto gov-ernment and those followed by the administration of President Zia ul-Haq was the emphasis on Pakistan's Middle East connection. President Zia seemed much less interested than Bhutto was in Third World politics; he was more willing to work closely with the United States and other Western powers; he was especially cold toward the Soviet Union; and he was happy to regard Mrs. Gandhi not as his equal in South Asia but as the leader of a premier power in the region. At the same time, however, Zia assiduously built on the links between Pakistan and the countries of the Middle East that were forged by his predecessor.

During the eight-year war between Iraq and Iran, it was important for Pakistan to adopt a careful posture toward the two parts of the Islamic world represented by that conflict: The Arabs were important for Pakistan not only for economic reasons but also because the type of Islam practiced on the Arabian peninsula was the one with which the more influential groups in Pakistan felt reasonably comfortable. At the same time, Pakistan had to be mindful of Shi'i Islam that revolutionized Iran. Approximately one quarter of the population of Pakistan professed faith in Shi'ism. The Shias had reacted very negatively to the imposition of *zakat* (tax on wealth collected for distribution to the poor) by the government of Zia ul-Haq. Their opposition to paying the tax had persuaded Zia to exclude the Shi'i community from being affected by the levy. Fear that Zia may not be mindful of Shi'i interests as he went about Islamizing the economy and society in Pakistan had raised the political profile of Tehrik-e-Nifaze Fiqh Jafreiya (TNFJ, Movement for the Introduction of Shi'i Laws). It was, therefore, prudent for Zia to walk the middle line between Iraq and Iran.

In the Kuwait crisis Pakistan took a more unequivocal position, however. It was quick to condemn Iraq's invasion of Kuwait and was equally quick to dispatch its troops to Saudi Arabia in support of the military mobilization spearheaded by the United States. The caretaker government of Ghulam Mustafa Jatoi as well as the successor government of Nawaz Sharif concluded that Pakistan's long-term interests would be served better if it continued to side with the conservative rather than the radical forces within the Arab world. Pakistan's nuclear weapons tests in May 1998 created difficulties with the West but won respect among the countries of the Muslim world.

Development of the Bomb

Two important foreign policy issues that remain to be analyzed concern Pakistan's attitude toward nuclear development and the use of its territory and that of neighboring Afghanistan by some Islamic fundamentalist groups to launch terrorist attacks against the West. For more than a decade, Pakistan denied it, often vigorously, but stories about nuclear-development efforts in a laboratory located at Kahuta, a few miles south of the capital city of Islamabad, continued to make newspaper headlines.

Pakistan made preparations to go nuclear in the teeth of opposition from Washington. The U.S. Congress made several attempts to block military sales to Pakistan unless the country openly and unequivocally disavowed its nuclear ambitions. The countries of Western Europe were even less enthusiastic, and India, of course, was openly hostile. Pakistan persisted with these efforts and exploded six nuclear devices seventeen days after India conducted its nuclear tests. The United

States viewed this action not as an open defiance by a trusted ally but more as a reaction to a difficult situation created by the Indian tests.

Since the explosion of India's nuclear device in 1974, membership in the nuclear club had remained limited to six nations—the United States, the Soviet Union, Britain, France, China, and India. However, a number of other countries remained poised at the threshold—namely, Israel, South Africa, Argentina, Brazil, and Pakistan. It was understood that any country crossing the threshold would bring with it a number of other aspirants. Such a move would therefore be considered highly irresponsible and would, no doubt, incur the wrath of the entire community of nations at a time when sentiment against nuclear proliferation was growing rapidly. In the early 1990s, especially after the collapse of the Communist states in Europe and the breakup of the Soviet Union, the international community sought to stop the spread of nuclear weapons by negotiating a Comprehensive Test Ban Treaty. Both India and Pakistan refused to sign the treaty thus continuing the stance they had adopted when the Nuclear Nonproliferation Treaty (NPT) was negotiated earlier. The two countries had adopted a simple logic in defying the international consensus that had developed on the issue of the spread of weapons of mass destruction. India maintained that the NPT was discriminatory in that it gave special privileges to the five recognized nuclear powers—the United States, Russia, the United Kingdom, France, and China. There was no reason for withholding the same recognition from India, given the size of its population, its geographic mass, and the fact that it had tested a nuclear device. In fact, the Indians wished to obtain a permanent seat in the UN Security Council. Pakistan's logic was simpler still: It wanted for itself what the international community was prepared to grant to India.

All this raised an important question: Why should Pakistan continue to seek nuclear equality with India? There were four possible reasons for Pakistan's position. The first of these had to do with Pakistan's interpretation of the South Asian military equation. Until 1971, Pakistan had sought military parity with India. In 1971, Pakistan lost Bangladesh and with it its perceived right to be considered India's equal. India, by going nuclear in 1974, further disturbed this equation. Two bitter wars with India, though fought only briefly, convinced Pakistani military planners that another confrontation could not be ruled out. In order to be prepared for such an eventuality, Pakistan would have to balance India's nuclear advantage—and it could accomplish that only by developing some nuclear-production capability of its own.

The second, even more complex, reason was embedded in the curious (in the sense of not having been officially articulated) military role that Pakistan was playing in the Middle East in the 1980s and 1990s. It was said that Pakistan's nuclear ambitions dated back to the early 1970s, when several Arab states began to worry about the possibility that Israel might equip itself with a nuclear device. An "Islamic bomb" had to be developed to counter Israel, the common belief being that the fear of Israel had led to some understanding between Libya and Pakistan.

In a statement smuggled out of the prison shortly before he was executed, Bhutto hinted that such an arrangement may indeed exist, if not with Libya, then with some other Arab states.[12]

The third possible reason for Pakistan's nuclear program was the country's very close ties with China. Again, only speculations can be made. Pakistan's plans to establish a uranium-enrichment plant began with the construction of a centrifuge facility based on a technology not known to many developing countries. As China's nuclear program used somewhat cruder methods for enriching uranium and obtaining weapon-grade plutonium, it may have been interested in acquiring a new form of technology if one had been successfully developed by Pakistan. China, by the same token, may have encouraged Pakistani scientists to keep on trying. The possibility of some understanding between Pakistan and China was hinted at in 1983, when the United States sought but failed to obtain an explicit understanding from the Chinese that they would not support nuclear-development programs in the developing world.

The fourth reason was articulated by President Zia ul-Haq to explain Pakistan's ongoing nuclear experiment. Because of its serious energy shortage, Pakistan had resorted to load-shedding (i.e., withholding electric power from domestic and industrial users during specified periods of time) since 1983, particularly during the winter months when the Tarbela and Mangla reservoirs ran low and could not produce enough power. In addition, Pakistan's other major source of energy—natural gas—had been seriously depleted through excessive use. Despite the establishment of a vast and expensive distribution network, the use of natural gas as a domestic and industrial fuel was being curtailed. At the same time, the consumption of energy continued to increase at a fast pace. In the 1980s, energy consumption increased at the rate of 15 percent per annum, whereas the GDP increased by only 6 percent. The result was a ratio of 2.5 (also called the elasticity-of-energy consumption measurement), which was much higher than the average for the Third World.

This mismatch between supply and demand created a considerable amount of anxiety among the planners. Development of nuclear energy seemed one way out, at least during this interim period, when additional investments were being made to produce hydropower. The plans for building another dam on River Indus at Kalabagh were being debated, but the power to be obtained from this source would not become available until the first decade of the next century. The economic policymakers in Pakistan, also mindful of developments in India, no doubt took note of the Indian plans to launch an ambitious program to close its own energy gap by emphasizing investments in nuclear plants, starting with the Seventh Five-Year Plan. The seventh plan was launched in India in April 1985, thus commencing a program of nuclear plant construction that, by the end of the century, will supply the country with a significant proportion of the electric power consumed. The program's backbone was a 260-megawatt nuclear power station that was designed and successfully tested in India. As this heavy-water plant used natural uranium, it operated independently of international controls and surveillance. The first such plant went into operation in March 1983. By the year 2000, India plans not only to have twenty similar plants in operation but will also have developed sufficient expertise in fast-breeder reactors. These developments in India encouraged Pakistani scientists and economic planners to persevere with their own nuclear programs. Not much work was done on the one nuclear power plant that was included in the Sixth Five-Year Plan (1983–1988), which was to be built on the Indus River at a site called Chasma. Pakistan could not obtain sufficient foreign technical cooperation. However, in the spring of 1990, Pakistan concluded a transfer of technology agreement with France signaling some thawing of industrial countries' attitudes toward Pakistan's nuclear policy.

This thaw did not last for long. In the fall of 1990, U.S. authorities all but announced to the world that Pakistan had achieved its goal of manufacturing a nuclear bomb. In a letter published in the *Nation* on November 19, 1990, Ambassador Robert Oakley said that the U.S. executive and legislative branches were agreed that "the fact of possession . . . applies to components of a nuclear device, not only to an assembled device."[13] The United States believed that Pakistan had also taken "various steps . . . in preparations for the deployment of nuclear bombs aboard U.S.–made F-16 fighter aircraft."[14]

There were, therefore, sufficiently good reasons for Pakistan to pursue plans to gain enough expertise to build nuclear reactors and if, need be, nuclear weapons.

Terrorism

One consequence of the Afghans' ten-year struggle against the Soviet Union's occupation of their country was to turn Pakistan into both a target of terrorism and a base for the training of terrorists. The ground for these developments was laid in the mid-1980s when the U.S. Central Intelligence Agency (CIA) worked with Pakistan's InterServices Intelligence (ISI) to establish training bases for the Afghan *mujahideen* on both sides of the Afghanistan-Pakistan border. The most important of these bases was in Khost, a small town south of Kabul, near the Pakistan border. The CIA built an elaborate network of training camps at Khost. Some of these facilities were lodged deep in the mountains to protect them against air attacks by the Soviet Union.

Following the departure of the Soviet Union from Afghanistan in 1989 and the withdrawal of CIA operators from Pakistan, the *mujahideen* training camps were taken over by a number of different groups that continued to fight in the prolonged civil war in Afghanistan. The camps on the Pakistani side helped train young graduates from the *madrasas* (religious schools) who were to form the backbone of the Taleban movement that gradually extended its sway over Afghanistan. The Khost facilities were acquired by Osama bin Laden, a Saudi millionaire, to train and equip hundreds of people to participate in various conflicts that pitched the forces of radical Islam against a variety of opponents. People trained in the camps run by bin Laden were said to have taken part in a number of conflicts around the globe, including those in Bosnia-Herzegovina, Chechnya, Kosovo, Kashmir, the Philippines, Somalia, and Sudan.

On August 7, 1998, terrorist bombs placed outside the U.S. Embassy in Kenya and in Tanzania killed nearly three hundred persons, including twelve Americans. On the same day, Pakistan arrested Muhammad Siddique Odeh, a young Palestinian, at the airport in Karachi while on his way from Nairobi to Peshawar. During interrogation, Odeh linked the bombings to Osama bin Laden. On August 20, the United States launched missile attacks on the bin Laden camps in Afghanistan and on a factory in Khartoum, the capital of Sudan, which was said to be producing chemicals that could be used in weapons of mass destruction. In explaining the missile attacks, President Bill Clinton linked bin Laden to a number of terrorist attacks, including those on U.S. and Pakistan troops in Somalia in October 1993; plans to bomb six American 747s over the Pacific; a plot to assassinate Egyptian president Hosni Mubarak in Ethiopia in June 1995; the bombing of the Egyptian embassy in Islamabad, Pakistan, in November 1995; and the gunning down of German tourists in Luxor, Egypt, in November 1997.

Osama bin Laden's support of the insurgency in Kashmir with the possible help from Pakistan's ISI brought Pakistan very close to being declared a terrorist state by the United States in 1996 and 1997. It was only after Pakistan gave a firm assurance to the United States that it would sever all contacts with Harakat Ansari, a shadowy group deeply involved in the Kashmir conflict, that the United States agreed to take Pakistan off the list of countries suspected of harboring terrorists. It was the need to establish a clean record for itself in the field of terrorism that persuaded Pakistan to arrest and extradite Ramzi Youseff, accused of masterminding the February 1995 bombing of the World Trade Center in New York, and Mir Jamal Kansi, accused of killing two CIA employees outside the agency's headquarters in Langley, Virginia. The arrest and extradition of Odeh in August 1998 was also a part of this effort.

Pakistani authorities believed that Osama bin Laden, a devout Sunni Muslim, might also have contributed to the escalation of the Sunni-Shia strife that claimed hundreds of lives in Pakistan in the 1990s. Terrorist activities in Pakistan were not confined to the work of Muslim fundamentalists, however. Several attacks that killed scores of people were often attributed by the authorities to the Indian intelligence agency, the Research and Analysis Wing (RAW). RAW operations in Pakistan were said to have been in retaliation for the alleged involvement of the Pakistani intelligence agencies in the Indian state of Punjab in the 1980s and in the Indian-occupied areas of Kashmir in the 1990s.

Conclusion

By the time Pakistan celebrated its fiftieth birthday on August 14, 1997, the world around it had changed dramatically. The breakup of the Soviet Union in 1991 and with it the collapse of communism in Eastern and Central Europe made the world a complex place for countries such as Pakistan. These countries had known only one compass—the Cold War—to use in finding their place in global affairs. Now the United States, the only remaining superpower, wanted an entirely different set of responses from its former client states. Fidelity and loyalty were now measured in terms of a country's contribution to U.S. strategic interests or its subscription to norms of behavior that the West, particularly Washington, expected of all civilized states.

United States strategic interests were now defined in terms considerably broader than those used during Cold War days. Maintaining unconstrained access to energy sources, particularly oil, was by far the most important. The United States had depleted domestic reserves to the point that a significant proportion of its domestic demand was met with imports from Venezuela, Mexico, the Middle East, and North Africa. Any threat of disruption of access would not be tolerated, as it demonstrated unambiguously when Iraq invaded Kuwait. The rhetoric surrounding the Gulf War only thinly disguised the main reason for the U.S. attack on Iraq: the fear that Baghdad, having taken Kuwait, would advance into the Arabian peninsula, thereby bringing a significant part of global oil reserves under its control. The same motive informed the U.S. approach toward the oil-rich countries of Central Asia. Pakistan's location close to the oil-rich states and the rise of Islamic fundamentalism in this area ensured that it would receive attention from Washington, but not the kind it had enjoyed during the days of the Cold War.

The United States was also concerned with China's increasing power in the Pacific area. In 1998, President Bill Clinton visited China after Washington had shunned the country for nearly a decade. This change in policy was produced by the appreciation that, the Tiananmen Square incident of June 1989 notwithstanding, the United States had to engage Beijing constructively. Once again, Pakistan, a longtime friend of China, was of some marginal interest to U.S. policymakers.

In the absence of a strong strategic interest, Washington began to define its relations with Pakistan in terms of Islamabad's willingness to play by the new rules of international behavior. Among them was the requirement that developing countries not acquire weapons of mass destruction; not violate human rights but respect the rights of children, women, and religious minorities; not tolerate terrorists on its territory, allow them sanctuary, or permit them to mount operations against other countries; and not export drugs or allow the laundering of money associated with the drug trade. Following the end of the Cold War, the international community began to define appropriate behavior in terms of international treaties. Countries that failed to subscribe to these treaties were threatened with sanctions.

With the Soviet Union gone, there was no longer a balancing force in the global political and economic system. It was inevitable that the collapse of the Soviet Union, and with it the collapse of communism in Europe, would lay the basis for the emergence of a new global order based on a number of principles to which policymakers in the United States strongly subscribed. In many ways Pakistan became the test of the new order, which required all countries to subject the exercise of their sovereignty to these governing principles.

Pakistan and India were subjected to this requirement in the months following their nuclear weapons tests in May 1998. These explosions did not violate any international treaty or obligation, since neither India nor Pakistan had signed the Nuclear Nonproliferation Treaty (NPT) or the Comprehensive Test Ban Treaty (CTBT). Nevertheless, the United States applied severe sanctions on the two countries, arguing that the nuclear tests were against an implicit understanding among all responsible nations that they would work against the spread of weapons of mass destruction. This understanding had the force of international law even if it was not fully reflected in international treaties. The United States also pointed to its own laws, which obliged the president to act unilaterally against countries that defied this understanding.

There was also an understanding (again, not included in an international treaty) that Pakistan would work assiduously against exporting Islamic fundamentalism or supporting its spread. By allowing the Taleban to gain control of Afghanistan and letting them introduce an extremely conservative Islam to the citizens of that country, Pakistan was once again defying international understanding. These facts were brought to the attention of Prime Minister Nawaz Sharif during his visit to Washington in early December 1998 and in his meetings with senior officials of the U.S. administration, including President Bill Clinton.

Even as it was sending these strong messages to the Pakistani prime minister, the U.S. government signaled some easing of the sanctions imposed on the country. This was done in recognition of another principle of the emerging global order: No major world economy would be allowed to collapse and thus threaten the entire international economic system. That such a thing could happen was made abundantly clear by the effects on the Western economies produced by the economic crises in East Asia in 1997–1998 and in Russia in the summer of 1998. When Nawaz Sharif visited Bill Clinton in Washington, Pakistan was close to economic collapse (see Chapter 3), and the International Monetary Fund was asked to put together a rescue operation for it. In sum, as Pakistan enters the second half century of its existence as an independent state, it is being required to live within the confines of a new global economic order.

7

AN UNCERTAIN
FUTURE

What lies in Pakistan's future? This question is asked routinely by scholars, politicians, and journalists. The answer to it depends on estimations of the country's
ability to survive by surmounting its several problems. But the fact that Pakistan
faces a number of economic, social, and political problems does not make it
unique; scores of other developing countries confront problems of equal or
greater gravity, but their ability to survive as nation-states is seldom doubted. The
important point about this question, then, is not that it has been answered in so
many different ways but that it is asked at all.

Pakistan's Historical Purpose

To understand why the question is asked, one must go back to the circumstances
that led to the creation of Pakistan in the first place as a separate state for the
Muslim diaspora of British India—a country in which the 70 million Muslims of
that time could live in security without being discriminated against by a much
larger non-Muslim majority. Today, the Muslim population of the subcontinent
of South Asia is on the order of 340 million, of which 100 million (80 percent out
of a population of 125 million) live in Bangladesh, 120 million remain in India
(12 percent out of a population of 980 million), and 120 million are in Pakistan
(92 percent out of a population of 130 million). By a strange historical quirk,
Pakistan, a country established to protect the rights of the Muslim community of
British India, was left with slightly more than one-third of the total descendant
population of that community. It is legitimate, therefore, to ask whether Pakistan
can continue to survive as a nation-state on the basis of its original raison d'être.

Though legitimate, this question is not an entirely serious one. Scores of today's independent countries were created for reasons that are no longer relevant. There are countries in Africa that call themselves nation-states without defining the meaning of "nation" as it would apply to their context, other than to specify the notion that the people who live within the boundaries of a country automatically constitute a nation. Many of these nation-states have problematic frontiers—they cut across tribes, cultures, and geography in a fashion much more improbable than the borders of today's Pakistan. New ministates are being established every year and are called independent nations for the simple reason that no other way exists for accommodating them elsewhere. In the current world, therefore, Pakistan is no longer a geographical, cultural, religious, or economic absurdity. In fact, if anything—and for historical reasons—it has become a viable entity.

After 1971, Pakistan was no longer a country "with two wings and no body." The eastern wing was now Bangladesh, and the western wing was the new Pakistan. Unlike the Pakistan of 1947, the new Pakistan was no longer a geographical deformity, although some of its boundaries, particularly those to the east and the northwest, remained contested. But even these boundaries were settled in one way or another. In 1973, the eastern frontier—the cease-fire line between the two parts of Kashmir—was redemarcated as a result of the Simla Agreement, with the tacit understanding between India and Pakistan that neither country would take steps, military or otherwise, to alter the status quo. In 1979, the Russian invasion of Afghanistan for all intents and purposes settled the boundary dispute between Pakistan and its northwestern neighbor. No matter how the Afghanistan situation is resolved, it does not seem likely that the demarcation of this border will ever again be a serious issue. Hence Pakistan appears, at last, to have a set of fixed borders rather than malleable frontiers.

Other changes have occurred since Pakistan appeared on the world's political map as an independent state, which must be factored in to reflections on the country's future. These factors include the Pakistanis' (including leaders and citizens) view of their place in the world; Islam's evolving role in building a Pakistani nation; the relationship among several communities of people that together make up the nation of Pakistan; the precarious condition of the economy; and the inability of the government to adequately serve a large and growing population. These issues must be examined in any speculations about the future of the country that was originally conceived to provide a safe haven for the Muslims of British India.

Pakistan's future will also be influenced by the policies that its neighbors adopt toward particularly India but also Afghanistan, Iran, and Saudi Arabia. It will also have to take serious cognizance of the wishes of the Western countries, in particular the United States, on matters such as the development of weapons of mass destruction, human rights, terrorism, drugs and money laundering, environment, and climate change. Issues that were considered outside the purview of foreign governments, no matter how much power they possessed, while the world was balanced between Eastern and Western blocs are now being treated as legitimate grounds for external pressure. Multilateral institutions such as the International Monetary Fund and the World Bank have begun to concern themselves with issues of corruption and governance. An important development since the collapse of communism in East Europe is the introduction of constraints on the behavior of nations around the globe. The advent of globalization has meant some loss of sovereignty by nation-states on issues about which the Western and industrial countries have reached a consensus. Pakistan is among a dozen or so countries whose future is closely tied to the enforcement of this consensus. It has already been forced to act against those who profit from the trade in drugs; it has had to provide repeated assurances that its territory will not be put at the disposal of terrorist groups; it has had to answer questions in regard to child labor, minorities, and corruption in government procurement. Donors would like to see Pakistan provide better social services to women. A positive response to these and other pressures would mean major structural changes in the economy, the society, and the organization of the political system.

One more development needs to be noted in any discussion of the more important external influences on Pakistan's future. The growth of the Pakistani diaspora since the birth of the country has already had a profound impact on the economy, particularly in reducing poverty and in improving the level of social development of the communities that exported labor to the outside world. By the close of the twentieth century the Pakistani expatriate communities in three parts of the globe—the Middle East, Great Britain, and North America—constitute one of the largest groups of expatriates in the world. They number about 4 million and their combined income is some 70 to 80 percent of their homeland's gross domestic product. They have begun to exert an influence on their homeland in many different ways. No Pakistani leader can afford to ignore them; both Benazir Bhutto and Nawaz Sharif traveled frequently to the Middle East, Great Britain, and North America to develop links with this community.

In short, there is not much resemblance between today's Pakistan and the Pakistan of 1947. It is now much smaller in size, its population is much more homogeneous, and its international borders are virtually settled. Its geopolitical situation is also very different from the one in which it found itself at the time of its birth. And nobody today questions the economic viability of the state of Pakistan. If anything, Pakistan, with a bit of luck and some careful economic management, may turn out to be one of the few countries to graduate from the ranks of low-income nations. For that to happen, policymakers in Islamabad will have to introduce deep structural changes in the economy. In view of all these developments, questions about Pakistan's future should perhaps not be raised in the context only of its initial purpose.

As previously noted, that purpose in 1947—the year Pakistan was born—was to safeguard the perceived interests of the majority of the Indian Muslim community by creating an independent Muslim state. In retrospect, that purpose appears to have been well served. It is highly unlikely that a solution other than the partition of India would have worked for the larger Indian Muslim community. India does indeed retain a sizable Muslim population: However, of the 340 million Muslims of South Asia, some 65 percent live in independent Muslim countries—Bangladesh and Pakistan. It can also be argued that, without partition, an independent India would have found it difficult to establish democratic institutions. The leadership would have had to contend with the communal problem arising from the presence of a large Muslim minority that would have numbered some 340 million by the closing years of the twentieth century if the British had not partitioned their domain in South Asia to accommodate most followers of Islam.

Pakistan's past purpose is therefore not very relevant in gauging its future prospects or even in defining the political and economic objectives that should be pursued. A new set of political, economic, and social goals are needed. In politics, the real challenge is to define a political framework in which to bring together a number of diverse interests. In economics, the real purpose should be to realize the country's great but partially untapped potential. In social development, the obvious goal is to improve the situation of those segments of the population, in particular women, that have not benefited from whatever economic growth has occurred in the past. Before any meaningful movement can occur in any of these areas, however, a consensus will have to emerge on the role of religion in Pakistani society. But to define this role, we must return once again to the history of the Pakistan movement.

The Role of Islam in Nation Building

The three Muslim communities of British India that campaigned for the creation of Pakistan did so in pursuit of different interests. For the urban community of Bihar, Uttar Pradesh, Delhi, Bombay, and other provinces of north-central India the objective was to find a way to overcome what was perceived as the Hindu majority's reluctance to grant the Muslims their due share in government and economy. The average per capita income of the Muslims of these provinces was perhaps the same as the average for the non-Muslims. They demanded the establishment of the state of Pakistan not so much to improve their relative position as to preserve it. It might have been possible for this community to settle for something less than the partition of British India, but once partition was accepted, they had to decide between staying on in India and migrating to the new country of Pakistan. Migration provided the ultimate solution to this perceived problem for several million of these Muslims.

The Muslims of Bengal and Assam also demanded the creation of Pakistan for economic reasons, but, unlike the Muslims of the north-central provinces, they wanted Pakistan not in order to gain opportunity for themselves equal to that of the non-Muslims but to improve the distribution of income between two different economic classes: the Hindu landlords and the Muslim peasants. Although they constituted a majority in Bengal, a very large proportion of the Muslims were concentrated among the poor. The only way they could significantly improve their economic well-being was to somehow engineer a profound structural change involving land redistribution and tenurial reform. Experience had taught this group that such a transformation would be difficult to bring about while the Hindu landlords remained the dominant political force. The Muslims of Bengal seceded three times—first in 1905, when the province of Bengal was partitioned into Muslim East Bengal and Hindu West Bengal; the second time in 1947, when Muslim East Bengal was separated from British India to become the eastern province of Pakistan; and the third time in 1971, when East Pakistan became Bangladesh. The first of these three secessions was temporary: In 1911 the British, under pressure from the non-Muslims, reunited the two parts of Bengal. The second secession was to lead to the third; it was a historical accident that Bangladesh had to wait for the creation and political maturation of Pakistan before emerging as an independent entity. It is doubtful whether the economic and social problems of the Muslim Bengali community could have been adequately addressed within a political entity in which the Bengalis did not exercise total political control.

It is also doubtful that the Muslim provinces of northwest British India—Balochistan, the Northwest Frontier Province, Punjab, and Sindh—could have stayed within an independent and predominantly Hindu India. But unlike the other two Muslim communities of British India, they sought secession for religious rather than economic reasons. The Muslims of these provinces constituted the majority of the population—as did the Muslims of Bengal—but, unlike the Bengali Muslims, they were economically comfortable. The large and powerful landed aristocracy was predominantly Muslim, as was the reasonably prosperous peasantry of the "canal colonies." The Muslims were also prominent among the urban professionals, and some of them had founded highly successful industrial and business enterprises during the economic boom produced by World War II. Economic well-being had not translated into a feeling of religious security, however.

It took a religious revival for the Muslims of present-day Pakistan to accept the idea of Pakistan. These Muslims had shown little interest in this idea for as long as the idiom of the Pakistan movement remained nonreligious. It was only after the idea for Pakistan came to be articulated in religious terms that the Pakistan movement gained the support of the people of Punjab, Sindh, and the Northwest Frontier Province. Having long remained indifferent to the campaign that the other two Muslim communities had launched to create a separate state for themselves, the Muslims of the northwestern provinces also joined in once they began to see that such a state could create for them an Islamic polity.

As long as Pakistan remained divided into two wings, the question of Islam's role in the affairs of the state remained unanswered. The people of East Bengal (later East Pakistan and still later the independent country of Bangladesh) were content to let Islam guide individual behavior rather than become the religion of the state. The most the Bengalis were prepared to do in this respect was to pass the Objectives Resolution in 1951 and let it become the preamble of the constitution of 1956. The resolution proclaimed, "Whereas sovereignty over the entire universe belongs to Allah Almighty alone and the authority which He has delegated to the State of Pakistan . . . Wherein the State shall exercise its powers and authority in through the chosen representatives of the people; Wherein the principles of democracy, freedom, equality, tolerance and social justice as enunciated by Islam shall be fully observed . . ." In other words, Pakistan was to be governed on the basis of the principles of liberal democracy as enunciated by the will of the people and exercised by their chosen representatives. It is useful to recall that it was under Khawaja Nazimuddin, a Bengali prime minister, that the government of Pakistan resisted with great force an attempt by proponents of conservative Islam to bring religion into politics. The Nazimuddin government chose to place parts of Pakistan under martial law rather than declare the Ahmadiya community a non-Muslim minority.

Field Marshal Ayub Khan, Pakistan's first military president, was inclined to limit democracy to what he described as its "basic form" but not because it was the will of Allah. He believed that the citizens of the country he governed were not literate enough to exercise full democratic rights. Ayub Khan's sole gesture toward the religious forces was to name Pakistan's new capital Islamabad. Only after Ayub Khan departed in 1969 and Pakistan broke up in 1971 did the leaders' resolve to keep religion out of politics begin to weaken. Prime Minister Zulfikar Ali Bhutto succumbed to the pressure of Islamic activists. The constitution of 1973, which he piloted, named Pakistan the "Islamic Republic of Pakistan." In 1974 the National Assembly declared the Ahmadiyas to be non-Muslims and adopted a number of other measures that included prohibiting the use of alcohol and making Friday rather than Sunday the weekly holiday.

The most significant changes in terms of bringing Islam formally into the affairs of the state occurred during the long rule of General Zia ul-Haq, Pakistan's third military president. Zia's attempt to do away with the directly elected national and provincial assemblies was thwarted by democratic elements (he would have liked to rule with the help of a Majilis-e-Shura, an appointed assembly of respected individuals), but he succeeded in some other ways. He introduced Islamic taxes—*zakat* and *ushr*—and interest-free banking. A Shariat court was established to examine whether the laws passed by the national and provincial legislatures conformed to the basic tenets of Islam. A blasphemy law was introduced that made any criticism of Muhammad, the prophet of Islam, a capital offense. The Hadood Ordinance reduced the status of women. In retrospect, the most far-reaching change during the Zia period was the flow of public sector funds to *madrasas*—religious schools run mostly by conservative Sunni groups who drew their inspiration from the brand of Islam followed by the ruling family in Saudi Arabia.

During Benazir Bhutto's first tenure as prime minister, December 1988–August 1990, Pakistan did not further the formal Islamization of the society. However, in spite of pressure from several women's groups and human rights activists, she did not repeal the blasphemy laws or the Hadood Ordinance, lacking the political authority and will to do so. By neglecting the social sectors, in particular education, she left a very large number of people in the care of the *madrasas*.

In the fall of 1990, Nawaz Sharif began his first tenure as prime minister at the head of a coalition that called itself the Islami Jamhoori Itehad, the Islamic Democratic Alliance. In May 1991, the IJI administration presented the Shariat bill to the National Assembly. The bill sought to introduce Islamic tenets into the Pakistani society and was readily approved by both houses of the parliament. With President Ghulam Ishaq Khan giving his assent, the bill became law in the summer of 1991. Despite the promulgation of the Shariat Act, the territory to be covered to Islamize the society remained uncharted; the precise meaning that should be attached to the concept of an Islamic state, an Islamic economy, and an Islamic social system remained unclear. In its original formulation, the Islamic parties wanted all laws of the land to be tested by a court of Islamic jurists. The Shariat Act reserves that judgment for the National Assembly.

Nawaz Sharif's second tenure as prime minister began in February 1997, and the government once again showed great willingness to accommodate religious interests. In January 1998, Farooq Ahmad Khan Leghari was succeeded by Muhammad Rafiq Tarar as president. Tarar had all the attributes Islamic activists considered necessary for the head of the state, including membership in religious organizations. Tarar was an active member of the Tablighi Jamaat, which devoted itself to proselytization. In the summer of 1998, Prime Minister Nawaz Sharif introduced the fifteenth amendment to the constitution. If approved, it will formally make Islam the law of the land.

Issues for the Future

In 1947, all three Muslim communities came together in the newly created state of Pakistan. But the reasons for which these communities had sought Pakistan were so different that the political, economic, social, and religious underpinnings of the new state could not be defined. One highly articulate faction in West Pakistan sought to fashion an Islamic Pakistan. Another, the East Pakistanis—the Muslims of East Bengal—wanted the state to concentrate instead on removing the social and economic barriers that had kept them impoverished for so long. A third group, the *muhajirs* from the north-central provinces, saw the creation of Pakistan as the achievement of their objective; all that remained to be done was to organize the state along modern lines.

In other words, of the three Muslim communities, the one that had been the most active exponent of Muslim separatism lost a great deal of its political dynamism once the objective of creating a separate state had been achieved. For the other two, the birth of Pakistan was only one step toward the realization of several additional goals: economic emancipation and economic betterment for the

Bengalis, and Islamization for a number of important political groups of West Pakistan. It was natural that the leadership of Pakistan should eventually pass on to these two communities, with the *muhajirs* being sidelined for a while. From 1956 on—that is, from the time of the framing of the first constitution—the main political conflict was waged between the groups that sought to resolve the problem posed by the unequal distribution of economic wealth among the provinces on the one hand, and those that wanted the country's political, economic, and social systems to be defined in Islamic terms on the other.

The departure of Bengal from Pakistan should have eased the tension between these two points of view. With the country no longer divided into two wings separated by a thousand miles of Indian territory, it should have been possible to evolve a political structure that satisfied the communities that now constituted the nation of Pakistan. These communities defined their entity in many different ways. Some did this on the basis of geography—those who lived in Balochistan, the Northwest Frontier Province, Punjab, Sariki, and Sindh. Some identified themselves on the basis of ethnicity—the *muhajirs*, the people who had migrated from the north-central provinces of India to Pakistan, wished to be treated separately, along with the Balochis, Pathans, Punjabis, Sarikis, and Sindhis. Still others saw themselves representing the modernizing populations living in the large cities, determined to wrest control of the political system from the hands of the feudal class that wanted to hold on to the levers of politics in spite of their declining numbers and economic strength. A new group made up of the Pakistani diaspora in the Middle East, Europe, and North America sought to find a suitable place for their homeland in the rapidly changing global economic and political system. Finally, the forces represented by conservative Islam tried hard to turn Pakistan into a fundamentalist Islamic state.

Had the leadership groups shown greater foresight, they would have devoted their energies to evolving a political and economic system that aimed to accommodate these diverse interests. The return of democracy in 1988, following the death of President Zia ul-Haq, offered such an opportunity, but it was frittered away by the intense rivalry between Benazir Bhutto and Nawaz Sharif. Each tried to destroy the other without paying any attention to the damage being done to fledging political institutions.

Whether the experiment that was launched in Pakistan will succeed depends on a number of circumstances—some internal, others external. Internally, the question of the role of the armed forces in politics will have to be decided, as will the question of political succession in what was for a very long time a garrison state. The issue of the distribution of political power between the federal government and the federating states will need to be resolved, as will the issue of meaningful participation in political decisionmaking on the part of the half dozen sociocultural communities that make up present-day Pakistan.

As always, external factors will play a role in Pakistan's future. The war in Afghanistan, the tensions created in the Middle East by Iraq's invasion of Kuwait, the continuing conflict between Israel and the Arabs, the process of maturation of the revolution in Iran, the question of the political legitimacy of the ruling families of Saudi Arabia and other states of the Gulf region—all could affect developments in Pakistan in many ways difficult to anticipate. But one thing is clear—and this has been the main thesis of this book—the Pakistan that emerges in the next decade or two will be very different from the country originally envisioned by its founder, Mohammad Ali Jinnah. It is already different—not only in the geographical sense but in many other ways as well—and this process of change will continue. It is important for the people of Pakistan to understand that the meaning of Pakistan need not be found in the context of the movement that made the birth of the country possible in the first place. It must be sought instead in the current situation, which is marked by internal and external circumstances very different from those that prevailed in 1947.

Indeed, history is no longer a very effective guide for defining Pakistan's raison d'être; too much has happened since 1947. The country is half its original size; culturally, socially, and economically, it is now less a part of South Asia than was the case in 1947. Religion is of much greater importance now than in 1947, not only in Pakistan but in the entire region to which it belongs. It is in these very changed circumstances that the people of Pakistan will need to look for a direction for themselves and for their country.

Notes

Introduction

1. For an excellent analysis of Pakistan's constitutional history, see Kamal Azfar, "Constitutional Developments During the Zia Period," in Shahid Javed Burki and Craig Baxter, *Pakistan Under the Military: Eleven Years of Zia ul-Haq* (Boulder: Westview, 1991), pp. 49–86.

2. For an analysis of the circumstances that led to the creation of Bangladesh, see Rounaq Jahan, *Pakistan: Failure in National Integration* (New York: Columbia University Press, 1972).

3. These estimates are based on data generated by the United Nations International Comparison Program (ICP) that has developed measures of real GDP on an internationally comparable scale using purchasing power parities (PPPs) instead of exchange rates as conversion factors. For a description of the methodology employed and the country estimates made by the program, see the World Bank, *World Development Report 1990* (Washington, D.C.: World Bank, 1990), pp. 246, 257–258, and Table 30 (pp. 236–237).

Chapter 1

1. The Great Indian Mutiny was to become one of the most written about events of the British rule in India. Among the better known works on the subject are R. C. Majumdar, *The Sepoy Mutiny and the Revolt of 1857* (Calcutta: Longmans, 1963) and Christopher Hibbert, *The Great Mutiny: India 1857* (New York: Viking, 1978).

2. Geoffrey Moorhouse, *India Britannica* (New York: Harper and Row, 1983), p. 128.

3. In his seminal work on the creation of Pakistan, Khalid bin Sayeed used the term "viceregal system" to describe Pakistan's basic political philosophy during the country's early years. See Khalid bin Sayeed, *Pakistan: The Formative Phase, 1857–1948* (London: Oxford University Press, 1968), pp. 270–300.

4. W. W. Hunter, *The Indian Mussulmans* (London: Trubner, 1871), pp. 179–180.

5. For an overview of the contribution made by Sir Sayyid Ahmad Khan to the political development of the Muslim community of British India, see David Lelyveld, *Aligarh's First Generation* (Princeton, N.J.: Princeton University Press, 1978).

6. Ayesha Jalal, *The Sole Spokesman: Jinnah, the Muslim League, and the Demand for Pakistan* (Cambridge, U.K.: Cambridge University Press, 1983).

7. Mohamed Ali, *My Life: A Fragment* (Lahore: S. M. Ashraf, 1946), pp. 17–18.

8. H. V. Hodson, *The Great Divide* (London: Hutchinson, 1969), p. 58.

9. Maulana Abdul Kalam Azad, *India Wins Freedom* (New York: Longmans, Green, 1960).

10. Quoted in M. H. Saiyid, *Mohammad Ali Jinnah: A Political Study* (Karachi: Elite Publishers, 1970), p. 5.

11. David Gilmartin, "Religious Leadership and the Pakistan Movement in the Punjab," *Modern Asian Studies* 13, no. 3 (July 1979): 498.

12. Ibid., p. 503.

13. A. K. Zainul Abedin, *Memorable Speeches of Sher-e-Bangla* (Barisal: AlHelal, 1978), p. 31.

14. Ibid., p. 138.

15. Salman Rushdie, *Shame* (London: Jonathan Cape, 1983), p. 87.

16. B. L. C. Johnson, *Pakistan* (London: Heinemann, 1979), p. 2.

17. Herbert Feldman, *Revolution in Pakistan: A Study of the Martial Law Administration* (London: Oxford University Press, 1967), p. 140.

18. For a discussion of the reaction of Pakistani women to the promulgation of the Hudood Ordinance, see Khawar Mumtaz and Farida Shaheed, *Women of Pakistan: Two Steps Forward, One Step Back?* (Lahore: Vanguard, 1987).

19. *Dawn*, "Will No One Ever Learn from History?" August 30, 1998.

CHAPTER 2

1. This excerpt is from the speech that Mohammad Ali Jinnah delivered in his capacity as president of the Constituent Assembly on August 11, 1947. See Muhammad Munir, *From Jinnah to Zia* (Lahore: Vanguard, 1979), pp. 29–30.

2. Zulfikar Ali Bhutto, *The Myth of Independence* (Karachi: Oxford University Press, 1969), p. 118.

3. Mahbub ul Haq, *The Poverty Curtain* (New York: Columbia University Press, 1976), p. 1.

4. Ibid.

5. Ibid.

6. A. R. Khan, *The Economy of Bangladesh* (London: Macmillan, 1972), p. 18.

7. Salman Rushdie, *Shame* (London: Jonathan Cape, 1983), p. 179.

8. Salamat Ali, "An Orderly Return to the Front," *Far Eastern Economic Review* (August 12, 1977).

9. General Zia ul-Haq, as quoted in the *Times* (London), September 8, 1977.

10. Quoted in Shahid Javed Burki, *Pakistan Under Bhutto: 1971–1977* (London: Macmillan, 1980), p. 202.

11. Benazir Bhutto, *Daughter of the East: An Autobiography* (London: Hamish Hamilton, 1988), p. 68.

12. "Who Killed Zia?" *Nation* (Lahore), August 4, 1989.

13. Zulfikar Ali Bhutto, *If I Am Assassinated . . .* (New Delhi: Vikas, 1979), passim.

14. Zia ul-Haq, *Pakistan Times* (Lahore), July 8, 1977.

15. Beverly Nichols, *Verdict on India* (Bombay: Thacker, 1946), pp. 58–59.

16. General Zia ul-Haq, as quoted in Tariq Ali, *Can Pakistan Survive?* (New York: Penguin, 1983), p. 133.

17. Fazlur Rahman, *Islam* (Chicago: University of Chicago Press, 1966), p. 124.

18. *Muslim* (Islamabad), December 1, 1984.

19. Mushahid Hussain, "President's Referendum Politicking: An Appraisal," *Muslim* (Islamabad), December 17, 1984.

20. Quoted in M. Aftab, "Low Turn-out in Zia Election Referendum," *Daily Telegraph* (London), December 21, 1984.

21. Mushahid Hussain, "Parties, Not Politicians, Bypassed in Polls," *Muslim* (Islamabad), February 28, 1985.

22. "Inshallah," *Wall Street Journal,* February 28, 1985.

23. Mahbub ul Haq, *Budget Speech, 1985* (Islamabad: Ministry of Finance, 1985).

24. "Anwarul Haq on Amendments: Basic Structure of 1973 Constitution Changed," *Muslim* (Islamabad), March 8, 1985.

25. "Ghafoor Criticizes Amendments: Call for 'Joint Action' to Restore Democracy," *Muslim* (Islamabad), March 6, 1985.

26. Ali Sikander, "Amendments Cancel Election Euphoria," *Muslim* (Islamabad), March 5, 1985.

27. "The President General," *Times* (London), March 8, 1985.

28. Mahbub ul Haq, as quoted in *Overseas Mashriq,* June 27, 1985.

29. "Almost Free," *Economist,* January 4, 1986, p. 30.

30. Quoted by Husain Haqqani, "Back to Barracks, But Keeping a Close Watch," *Far Eastern Economic Review,* January 9, 1986, p. 24.

31. Mahbub ul Haq joined the cabinet later, but not as finance minister. On February 12, 1986, he was assigned the portfolio of planning and development.

32. For Gen. F. A. Chishti's account of "Operation Fair Play," see his book, *Betrayals of Another Kind: Islam, Democracy, and the Army in Pakistan* (Delhi: Tricolour Books, 1989), pp. 29–78.

33. Ibid., p. 63.

34. Rasul B. Rais, "Pakistan in 1988: From Command to Conciliation," *Asian Survey* 29 (February 1989): 201.

35. President Ghulam Ishaq Khan's address to the nation was carried by all newspapers on August 7, 1990. See *Muslim* (Islamabad), *Nation* (Lahore), *Dawn* (Karachi) for August 7, 1990.

36. Ibid.

37. Ayaz Amir, "Another Kind of Election . . . ," *Herald* (Karachi), October 1990, p. 6.

38. Conversation with the author on July 18, 1993.

CHAPTER 3

1. World Bank, *World Development Report, 1990* (Washington, D.C.: World Bank, 1990), p. 178.

2. All the major newspapers published the text of President Ghulam Ishaq's television and radio address in full on August 7, 1990. See the *Muslim* (Islamabad), the *Nation* (Lahore), and *Dawn* (Karachi).

3. See President Ghulam Ishaq Khan's presidential order dissolving the National Assembly, *Dawn* (Karachi), August 7, 1990.

4. Steve Col, "Bhutto's Husband Arrested," *Washington Post,* September 13, 1990.

5. World Bank, *World Development Report, 1997,* Table 13, pp. 238–239.

6. These data are from World Bank, *World Development Report, 1990* (Washington, D.C.: World Bank, 1990).

7. Gustav F. Papanek, *Pakistan's Development: Social Goals and Private Incentives* (Cambridge: Harvard University Press, 1967), pp. 56–74.

8. George Rosen, *Western Economists and Eastern Societies: Agents of Change in South Asia, 1950–1970* (Baltimore: Johns Hopkins University Press, 1985), pp. 146–200.

9. World Bank, *IDA in Retrospect: The First Two Decades of the International Development Association* (Washington, D.C.: World Bank, 1982), pp. 1–9.

10. See Rounaq Jahan, *Pakistan: Failure in National Integration* (New York: Columbia University Press, 1972), for a detailed account of the debate between East and West Pakistan on the question of resource transfer between the two provinces.

11. Peter Montagnon, "Sharp Blow to the Most Vulnerable," *Financial Times,* September 7, 1990.

12. David Housego, "Pakistan Seeks Help to Ease Gulf Shocks," *Financial Times,* September 14, 1990.

13. For a detailed analysis of the potential of the Indus River system and the dispute between India and Pakistan on the distribution of the waters of the system, see Aloys A. Michel, *The Indus Rivers* (New Haven: Yale University Press, 1967).

14. Shahid Javed Burki, *Pakistan: The Continuing Search for Nationhood* (Boulder: Westview, 1991), p. 136.

15. John Cool, "Indus: The Grain Machine" (Cambridge: Harvard University Development Advisory Service files, mimeograph, 1967).

16. See Shahid Javed Burki, *Pakistan Under Bhutto, 1971–1977* (London: Macmillan, 1988), for an analysis of the Bhutto period.

17. For analysis of the reform efforts in Latin America, see Sebastian Edwards, *Crisis and Reform in Latin American: From Despair to Hope* (New York: Oxford University Press, 1995).

18. For a discussion of the policy options available to the leaders of Pakistan in 1999 see Shahid Javed Burki, Pakistan in crisis: "A diagnosis of its causes and an approach for resolving it" lecture delivered at the Pakistan Institute for Development Economics, Islamabad, November 18, 1998.

Chapter 4

1. The "cumulative causation" thesis was developed by Paul Streeten et al. in *First Things First: Meeting Basic Human Needs in Developing Countries* (New York: Oxford University Press, 1981), pp. 46–67.

2. James Grant, *The State of the World's Children, 1984* (New York: UNICEF, 1984), p. 18.

3. For a description of the educational policies pursued by the government of Zulfikar Ali Bhutto, see Dawn E. Jones and Rodney W. Jones, "Nationalizing Education in Pakistan: Teachers Association and the People's Party," *Pacific Affairs* 50, no. 4 (Winter 1974–1975): 570–581.

4. Government of Pakistan, *The Sixth Five-Year Plan, 1983–1988* (Islamabad: Planning Commission, 1983), p. 302.

5. Government of Pakistan, *The Seventh Five-Year Plan, 1988–1993, and Perspective Plan, 1988–2003* (Islamabad: Planning Commission, 1988), p. 23.

6. Mahbubul Haq persuaded the United Nations Development Program (UNDP) to publish an annual *Human Development Report.* The first report was published in 1990 and

included an index on human development that measured the progress made by countries not only in terms of their gross domestic product but also in terms of a number of indices that measured the quality of life.

7. S. Akbar Zaidi, "The Urban Bias in Health Facilities in Pakistan," *Social Sciences and Medicine* 20, no. 5 (1985): 473–482.

8. Government of Pakistan, *The Fifth Five-Year Plan, 1978–1983* (Islamabad: Planning Commission, 1978), p. 614.

9. World Bank, *Health: Sector Policy Paper* (Washington, D.C.: World Bank, 1980), pp. 13–23.

10. Government of Pakistan, *The Fifth Five-Year Plan, 1978–1983*, p. 593.

11. "Zayed Hospital to Become Fully Operational Soon," *Muslim* (Islamabad, August 5, 1985).

12. Government of Pakistan, *Pakistan National Impact Study: 1968–1969* (Islamabad: Population Planning Council, 1971), p. 83.

13. Government of Pakistan, *Seventh Five-Year Plan*, p. 273.

14. Willy Brandt et al., *North-South: A Program for Survival* (Cambridge, Mass.: MIT Press, 1980), pp. 78–89.

15. For one speculation, see Shahid Javed Burki, "Poverty in Pakistan: Myth or Reality," in *Rural Poverty in South Asia*, ed. T. N. Srinivasan and Pranab K. Bardhan (New York: Columbia University Press, 1988), pp. 69–88.

16. Ann Duncan, *Women in Pakistan: An Economic and Social Strategy* (Washington, D.C.: World Bank, 1989), p. xxi.

17. Khawar Mumtaz and Farida Shaheed, *Women of Pakistan: Two Steps Forward, One Step Back?* (Lahore: Vanguard, 1987), p. 75.

18. Government of Pakistan, *Seventh Five-Year Plan*, p. 17.

CHAPTER 5

1. See Makhdoom Ali Khan, *The Constitution of the Islamic Republic Pakistan* (Karachi: Pakistan Publishing House, 1986), p. 40.

2. During the tenure of the caretaker administration, Ardeshir Cowasjee published a series of articles in *Dawn*, Pakistan's largest English-language newspaper, under the title of *Ehtesab Before Itikhab*.

3. For a fairly thorough analysis of the unfolding events in the case against Benazir Bhutto and her husband, Asif Ali Zardari, see Farhan Bukhari, "Bhutto: 'I Am Not a Criminal,'" *Financial Times*, September 12, 1997, p. 6; and Jimmy Burns, "$3.6 Billion Left Pakistan Illegally," *Financial Times*, September 25, 1997, p. 14.

4. Zafar Abbas, "The Swiss Connection," *Herald* (Karachi), October 1997, pp. 31–39.

5. Jimmy Burns, "Pakistan Refused Help by UK Over Bhutto," *Financial Times*, September 18, 1977, p. 14.

6. *Link* (Los Angeles), November 3, 1997, p. 13.

7. The SGS-Cotecna story was extensively covered by the Western press, in particular, the *Financial Times* and the *New York Times*.

8. World Bank, *Governance and Development* (Washington, D.C.: World Bank, 1992), p. 3.

9. Mahbubul Haq, *Human Development in South Asia, 1997* (Karachi: Oxford University Press, 1997). p. 37.

10. Shahid Javed Burki, "Governance, Corruption, and Development: Some Major Obstacles to Growth and Development," *The Banker* (Lahore), Spring 1998.

11. World Bank, *Helping Countries Combat Corruption: The Role of the World Bank* (Washington, D.C.: World Bank, 1997), p. 8.

12. Ibid., p. 8.

13. Martin Wolf, "Corruption in the Spotlight," *Financial Times*, September 16, 1997, p. 15.

14. See, for instance, Paulo Mauro, "The Effects of Corruption on Growth, Investment, and Government Expenditure: A Cross-Country Analysis," in *Corruption and the Global Economy*, ed. Kimberley Ann Elliot (Washington, D.C.: Institute for International Economics, 1997); Susan Rose-Ackerman, "Corruption and Development" (paper presented at the World Bank Annual Conference on Development, Washington D.C., April 30–May 1, 1997); and Daniel Kaufman, "Corruption: The Facts," *Foreign Policy*, Summer 1997.

15. This term was first used by Shahid Javed Burki, *Pakistan Under Bhutto, 1971–1977* (London: Macmillan, 1980).

16. Perhaps the best account of the ICS rule of India is to be found in a two-volume work by Philip Woodruff, himself a member of the ICS. See *Men Who Ruled India: The Founders* and *Men Who Ruled India: The Guardians* (London: Jonathan Cape, 1965).

17. See Ardeshir Cowasjee, "Fascism on the March," *Dawn*, December 7, 1997, p. 13.

18. See Jeab Tirole, "A Theory of Collective Reputations," *Review of Economic Studies* 63, no. 1 (January 1966): 1–22.

19. For a description of these reforms in the context of the region of Latin America and the Caribbean, see Shahid Javed Burki and Guillermo Perry, *The Long March: A Reform Agenda for Latin America and the Caribbean in the Next Decade* (Washington, D.C.: World Bank, 1997).

CHAPTER 6

1. N. Mansergh and Penderel Moon, *Constitutional Relations Between Britain and India: The Transfer of Power, 1944–1947* (London: Her Majesty's Stationery Office, 1982).

2. See Benazir Bhutto, *Daughter of the East: An Autobiography* (London: Hamish Hamilton, 1988), for a firsthand account of the deliberations that led to the signing of the Simla accord between Zulfikar Ali Bhutto, her father, and Indira Gandhi, the prime minister of India.

3. Ravi Rikhye, *The War That Never Was* (Delhi: Chanakya, 1988), p. 31.

4. Leonard S. Spector, "If India and Pakistan Went to War?" *International Herald Tribune*, June 8, 1990.

5. James Rupert, "Fighting Reported Near Afghan Capital in New Offensive," *Washington Post*, October 13, 1990.

6. *The Economist*, "Afghanistan and Iran: War Cries," September 19, 1998, p. 52.

7. Zulfikar Ali Bhutto spelled out his approach toward Pakistan's foreign relations in a book he wrote after leaving the administration of President Muhammad Ayub Khan. See *The Myth of Independence* (Karachi: Oxford University Press, 1967).

8. "Straight Talk on Pakistan," *New York Times*, September 12, 1990.

9. Barbara Crossette, "U.S. Aid Judgment Upsets Pakistani Leaders," *New York Times,* October 16, 1990.

10. Zulfikar Ali Bhutto, *Myth of Independence,* p. 13.

11. Zulfikar Ali Bhutto, *Speeches* (Islamabad: Government of Pakistan, Ministry of Information, 1973), p. 13.

12. See Zulfikar Ali Bhutto, *If I Am Assasinated* (New Delhi: Vikas, 1979).

13. Robert Oakley, "Pakistan's Nuclear Program," *Nation* (Lahore), November 19, 1990.

14. R. Jeffrey Smith, "U.S. Stiffens Policy on Nuclear Arms, Pakistan Aid," *Washington Post,* November 20, 1990.

Bibliography

THE BRITISH PERIOD IN INDIA

Andrew, Ward. *Our Bones Are Scattered: The Cawnpore Massacres and the Indian Mutiny.* New York: Holt, 1996.

French, Patrick. *Liberty or Death: India's Journey to Independence and Division.* London: HarperCollins, 1997.

Hibbert, Christopher. *The Great Mutiny: India, 1857.* New York: Viking, 1978.

Majumdar, R. C. *The Sepoy Mutiny and the Revolt of 1857.* Calcutta: Longmans, 1963.

Moorhouse, Geoffrey. *India Britannica.* New York: Harper and Row, 1983.

Morris, James. *Pax Britannica: The Climax of an Empire.* New York: Harcourt, Brace, and World, 1968.

Schweiniitz, Karl de. *The Rise and Fall of British India.* London: Methuen, 1983.

Woodruff, Philip. *The Men Who Ruled India: The Founders* London: Jonathan Cape, 1953.

————. *The Men Who Ruled India: The Guardians.* London: Jonathan Cape, 1954.

THE MUSLIMS OF BRITISH INDIA

Hardy, P. *The Muslims of British India.* Cambridge, U.K.: Cambridge University Press, 1972.

Ikram, S. M. *Muslim Civilization in India.* New York: Columbia University Press, 1964.

Lelyveld, David. *Aligarh's First Generation: Muslim Solidarity in British India.* Princeton, N.J.: Princeton University Press, 1978.

Minault, Gail. *The Khilafat Movement: Religious Symbolism and Political Mobilization in India.* New York: Columbia University Press, 1982.

Mujeeb, M. *The Indian Muslims.* London: George Allen and Unwin, 1967.

Shaikh, Forzana. *Community and Consensus in Islam: Muslim Representation in Colonial India.* Cambridge, U.K.: Cambridge University Press, 1989.

THE FREEDOM MOVEMENT AND THE PARTITION OF BRITISH INDIA

Collins, Larry, and Dominique Lapierre. *Freedom at Midnight.* New York: Simon and Schuster, 1975.

Hamid, Abdul. *Muslim Separatism in India.* Karachi: Oxford University Press, 1967.

Hamid, Shahid, *Disastrous Twilight: A Personal Record of the Partition of India.* London: Leo Cooper, 1986.

Hodson, H. V. *The Great Divide.* London: Hutchinson, 1969.

Jalal, Ayesha. *The Sole Spokesman: Jinnah, the Muslim League, and the Demand for Pakistan.* Cambridge, U.K.: Cambridge University Press, 1985.

Azad, Maulana Abdul. *India Wins Freedom.* London: Longman, 1960.

Moon, Penderel. *Divide and Quit.* London: Chatto and Windus, 1964.

Philips, C. M., and Mary Doran, eds. *The Partition of India: Policies and Perspectives, 1935–1947.* Cambridge, Mass.: MIT Press, 1970.

PAKISTAN'S HISTORY

Burki, Shahid Javed. *Historical Dictionary of Pakistan.* Metuchen, N.J.: Scarecrow, 1991.

Khan, Roedad. *Pakistan: A Dream Gone Sour.* Karachi: Oxford University Press, 1997.

Khan, Sardar Shaukat Hayat. *Memoirs: The Nation That Lost Its Soul.* Lahore: Jang, 1995.

Ziring, Lawrence. *Pakistan in the Twentieth Century: A Political History.* Karachi: Oxford University Press, 1997.

PAKISTAN'S EARLY YEARS

Ahmad, Syed Nur. *From Martial Law to Martial Law: Politics in the Punjab, 1919–1958.* Boulder: Westview, 1985.

Ali, Chaudhri Muhammed. *The Emergence of Pakistan.* New York: Columbia University Press, 1967.

Callard, Keith. *Pakistan: A Political Study.* London: Macmillan, 1957.

Jalal, Ayesha. *The State of Martial Rule: The Origins of Pakistan's Political Economy of Defense.* Cambridge, U.K.: Cambridge University Press, 1990.

Sayeed, Khalid bin. *Pakistan: The Formative Phase, 1857–1948.* London: Oxford University Press, 1968.

Symonds, Richard. *The Making of Pakistan.* London: Faber and Faber, 1950.

Zaheer, Hasan. *The Times and Trial of the Rawalpindi Conspiracy, 1951: The First Coup Attempt in Pakistan.* Karachi: Oxford University Press, 1998.

THE AYUB KHAN ERA

Feldman, Herbert. *From Crisis to Crisis: Pakistan, 1962–1969.* London: Oxford University Press, 1972.

———. *Revolution in Pakistan: A Study of the Martial Law Administration.* London: Oxford University Press, 1967.

von Vorys, Karl. *Political Development in Pakistan.* Princeton, N.J.: Princeton University Press, 1965.

Wheeler, Richard S. *The Politics of Pakistan: A Constitutional Quest.* Ithaca, N.Y.: Cornell University Press, 1970.

Williams, L. F. Rushbrook. *The State of Pakistan.* London: Faber and Faber, 1966.

Ziring, Lawrence. *The Ayub Khan Era: Politics in Pakistan, 1958–1969.* Syracuse, N.Y.: Syracuse University Press, 1971.

The Yahya Khan Era and the Breakup of Original Pakistan

Ali, Tariq. *Pakistan: Military Rule or People's Power.* London: Jonathan Cape, 1970.
Choudhury, G. W. *Last Days of United Pakistan.* Bloomington: Indiana University Press, 1974.
Feldman, Herbert. *The End and the Beginning: Pakistan, 1969–1971.* London: Oxford University Press, 1976.
Wriggins, W. H., ed. *Pakistan in Transition.* Islamabad: University of Islamabad Press, 1975.

The Zulfikar Ali Bhutto Era

Bhutto, Benazir. *Daughter of the East: An Autobiography.* London: Hamish Hamilton, 1988.
Burki, Shahid Javed. *Pakistan Under Bhutto: 1971–1977.* London: Macmillan, 1980.
Khan, Lt. General Gul Hasan. *Memoirs.* Karachi: Oxford University Press, 1993.
Sayeed, Khalid bin. *Politics in Pakistan: The Nature and Direction of Change.* New York: Praeger, 1980.
Yusuf, Hamid. *Pakistan in Search of Democracy, 1947–1977.* Lahore: Afroasia, 1980.
Ziring, Lawrence. *Pakistan: The Enigma of Political Development.* Boulder: Westview, 1980.
Ziring, Lawrence, Ralph Braibanti, and W. Howard Wriggins, eds. *Pakistan: The Long View.* Durham, N.C.: Duke University Press, 1977.

The Zia Ul-Haq Era

Ali, Tariq. *Can Pakistan Survive? The Death of a State.* London: Penguin, 1983.
Baxter, Craig, ed. *Zia's Pakistan: Politics and Stability in a Frontline State.* Boulder: Westview, 1985.
Burki, Shahid Javed, and Craig Baxter. *Pakistan Under the Military: Eleven Years of Zia ul-Haq.* Boulder: Westview, 1991.
Chishti, Faiz Ali. *Betrayals of Another Kind: Islam, Democracy, and the Army in Pakistan.* Delhi: Tricolour Books, 1989.
Choudhury, Galam W. *Pakistan: Transition from Military to Civilian Rule.* London: Scorpion, 1988.
Choudhury, Hassan, and Jamil Rashid, eds. *Pakistan: The Roots of Dictatorship.* London: Zed, 1983.
Munir, Muhammad. *From Jinnah to Zia.* Lahore: Vanguard, 1979.

The Breakup of Pakistan

Jahan, Rounaq. *Pakistan: Failure in National Integration.* New York: Columbia University Press, 1972.
Niazi, Lt. General A. A. K. *The Betrayal of East Pakistan.* Karachi: Oxford University Press, 1998.
Salik, Hasan. *The Separation of East Pakistan: The Rise and Realization of Bengali Muslim Nationalism.* Karachi: Oxford University Press, 1994.
Salik, Siddiq. *Witness to Surrender.* Karachi: Oxford University Press, 1977.

PAKISTAN'S ECONOMY

Amjad, Rashid. *Private Industrial Investment in Pakistan, 1960–1970.* London: Cambridge University Press, 1982.

Andrus, J. Russel, and Azizali F. Mohammed. *The Economy of Pakistan.* London: Oxford University Press, 1958.

Burki, Shahid Javed, and Robert Laporte Jr., eds. *Pakistan's Development Priorities: Choices for the Future.* Karachi: Oxford University Press, 1984.

Haq, Mahbub ul. *The Strategy of Economic Planning: A Case Study of Pakistan.* Karachi: Oxford University Press, 1963.

LaPorte, Robert, Jr., and Muntazar Bashir Ahmad. *Public Enterprises in Pakistan.* Boulder: Westview, 1989.

Lewis, Stephen R. *Economic Policy and Industrial Growth in Pakistan.* London: George Allen and Unwin, 1969.

Michel, Aloys A. *The Indus Rivers.* New Haven: Yale University Press, 1967.

Nabi, Ijaz, Naved Hamid, and Shahid Zahid. *The Agrarian Economy of Pakistan: Issues and Policies.* Karachi: Oxford University Press, 1986.

Noman, Omar. *Pakistan: Political and Economic History Since 1947.* New York: Kegan Paul, 1990.

Papanek, Gustav F. *Pakistan's Development: Social Goals and Private Incentives.* Cambridge: Harvard University Press, 1967.

Parvez, Hasan. *Pakistan's Economy at the Crossroads: Past Policies and Present Imperatives.* Karachi: Oxford University Press, 1998.

Rosen, George. *Western Economists and Eastern Societies: Agents of Change in South Asia, 1950–1970.* Baltimore: Johns Hopkins University Press, 1985.

Stevens, Robert D., Hamza Alavi, and Peter J. Bertocci. *Rural Development in Bangladesh and Pakistan.* Honolulu: University Press of Hawaii, 1976.

White, Lawrence J. *Industrial Concentration and Economic Power in Pakistan.* Princeton, N.J.: Princeton University Press, 1974.

PAKISTAN'S GOVERNING ELITES

Ahmad, Muneer. *The Civil Servant in Pakistan.* Karachi: Oxford University Press, 1966.

Cohen, Stephen P. *The Pakistan Army.* Berkeley: University of California Press, 1989.

Kochanek, Stanley A. *Interest Groups and Development.* New Delhi: Oxford University Press, 1983.

LaPorte, Robert, Jr. *Power and Privilege: Influence and Decisionmakers in Pakistan.* Berkeley: University of California Press, 1975.

Mason, Philip. *A Matter of Honour: An Account of the Indian Army, the Officers and Men.* New York: Holt, Rinehart, and Winston, 1974.

Naipaul, V. S. *Among the Believers: An Islamic Journey.* New York: Knopf, 1981.

PAKISTAN'S FOREIGN RELATIONS

Brown, W. Norman. *United States and India and Pakistan.* Cambridge: Harvard University Press, 1963.

Burke, S. M. *Pakistan's Foreign Policy: An Historical Analysis.* London: Oxford University Press, 1973.
Gupta, Sisir. *Kashmir: A Study in India-Pakistan Relations.* London: Asia, 1966.
Korbel, Joseph. *Danger in Kashmir.* Princeton, N.J.: Princeton University Press, 1966.
Pran, Chopra. *India, Pakistan, and the Kashmir Tangle.* New Delhi: Vikas, 1994.
Schfield, Victoria. *Kashmir in the Crossfire.* London: Tauris, 1996.
Shahi, Agha. *Pakistan's Security and Foreign Policy.* Lahore: Progressive, 1988.
Sisson, Richard, and Leo E. Rose. *Pakistan, India, and the Creation of Bangladesh.* Berkeley: University of California Press, 1990.

PAKISTAN'S LEADERSHIP

Bhutto, Zulfikar Ali. *If I Am Assassinated.* New Delhi: Vikas, 1979.
Bolitho, Hector. *Jinnah: Creator of Pakistan.* London: John Murray, 1954.
Khan, Mohammed Ayub. *Friends, Not Masters: A Political Autobiography.* London: Oxford University Press, 1967.
Malik, Hafeez, ed. *Iqbal: Poet-Philosopher of Pakistan.* New York: Columbia University Press, 1971.
Taseer, Salmaan. *Bhutto: A Political Biography.* London: Ithaca, 1979.
Wolpert, Stanley. *Jinnah of Pakistan.* New York: Oxford University Press, 1984.

REGIONAL ISSUES

Ahmed, Akbar S. *Millennium and Charisma Among Pathans: A Critical Essay in Social Anthropology.* London: Routledge and Kegan Paul, 1976.
———. *Pakhtun Economy and Society: Traditional Structure and Economic Development in a Tribal Society.* London: Routledge and Kegan Paul, 1980.
Ali, Imran. *The Punjab Under Imperialism, 1885–1947.* Princeton, N.J.: Princeton University Press, 1988.
Awan, A. B. *Baluchistan: Historical and Political Processes.* London: New Century, 1985.
Fox, Richard G. *Lions of the Punjab: Culture in the Making.* Berkeley: University of California Press, 1985.
Harrison, Selig S. *In Afghanistan's Shadow: Baluch Nationalism and Soviet Temptations.* Washington, D.C.: Carnegie Endowment for International Peace, 1981.
Khuhro, Homeeda. *The Making of Modern Sind.* Karachi: Indus, 1978.
Korbel, Josef. *Danger in Kashmir.* Princeton, N.J.: Princeton University Press, 1966.
Lambrick, H. T. *Sind: A General Introduction.* Hyderabad: Sindhi Adabi Board, 1964.
Mayne, Peter. *Saints of Sind.* London: John Murray, 1956.
Saeed, Muhammad. *Lahore: A Memoire.* Lahore: Vanguard, 1989.

PAKISTAN'S SOCIAL DEVELOPMENT

Brandt, Willy, et al. *North-South: A Program for Survival.* Cambridge, Mass.: MIT Press, 1980.
Duncan, Ann. *Women in Pakistan: An Economic and Social Strategy.* Washington, D.C.: World Bank, 1989.

Mumtaz, Khawar, and Farida Shaheed. *Women of Pakistan: Two Steps Forward, One Step Back?* Lahore: Vanguard, 1987.

Pervez, Hoodbhoy, ed. *Education and the State: Fifty Years of Pakistan.* Karachi: Oxford Univeristy Press, 1997.

Rikhye, Ravi. *The War That Never Was.* Delhi: Chanakya, 1988.

Shah, Nasra M., and Muhammad Anwar. *Basic Needs, Women and Development: A Survey of Squatters in Lahore, Pakistan.* Honolulu: East-West Center, 1986.

Srinivasan, T. N., and Pranab K. Bardhan, eds. *Rural Poverty in South Asia.* New York: Columbia University Press, 1988.

ISLAMIZATION

Ahmad, Khurshid, and Zafar Ishaq Ansari, eds. *Islamic Perspectives: Studies in Honor of Mawlana Sayyid Abdul Ala Mawdudi.* London: Islamic Foundation, 1979.

Donohue, John L., and John L. Esposito, eds. *Islam in Transition: Muslim Perspectives.* New York: Oxford University Press, 1982.

Esposito, John L., ed. *Islam and Development: Religion and Social Change.* Syracuse, N.Y.: Syracuse University Press, 1980.

Syed, Anwar. *Pakistan: Islam, Politics, and National Solidarity.* Lahore: Vanguard, 1984.

Weiss, Anita M. *Islamic Reassertion in Pakistan.* Syracuse, N.Y.: Syracuse University Press, 1986.

FICTION

Rushdie, Salman. *Midnight's Children.* New York: Knopf, 1981.
———. *Shame.* London: Jonathan Cape, 1983.
Scott, Paul. *The Raj Quartet.* London: Heinemann, 1978.

About the Book and Author

Pakistan came into being as the result of a movement that sought to establish a separate national identity for the Muslims of British India. Although it achieved independence in 1947, Pakistan has not yet succeeded in integrating its diverse population into a nation—as its short yet turbulent history vividly demonstrates.

This revised and updated introduction to Pakistan's political, economic, and social development includes a thorough analysis of the performance of a number of administrations that were inducted into office in the last decade. Burki assesses the implications of some recent developments, including the testing of nuclear devices by both Pakistan and India, the consolidation of the rule of Taleban in Afghanistan, and the increasing influence of Islam in Pakistan.

Shahid Javed Burki was minister of finance, planning, and economic affairs in the caretaker administration that took office following the dismissal of Benazir Bhutto in November 1996. He is at present regional vice president at the World Bank in charge of Latin America and the Caribbean.

Index

6045